A PRACTICAL GUIDE FOR OWNERS AND BREEDERS

GERMAN SHEPHERDS

A PRACTICAL GUIDE FOR OWNERS AND BREEDERS
GERMAN SHEPHERDS

ALLISON CLARKE
AND LIZZY BROWN

THE CROWOOD PRESS

First published in 2016 by
The Crowood Press Ltd
Ramsbury, Marlborough
Wiltshire SN8 2HR

www.crowood.com

British Library Cataloguing-in-Publication Data
A catalogue record for this book is available from the British Library.

ISBN 978 1 78500 090 4

Typeset by Jean Cussons Typesetting, Diss, Norfolk

Printed and bound in Singapore by Craft Print Pte Ltd

CONTENTS

INTRODUCTION

Having never written, or even considered writing a book, imagine our surprise when we were asked to write *German Shepherds – A Practical Guide for Owners and Breeders*.

Although we come from very different backgrounds and from the opposite ends of the country, we share a common passion: our love for animals, and we have both owned German Shepherds throughout our lives. We met through the world of dog rescue many years ago, when we were both volunteers for a German Shepherd rescue, each co-ordinating the rescue and re-homing of dogs in our own part of the country.

But we wanted to do more: we wanted to be proactive in trying to change the way dogs are treated as a disposable commodity in modern times, rather than just being there to pick up the pieces. We believed that every dog that came through a rescue should be neutered, microchipped and vaccinated. Therefore in 2012 German Shepherd Rescue Élite came into existence with these goals, and we were very proud to achieve registered charity status within six months.

With our remarkable team of volunteers, all of whom give up their time and money for this wonderful breed, we have been able to help hundreds of German Shepherds. We give every dog a chance however young or old, and take in many from the numerous pounds across the country, many of which operate their lawful requirement of keeping a stray dog for seven days, and if it is not reclaimed, putting it to sleep. This is the harsh reality of modern-day life, and with the increasing number of back-street breeders, and dogs coming in from abroad, the problems are further exacerbated. We have also been known to stray from our beloved breed, and have helped many others that would otherwise have lost their lives simply because they were no longer wanted. We act as social services for these dogs.

Writing this book has been tough going at times, mainly from the time aspect of fitting in the research and the writing alongside running a rescue, and also, of course, around the normal routine of everyday life. But we have learnt an incredible amount along the way, in areas we have not been involved in previously, such as breeding and showing. We are great believers that you can never stop learning.

We hope you will enjoy reading our book as much as we have enjoyed its creation, and we hope that along the way we have highlighted the issues faced by dog rescues across the country. With power in numbers, we would like to believe that one day our dogs will receive the proper legal status and protection they deserve, and we will continue to fight for change wherever we can.

www.gsrelite.co.uk

1 A BRIEF HISTORY OF THE BREED AND BREED STANDARDS

EVOLUTION OF THE GERMAN SHEPHERD

The German Shepherd is remarkably similar in appearance to its ancestor the wolf, from which all today's breed of dogs have evolved.

The relationship between man and dog has existed since prehistoric times, with dogs being bred predominantly for the roles they could fulfil, and not how they looked. But due to the dramatic rise in pet ownership in the last century the shift of emphasis has been towards a dog's appearance and social temperament, and this shift is probably at the root of many of the physical and behavioural problems now seen in many modern breeds of dog. However, the German Shepherd dog has predominantly made the change from a working role to a pet and companion with few problems.

Animals change physically, triggered by changes in environment, and make behavioural adaptations to ensure survival. The domestication of the wolf to a dog occurred when man began to adopt a village way of life. The wolf soon realized that the village gave a continual supply of food if it lived close enough to exploit the situation, with rubbish dumps being a good place to scavenge and a safe place to leave their young. Therefore these youngsters soon learnt to live and survive close to man.

With man's switch from hunter/gatherer to crop farmer, the wolf provided man with a source of easily obtainable meat, so their presence would have been tolerated. And as the resident population reached maturity, breeding would have been encouraged to ensure future supplies.

The direct physical contact and socialization

SURVIVAL INSTINCTS

Survival imperatives for any animal are feeding, reproducing, and staying out of trouble.

The dog's ancestor, the wolf.

The modern German Shepherd dog.

of village-born pups occurred as a crucial part of the taming and domestication process. Indirectly the pups would have been encouraged to retain playful characteristics, and not to develop the fully dominant or predatory behaviours typical of adult wolves. These characteristics would then become established in the adult population of the village dogs. Approximately 60 per cent of the human race still has a cultural attachment to eating dog meat to some degree.

Dogs later became prized as hunter/guard working companions, and were transported around the world via trade routes to places where they had not evolved through the village domestication process. As working animals, dogs became much valued, though the dog type that excelled at herding in one settlement may have looked entirely different to the dog evolved for the same job in another settlement. Selection for breeding was based on the dog's ability to do the job required, and this is what established the appearance of his type and his physical characteristics, according to whether his job was hunting, herding, guarding or retrieving.

Captain Max von Stephanitz.

HISTORY OF THE GERMAN SHEPHERD

In Europe dogs were bred to preserve traits that assisted in their job of herding and guarding sheep. In Germany this was done by selecting and breeding dogs that the villagers felt had the skills necessary, such as intelligence, speed, strength and a keen sense of smell. This resulted in dogs with the skill set required, but from one community to another the dogs would differ significantly in appearance and ability.

The Phylax Society was formed in 1891 with the aim of standardizing the dog breeds in Germany. The society was disbanded after only a few years due to internal conflicts as to whether working ability in dogs was more important than appearance when breeding, but its legacy was to encourage individuals to pursue standardization. One of the ex-members, Max von Stephanitz, believed strongly that dogs should be bred for working. Von Stephanitz was an ex-cavalry captain and had been a student of the Berlin Veterinary College.

Von Stephanitz attended a dog show in 1899 where he was shown a dog named Hektor Linksrhein, the product of a few generations of selective breeding. Hektor was everything Von Stephanitz believed a working dog should be, possessing strength, intelligence, loyalty and appearance. He purchased Hektor, changing his name to Horand von Grafrath, and along with his friend Artur Meyer, founded the first society for German Shepherds, the Verein Für Deutsche Schäferhunde (the SV), with Horand the first dog to be registered. Along with establishing a breed standard, the SV also developed a breed register, or Zuchtbuch. Looking back in the original Zuchtbuch, there are four wolf crosses within two pages of entries, from forty-one to seventy-six. Since the breed draws its original genetic link from this time, its similarity to its ancestor, the wolf, is not so surprising.

Hektor Linksrhein, renamed Horand von Grafrath.

Horand became the focal point of breeding programmes, and was only bred to society members displaying desirable traits. Horand's most successful son was Hektor von Schwaben, who won the Sieger (top male) title in 1900 and 1901. Hektor was inbred with another of Horand's offspring, producing Beowulf who sired eighty-four pups, mostly through inbreeding with Hektor's other offspring. Beowulf's progeny was also inbred, and it is from these pups that all German Shepherds draw a genetic link. The society had achieved its goal due to Von Stephanitz's determination, and he is therefore credited with being the creator of the German Shepherd Dog.

THE KÖRBUCH

Along with establishing a breed standard, indiscriminate breeding was becoming a problem, so in 1921 Von Stephanitz established the breed survey book, or Körbuch, which determined a dog's suitability for breeding based on physical and mental characteristics, rather than show wins. This practice has been continued ever since.

When the UK Kennel Club first accepted registrations for the breed in 1919, fifty-four dogs were registered, with the number growing to over 8,000 by 1926. The German Shepherd breed gained international recognition at the end of World War I when soldiers returned with tales of dogs performing heroic deeds; and animal actors such as Strongheart and Rin Tin Tin popularized the breed still further. Strongheart had originally been trained as a police dog in Germany, but was taken to the US to become one of the first canine stars. Strongheart paved the way for the much better remembered Rin Tin Tin, rescued from a German battlefield during World War I by an American soldier, Lee Duncan.

Strongheart.

Rin Tin Tin.

The breed had been named Deutscher Schäferhund by Von Stephanitz, which translated to German Shepherd Dog. However, as the breed's original purpose had been to herd and protect sheep, all herding dogs in Germany were referred to by this name, so the German Shepherd became known as the Altdeutsche Schäferhunde, or Old German Shepherd Dog.

THE BREED NAME

Due to anti-German sentiment after World War I, the breed was officially renamed Alsatian Wolf Dog, instead of German Shepherd Dog, by the UK Kennel Club, with the appendage of Wolf Dog eventually being dropped. The Alsatian name remained until 1977, when enthusiasts successfully campaigned the UK Kennel Club to allow the breed to be registered once again as German Shepherd Dog. Thus the word Alsatian can still appear as part of the formal breed name in parentheses, and was only removed in 2010.

The modern German Shepherd has been criticised for straying away from Von Stephanitz's original ideology that the breed is primarily a working dog and breeding should be controlled to eliminate defects quickly. It is careless breeding that has promoted disease and defects, and non-regulation of breeding means that genetic problems such as hip dysplasia and weakness of temperament are much too common in our modern dogs.

THE VERSATILITY OF THE GERMAN SHEPHERD

The German Shepherd is a very popular breed as a working dog, and is especially well known for working with the police tracking criminals and patrolling troubled areas, and in detecting and holding suspects. In addition the German Shepherd has been used in the thousands by the military, when it is trained for patrol duty and detection. Some dogs are also trained by the military to parachute from an aircraft.

The German Shepherd is the most widely used breed in the British police due to its effectiveness as a versatile and courageous protection dog. Some police forces have breeding programmes in place to ensure suitable dogs, whilst others

Police dog tracking: Jack with handler Steve Butcher. (Photo: Surrey Police Dog Training School)

Police dog in training: Jake with instructor Pete Grimmett impersonating a criminal. (Photo: Surrey Police Dog Training School)

will buy, and some police dogs are gifted. If a dog is accepted by the police it is allocated to a handler and will commence a lengthy training course of thirteen weeks, which it must pass in order to become a fully fledged police dog. The dog's adaptability and temperament are paramount, as it may need to face a criminal with a weapon, undertake crowd control or search for a lost child.

The German Shepherd is one of the most widely used breeds in scent work roles, including search and rescue, cadaver search, and detection of narcotics, explosives, accelerant and mines. They are suited to this line of work because of their keen sense of smell and their ability to work regardless of distraction, whilst covering a wide area quickly. Sniffer dogs undergo a rigorous training programme. Search and rescue dogs will work in countries all round the world in hazardous conditions such as earthquakes, explosions or on the side of a mountain. This is where courage is also required.

Due to their strong sense of duty, their mental abilities, their fearlessness and attachment to their owner, German Shepherds excel as guide dogs and at one time was the breed chosen almost exclusively for this role. In more recent years Labradors and Golden Retrievers have been used more widely; however, the German Shepherd still makes up one third of the guide dogs in the UK. The breed is also trained to be support dogs for the disabled, a rapidly growing role in this country. The dogs are specially trained and allocated to a particular owner.

Many a German Shepherd has become a PAT (Pets As Therapy) dog, having passed a thorough assessment. There are over 5,000 active PAT dogs in the UK, visiting both the young and the old and giving them the opportunity to stroke and talk to one of these calm friendly dogs. These dogs bring comfort and companionship to thousands of people every week. The charity, Pets As Therapy, also runs a 'Read2Dogs' programme, which helps children in the classroom improve their reading ability by helping to increase their confidence and enjoyment of reading. We have seen this at first hand with Olly: owned by Allison and a registered PAT dog, Olly was one of the

Olly at school.

first dogs on this scheme. The children love Olly visiting and will read to him when they do not have the confidence to read to a teacher or parent.

The breed is still used to herd sheep in many parts of the world, and is expected to patrol boundaries to keep sheep from trespassing on to crops and damaging them. In Germany these skills are tested in herding utility dog trials known as Herdengebrauchshund.

German Shepherds are also a popular breed trained for protection work, be it general or personal, and these dogs can change hands for large amounts of money. Schutzhund, which means protection dog, originated in Germany in the 1800s: at this time German police were called Schutzmann and his canine companion Schutzhund.

Of course we must not forget the German Shepherd's most common role as a companion dog. The majority of the dogs today reside in a family environment as a family pet and companion.

THE IDEAL GERMAN SHEPHERD OWNER

The German Shepherd is not the ideal pet for all homes as it is a highly active dog, curious, intelligent and protective, and it can be very self assured. The ideal German Shepherd owner is one who has researched the breed and understands its characteristics and traits, and can give the dog the right environment where it will thrive and become a loving and loyal family member.

THE BREED STANDARD

The German Shepherd falls under the 'Pastoral Breed Group', which consists of herding dogs that are associated with working cattle, sheep, reindeer and other cloven-footed animals. Usually this type of dog has a weatherproof double coat to protect it from the elements when working in severe conditions. Other breeds that fall into the Pastoral Breed Group include the Collie family, Old English Sheepdogs and Samoyeds.

As cited by the Kennel Club (UK):

A Breed Standard is the guideline which describes the ideal characteristics, temperament and appearance of a breed and ensures that the breed is fit for function. Absolute soundness is essential. Breeders and judges should at all times be careful to avoid obvious conditions or exaggerations which would be detrimental in any way to the health, welfare or soundness of this breed. From time to time certain conditions or exaggerations may be considered to have the potential to affect dogs in some breeds adversely, and judges and breeders are requested to refer to the Breed Watch section of the Kennel Club website for details of any such current issues. If a feature or quality is desirable it should only be present in the right measure. However, if a dog possesses a feature, characteristic or colour described as undesirable or highly undesirable it is strongly recommended that it should not be rewarded in the show ring.

General Appearance
Slightly long in comparison to height; of powerful, well muscled build with weather-resistant coat. Relation between height, length, position and structure of fore and hindquarters (angulation) producing a far-reaching, enduring gait. Clear definition of masculinity and femininity essential, and working ability never sacrificed for mere beauty.

Characteristics
Versatile working dog, balanced and free from exaggeration. Attentive, alert, resilient and tireless, with keen scenting ability.

Temperament
Steady of nerve, loyal, self-assured, courageous and tractable. Never nervous, over-aggressive or shy.

Head and Skull
Proportionate in size to body, never coarse, too

fine or long. Clean cut; fairly broad between ears. Forehead slightly domed; little or no trace of central furrow. Cheeks forming softly rounded curve, never protruding. Skull from ears to bridge of nose tapering gradually and evenly, blending without too pronounced stop into wedge-shaped powerful muzzle. Skull approximately 50 per cent of overall length of head. Width of skull corresponding approximately to length, in males slightly greater, in females slightly less. Muzzle strong, lips firm, clean and closing tightly. Top of muzzle straight, almost parallel to forehead. Short, blunt, weak, pointed, overlong muzzle undesirable.

Eyes

Medium-sized, almond-shaped, never protruding. Dark brown preferred, lighter shade permissible, provided expression good and general harmony of head not destroyed. Expression lively, intelligent and self-assured.

Ears

Medium-sized, firm in texture, broad at base, set high, carried erect, almost parallel, never pulled inwards or tipped, tapering to a point, open at front. Never hanging. Folding back during movement permissible.

Mouth

Jaws strongly developed. With a perfect, regular and complete scissor bite, ie upper teeth closely overlapping lower teeth and set square to the jaws. Teeth healthy and strong. Full dentition of forty-two teeth is desirable.

Neck

Fairly long, strong, with well developed muscles, free from throatiness. Carried at 45 degrees angle to horizontal, raised when excited, lowered at fast trot.

Forequarters

Shoulder blade and upper arms are equal in length, well muscled and firmly attached to the body. Shoulder blades set obliquely (approximately 45 degrees) laid flat to body. Upper arm strong, well muscled, joining shoulder blade at

Good conformation is a good start towards having a healthy dog.

approximately 90 degrees. Seen from all sides, the forearms are straight and, seen from the front, absolutely parallel. Bone oval rather than round. The elbows must turn neither in nor out while standing or moving. Pasterns firm, supple, with a slight forward slope. An over long, weak pastern, which would affect a dog's working ability is to be heavily penalised. Length of foreleg slightly exceeds the depth of chest.

Body

Length measured from point of shoulder to point of buttock, slightly exceeding height at withers. Correct ratio 10 to 9 or 8 and a half. Undersized dogs, stunted growth, high-legged dogs, those too heavy or too light in build, overloaded fronts, too short overall appearance, any feature detracting from reach or endurance of gait, undesirable. Chest deep (45–48 per cent) of height at shoulder, not too broad, brisket long, well developed. Ribs well formed and long; neither barrel-shaped nor too flat; allowing free movement of elbows when gaiting. Relatively short loin. Belly firm, only slightly drawn up. Back between withers and croup, straight, strongly developed, not too long. Overall length achieved by correct angle of well laid shoulders, correct length of croup and hindquarters. The topline runs without any visible break from the set on of the neck, over the well defined withers, falling away slightly in a straight line to the gently sloping croup. The back is firm, strong and well muscled. Loin broad, strong, well muscled. Weak, soft and roach backs undesirable and should be heavily penalised. Croup slightly sloping and without any break in the topline, merges imperceptibly with the set on of the tail. Short, steep or flat croups highly undesirable.

Hindquarters
Overall strong, broad and well muscled, enabling effortless forward propulsion. Upper and lower thigh are approximately of equal length. Hind angulation sufficient if imaginary line dropped from point of buttocks cuts through lower thigh just in front of hock, continuing down slightly in front of hindfeet. Angulations corresponding approximately with front angulation, without over-angulation. Seen from rear, the hind legs are straight and parallel to each other. The hocks are strong and firm.

The rear pasterns are vertical. Any tendency towards over-angulation of hindquarters, weak hocks, cow hocks or sickle hooks, is to be heavily penalised as this reduces firmness and endurance in movement.

Feet
Rounded toes well closed and arched. Pads well cushioned and durable. Nails short, strong and dark in colour.

Tail
Bushy-haired, reaches at least to hock – ideal length reaching to middle of metatarsus. At rest tail hangs in slight sabre-like curve; when moving raised and curve increased, ideally never above level of back. Short, rolled, curled, generally carried badly or stumpy from birth, undesirable.

Gait/Movement
Sequence of step follows diagonal pattern, moving foreleg and opposite hindleg forward simultaneously; hindfoot thrust forward to mid-

Strong hindquarters are needed for a large working breed.

point of body and having equally long reach with forefeet without any noticeable change in backline. Absolute soundness of movement essential.

Coat

Outer coat consisting of straight, hard, close-lying hair as dense as possible; thick undercoat. Hair on head, ears, front of legs, paws and toes short; on back, longer and thicker; in some males forming slight ruff. Hair longer on back of legs as far down as pasterns and stifles and forming fairly thick trousers on hindquarters. No hard and fast rule for length of hair; mole-type coats undesirable.

Colour

Black or black saddle with tan, or gold to light grey markings. All black, all grey, with lighter or brown markings referred to as Sables. Bi-colour: Predominantly black, may have tan or gold markings on head, chest, legs and feet; black markings may be present on toes and rear pasterns. Nose black. Light markings on chest or very pale colour on inside of legs permissible but undesirable, as are whitish nails, red-tipped tails or wishy-washy faded colours defined as lacking in pigmentation. Blues, livers, albinos, whites (i.e. almost pure white dogs with black noses) and near whites highly undesirable. Undercoat, except in all black dogs, usually grey or fawn. Colour in itself is of secondary importance having no effect on character or fitness for work. Final colour of a young dog only ascertained when outer coat has developed.

Size

Ideal height (from withers and just touching elbows): dogs: 63cm (25in); bitches: 58cm (23in). 2.5cm (1in) either above or below ideal permissible.

Faults

Any departure from the foregoing points should be considered a fault and the seriousness with which the fault should be regarded should be in exact proportion to its degree and its effect upon the health and welfare of the dog.

Note

Male animals should have two apparently normal testicles fully descended into the scrotum.

Copyright The Kennel Club Limited
Reproduced with their permission

The pedigree of a dog is a gateway to the past, and we shall look at this in more detail in Chapter 9 'Breeding and Pregnancy'.

Solid black.

Solid white (undesirable).

Dark sable.

Light sable.

Bi-colour.

Black and tan blanket.

Black and gold saddle.

2 CHOOSING YOUR GERMAN SHEPHERD

IS A GERMAN SHEPHERD THE RIGHT DOG FOR YOU?

The decision you are about to make needs very careful consideration, as taking on a German Shepherd dog is a huge responsibility and commitment – as in fact it is to take on any breed of dog, whether a puppy or an older dog: so please take time to do your research.

Key Considerations

Lifestyle: Think about your lifestyle, as German Shepherds are social animals and do not like being left alone for long periods of time. The general rule of thumb is that your dog should not be left for more than four hours in a day, although this will vary with his age.

Space: Think about your home and whether it can accommodate a large breed dog. Not only will your dog like to have his own space within the home, but a German Shepherd is not well suited if you live in a flat with no outdoor space where he can stretch his legs in between walks – and where will he go to the toilet on that occasional day you feel too unwell to take him out

German Shepherds need space to exercise.

for a walk? If in a flat, what floor are you on, and do you have stairs or a lift? Older Shepherds can struggle with stairs.

Money: Apart from the initial cost of obtaining your German Shepherd, and essential equipment such as collars, leads, bowls and bedding, the ongoing costs can soon add up, bearing in mind that these dogs can live to an average of twelve years. Consider the following:

- *Food:* Look into the costs of good quality dog food.
- *Insurance:* Ensure you have a minimum of third party cover for your dog, and look into the options that are on offer to cover accidental and medical health problems. Check out what excesses apply. Most insurers will allow you to pay by monthly direct debit at no additional cost.
- *Vet bills:* Insurance will not cover you for routine healthcare for your dog such as yearly vaccinations, having your dog neutered, or having his teeth cleaned. And if you have not taken out insurance, will you have the finances to cover an emergency operation if required, which can run into hundreds and sometimes thousands of pounds. Does your vet offer a health plan payable monthly?
- *Kennels or pet sitter:* Where will your dog go when you are on holiday? If he is lucky enough to go with you, then this is not so much of an issue, but if you jet off regularly once a year to warmer climates, consider the care costs.

Time: German Shepherds are active animals and need a considerable amount of exercise every day depending on their age. Your dog will need

training, and socialization with people and other animals. Media hype means that many people are wary of them when out in public, and whilst much of the press is exaggerated and inaccurate, it is our responsibility as German Shepherd owners to dispel these fears by ensuring that our dog is well mannered and obedient when out and about.

Cleanliness: Despite regular grooming, your German Shepherd will moult, and sometimes it can feel that this occurs 365 days of the year. They also have a tendency to love water and mud, and always save shaking themselves off until they are in the house. If you are house proud, this is not the dog for you.

TO BUY OR TO RESCUE?

Wherever you get your German Shepherd from, there are some very simple rules to follow:

- Never buy a dog from an advert where more than one breed is advertised, as it is very likely that the advertiser is breeding unscrupulously, purely for financial gain
- Never buy from an advert where an individual is selling or giving up their dog due to a change in circumstances, unless you are sure they will allow you several visits and will take

Consider adopting a rescue dog.

the dog back should there be a problem. Unfortunately the reality is that many people use this form of advertising to offload a 'difficult' dog, with problems usually of their own making

- Never buy from a pet shop as these are outlets for 'puppy farms', again unscrupulous breeders whose only interest is in money, and not the welfare of the dogs
- Never buy a dog on an impulse – for example, from the man down the pub who has to sell his dog

The reality is that a large number of dogs that end up in rescues started life through one of these outlets, resulting in a dog with medical or behavioural problems due to their poor start in life. Every day hundreds of dogs are put to sleep in the UK because so many are unwanted, having been bred purely for financial gain. However, this should not put you off considering taking on a dog from a rescue, as many dogs have just been misunderstood, or they are the victims of circumstance and turn out to be the most rewarding pets.

To buy or to rescue really depends on exactly what you are looking for in your German Shepherd, and on your personal circumstances. It is often stated that buying a puppy is the best option, as you know it will not have any 'issues' and therefore should fit in with children and other pets. But you should consider the following:

- Puppies have sharp little teeth, and use them in exploring the world in their first few months. This can mean young children get hurt accidentally and their toys destroyed by a puppy
- Puppies will need house training, and you will need to ensure your young child does not walk or crawl into their toilet areas before you have had a chance to clear up
- As puppies get larger they will become quite boisterous in their play, and many a young child has been knocked over by an over-zealous young dog, with the result that the child is then scared of the dog. Of course, no child

should be left alone with a dog of any age or breed, and ultimately it is the parent's responsibility to ensure both children and dogs are safe
- You may have an older dog or cat, and feel that they will find it easiest to accept a puppy into their home. But does your older pet really want a young puppy hanging off the scruff of its neck?
- You may already have a dog that does not get on with other dogs, but you think he will be fine with a puppy. However, this is the worst thing you could do for either dog, as exposing a puppy to such negative behaviour at this crucial age more often than not means that you end up with two dogs with the same issue. Help your own dog by socializing him on walks with others, and help him to gain his confidence
- Your own age is a big consideration. Are you still very fit and active, and do you have people close to you who will take care of your dog should you be taken unwell? Unfortunately many older people who have had German Shepherds all their life, take on a puppy and then realize they had forgotten how much time and energy a puppy consumes. By the time it is around a year old, they are also then struggling to hold such a strong dog and give it the exercise it needs

All too often rescues are asked to help to find new homes for German Shepherds from such scenarios, which is why you may be better off looking at adopting one of the many rescue dogs out there in need of a new 'forever' home. Many of these dogs are looking for a home through no fault of their own, but due to a change in their owner's circumstances. The most common are:

- The owner has died
- Marital or relationship breakdown
- Moving into accommodation where dogs are not allowed
- Long-term illness, making it impossible to exercise and care for the dog
- Long working hours, so the dog is being left alone for too long

These are usually responsible owners who have loved and cared for their dog to the best of their capabilities, so the dog has had a good start to its life. Many of these dogs will already be well socialized with children and other animals, and understand the general rules in the house and out in public. It may be better to consider a middle-aged rescue dog that has lived with young children as your first family German Shepherd. And of course there are many older dogs out there that no longer want to hike for miles, and would fit happily into a life of retirement with older owners.

FINDING A SUITABLE BREEDER

If after some thought you have decided that your lifestyle would accommodate having a puppy, then finding the right breeder is paramount.

The best place to start is on the Kennel Club website, as they offer a lot of advice on buying the right puppy, and have a list of Assured Breeders. Also they have regulations in place to help ensure that dogs registered with them do not come from puppy farmers. Word of mouth from a reliable source is another common way for people to find a reputable breeder.

The Kennel Club is endeavouring to set the benchmark for breeding standards by its Assured Breeder Scheme, which was established in 2004. There are set requirements that assured breeders must agree to follow to encourage the breeding of healthy, well adjusted puppies. Such breeders have agreed to an ethical code of practice, tested their dogs for hereditary diseases, and raise their pups in ideal conditions.

A good breeder will want to ensure their puppy is going to the right environment, and you may well feel under interrogation – but this shows they care. They should want to know if you have carefully considered buying a German Shepherd puppy, they will question your lifestyle and home environment (some may even ask to visit your home), they may want to meet all the

All puppies are cute, but how they started life is important.

family including children, and they may ask your long-term plans for puppy – such as: is puppy just a pet, will you be competing in any of the many disciplines available, do you intend to breed from him/her in the future?

Whichever route you take in buying your German Shepherd puppy, there are some simple guidelines that you should follow:

- The breeder should allow you to see mum with her litter of pups. This is very important, and you should never buy a puppy from anywhere you are not allowed to meet mum, whatever reason they give. Seeing the mother and assessing her temperament will give you an idea of how the pups should be in terms of temperament, size and characteristics
- If dad is also owned by the same breeder, you should ask to meet him. This is not always possible, as stud dogs are not always owned by the same person. However, breeders of good repute will be happy to show off one or both parents
- Ideally pups should have been raised in the home of the person selling them, rather than in a kennel or barn, otherwise they cannot have had enough experience of everyday life, or contact with people and the domestic environment
- You should be allowed to handle and meet the whole litter rather than just being shown the pup that may be intended for you. This allows you to assess your pup against its siblings in terms of size, characteristics and confidence. This is also a good test of mum's temperament as she should be happy to allow visitors to handle her pups and not be worried when you pick them up and play with them

A good breeder will let you visit mum with her litter.

- Visiting a number of times should also be welcomed by a breeder – though remember that too many visits can become an inconvenience
- Ask the breeder for a copy of their contract of sale. A reputable breeder will provide this, and it should include details of both the breeder's and your responsibilities to the puppy. It should also list any Kennel Club endorsements (restrictions) that have been placed on the pup's record, and under what conditions they may be prepared to remove them. Such endorsements may include that your puppy is not for breeding, or not for export
- Take time to chat with the breeder about vaccinations, microchipping, worming, flea treatments, feeding and exercise. Written advice on all of this should be supplied by the breeder, but it is good to go through it to ensure you are totally clear on when and if pup may need his next vaccination
- The breeder should also provide you with a pedigree detailing your pup's ancestry; this can be hand written or printed from the breeder, or an official one from the Kennel Club
- Breeders should also supply copies of any additional health certificates held for mum and dad. German Shepherds are prone to a number of hereditary diseases and it is important you are aware of these conditions so know the right questions to ask. Nowadays some dogs are also DNA tested for certain conditions
- Ask at what age you can take your puppy home. The ideal age is eight weeks, but many breeders will let you take pup home from six weeks. A pup should never leave its mother or siblings any younger than this

If the breeder appears uncomfortable about any of your questions or requests, then maybe they are not right for you. Never be afraid to walk away. Be patient for the right pup from the right breeder.

The more that pup has experienced before he comes home with you, the more confident, outgoing and steady he is likely to be. Sometimes the one-off pet breeders, or the breeders who only produce one or two litters a year, can be best at this, as they have more time to invest in the litter's socialization during that crucial time when pup's behaviour and character can be determined – between three to twelve weeks of age.

FINDING A SUITABLE RESCUE

The number of rescues to choose from has risen dramatically in recent times, so you really do need to be careful as to which ones you consider using. The Kennel Club also has a directory of breed-specific rescues and charities to help you. To be on this directory, all rescues and charities will have had to provide a letter from a vet they use regularly, or a breed club they have attended over a period of time, to provide proof that they do not put a healthy dog to sleep (a 'no PTS' policy), and that their sole intention is to provide help and care for that breed. A charity will also have been checked and accepted by the Charities Commission, and will have to adhere to their stringent guidelines. They will have to provide detailed annual accounts so you can then see where every penny goes. A reputable charity will ensure that all money donated is funded into helping the dogs – which is what we believe a true rescue should be all about.

One of the first things you can do is check the rescue's website, which will give you a very good indication as to what kind of organization they are, and how they operate. If they are a registered charity this should be indicated, and you can check their charity number on the Charity Commission's website. You can glean a lot from websites, and it is absolutely free!

There are mainly two types of rescue: the centres that you can actually visit and where you can view the dogs, and the internet-based rescues – these may have more dogs to adopt, but the dogs will be dotted around the country, some in commercial boarding kennels or foster homes, and some still in their original homes. Each person will have a view on which they prefer.

The centres will take your details and then happily show you dogs they feel will suit you and your family; and if everyone is happy with a particular dog they will hopefully then arrange a home check to make sure your home is ready and safe for the dog to go to. Unfortunately many of the larger charities have stopped doing home checks due to lack of resources, so it becomes very difficult for them to ascertain if your environment is right for the dog. This is why the larger charities tend to see a large number of dogs coming back into their care, due to an unsuitable matching. However, this does mean that you can very often walk into a centre and walk out the same day with a new dog. If you have other dogs in the home, you should be asked to bring them to meet your potential new dog before going home, and some centres ask that this be done a couple of times.

The internet-based rescues work slightly differently. The reputable rescues will ask you to complete an adoption form application, and you will then be screened over the telephone for suitability; where possible the rescue will obtain

Rescue volunteers out fundraising.

a reference from your vet. If all is clear to this stage, a home check will be arranged by a local volunteer. On receiving the home check report you should then be contacted by a senior volunteer or co-ordinator to let you know the outcome of the report; you should be in a position to discuss dogs that you and they have decided may be suitable candidates. Certain guidelines should be followed: for example, a dog picked up as a stray with no history should not be re-homed with children.

Once a dog is selected, a meeting is set up at the dog's location, or close to where the dog resides. This is your opportunity to take any other dogs you may own to meet the potential new member of your family and spend some time together. If the dog is in commercial kennels or a foster home it may be that if all has gone well, you can then return to collect your new dog, rather than travel the two together immediately. If the dog is still with its current owner, the meeting would have been arranged close to the dog's home with a volunteer, for data protection and neutrality. In these circumstances it is often kinder on both the dog and the previous owner that if the meet goes well, the dog is taken home there and then.

You should be asked to complete an adoption contract, which will state the responsibilities the rescue has to you and the dog, and the conditions under which they are allowing you to adopt the dog. A good rescue will state that you have full rescue support once you have adopted a dog, and if for any reason it becomes necessary for you to find the dog a new home in the future, then you must approach the rescue to assist in this. Basic conditions relate to the long-term welfare of the dog, and your responsibilities to the dog and the law. You should have been given a copy of the contract before meeting the dog so you have time to fully understand it and raise any questions with your co-ordinator.

Whichever route you take, find out as much as you can about the dog and his history. Rescued dogs are usually more than six months old, are housetrained, past the chewing stage, and happy to be placed in a good home. However, there are also dogs that have been abused or neglected,

Poppy

Location: Coventry
Sex: Female
Age: 3
Neutered: Yes
Children: Yes - Older Only
Other dogs: Careful introduction
Cats: No

Tag

Location: Oxon
Sex: Male
Age: 7 years
Neutered: No
Children: Yes - Older Only
Other dogs: Yes
Cats: Yes

Cleo

Location: Essex
Sex: Female
Age: 9
Neutered: Yes
Children: Yes
Other dogs: Yes
Cats: Yes

Bella

Location: Fleetwood
Sex: Female
Age: 8
Neutered: Yes
Children: No
Other dogs: Careful introduction
Cats: No

Shan

Location: Notts
Sex: Female
Age: 10
Neutered: No
Children: Yes - Older Only
Other dogs: Selective
Cats: Unknown

Roxy

Location: Birmingham
Sex: Female
Age: 4
Neutered: No
Children: Yes - Older Only
Other dogs: Careful introduction
Cats: No

A rescue website showing some of the dogs in their care.

and these will need a lot of patience and care to help them overcome their trauma. A reputable rescue will tell you all they know about the dog, including any issues the dog may have and any ongoing medical conditions. A good rescue will have endeavoured to ensure that the dogs leaving their care are neutered, microchipped and vaccinated. Check their policies. You should also receive guidelines on how to care for your adopted German Shepherd dog, and how to introduce him into your home and life.

WHICH ONE FOR YOU?

It is said that females are easier to train and less competitive in a family environment than males, but this will depend on the female in question and the environment she is going into. There are no set rules for this breed, one of whose characteristics we adore is their individuality.

Do not necessarily pick the puppy who jumped on you first, as this pup could be demanding and end up wanting to rule the roost; but he could be the one for you if you were considering competing in working trials or agility in the future. Equally, it may not be a good idea to pick the pup who did not want to come out of hiding because he was too shy, as this may be an indication of future problems of nervousness or anxiety – although some of these fearful pups turn out to be highly intelligent, using brain over brawn. Pups should be happy to meet you, and to be picked up, handled and played with. They should not be worried by sudden sounds, and should play well with their siblings. Pick the average pup, stay sensible, and stick to the brief you have given yourself considering all of the above factors. Make sure your selection will be the best end result for both of you.

Never be tempted or persuaded to take two pups from the same litter, however cute they are or just because one will be left. At this time in their life a pup needs to learn the bond with people rather than the dog/dog bond, which can be very difficult with two as they may interact more with each other, often to the exclusion of people and sometimes other breeds of dogs. If you are looking at buying two puppies, in the long term it is best to buy one first and make sure it is well socialized and train it before buying the second.

DO NOT LET YOUR HEART RULE YOUR HEAD

Please do not let your heart rule your head when making your final choice, as you may not get the happy ending you expected. Take into consideration your working hours, other pets you already have, your family life and subsequent others, age, temperament, expectations, acceptable issues if any, and your own German Shepherd dog experience.

If adopting from a breed-specific rescue all the people you deal with should have German Shepherd dog experience. Use their experience and take your time in making any decisions. Follow their guidelines and advice, and hopefully this will ensure you get the right partner, friend and new family member for life. Remember, however, that they can only advise you on what they have seen and know about these dogs, and dogs can react differently in new environments, and some will take longer than others to settle in and find their feet. Never be afraid to ask for help if an issue arises, as many rescues have a wealth of knowledge among them, and many a time can help you resolve a problem very quickly.

3 BRINGING YOUR GERMAN SHEPHERD HOME

PLANNING FOR THE ARRIVAL OF YOUR PUPPY

So you have chosen your new addition and the breeder should have given you a date when your puppy can be collected, and ensured you are prepared at home.

Where will Puppy be Sleeping?

Puppies like to 'bundle' amongst each other where they feel safest and warm. Some people suggest using a large cardboard box as a bed, but with a German Shepherd puppy that will not last long! There are many good plastic beds on the market, which should be well padded with towels or blankets for puppy to snuggle into. This type of bed should be in a restricted area of the home as puppy is likely to wake up in the night and go to the toilet, and may well explore things with his teeth.

Another option is to use a dog crate as your puppy's bed. Not only will puppy learn that this is his safe spot, but it will help ensure that he is safe and isn't chewing anything he shouldn't be during the night, and will assist in house training. Nobody likes to sleep in their own mess and most puppies will

try to hold on until morning as well. If associated with food and toys, puppies usually accept a crate very quickly and regard it as a cosy den. Many adult dogs will still choose their crate, if the door is left open, in favour of a bed on the floor.

Having decided on your bed type, where in the house will puppy's bed be? We used to be told to leave puppy downstairs and ignore any crying he made for the first few nights, and then all would be fine. But a crying puppy is not a naughty puppy, but usually one that is very stressed and anxious, so this method is actually quite cruel, as not only has puppy been taken away from his mum and siblings, but is now also in a completely strange environment and will feel very lonely and isolated. If possible, look out an old blanket or towel with your smell on it, and take it to the breeder before you collect puppy, and ask the breeder to put it in with mum and the puppies

Where will puppy sleep?

TOP TIPS

Remember, if you let puppy get in or on your bed he will expect the same when an adult.

Remember, crates should never be used for long-term confinement other than at bed time.

---

so it can gather up the puppy's family smells. This can be a comforter to a puppy on its first few nights, as not only will it have got used to your scent, but it will have its family's scent as well, which will help it to relax.

If you have other dogs in the family then puppy should sleep within their bedroom area, though of course ensuring he is safe from the other dogs, who may get frustrated with him if their sleep is disturbed. If there are no other dogs in the family then consider having puppy's crate with you in the bedroom. You are not encouraging puppy to sleep in the bedroom as he will see his crate as his bed, but having the company will help to ease his stress so everyone gets a good night's sleep. Once puppy is more confident in his new home, his crate can be moved into what will be his normal bedroom area in the house.

Where will Puppy be Allowed in the House?
Boundaries should be established from the start as to where puppy will be allowed in the house, and that means not just which rooms, but whether he will be allowed on furniture or not. There is no given rule as to where a dog should be allowed, and as a family pet it is up to the family to decide the boundaries for their new addition. The important thing to remember is that if puppy is given free rein to start, he will always expect it. If firm boundaries are instilled from the start, they can always be removed as puppy gets older or if the family feels they are no longer needed.

To start with it is best to ensure puppy does not go upstairs (unless at nights as explained previously), not only for boundary reasons but because it is not good for their young legs bounding up and down stairs. Puppy should only be allowed in the main living room if supervised, again not just for boundary reasons but because he could

be chewing all sorts of wires and furniture, not to mention leaving you 'presents'. Most people will keep puppy in their kitchen area as the flooring is usually such that it is easy to clear up any mistakes, and the back door is generally close for puppy to use after eating his meals.

A playpen can be used for keeping puppy in a confined area, however it does need to be of substantial quality in order for a German Shepherd puppy not to dismantle it, and it won't be long before he can jump/scrabble over a fair height if he is determined enough. Baby gates can be useful to keep puppy in a particular room whilst not shutting him away from the rest of the house, or to prevent him going upstairs, however the same applies in that the pup may quite soon be big enough to escape and so it may well be worth investing in a proper dog gate, as these are taller than a typical baby gate and therefore can be used even when puppy has grown up if needed.

What will Puppy be Eating?
A good breeder will have ensured that you know what to stock up on so puppy has a continuous diet in order not to upset his tummy. Some breeders will send you away with a small quantity of the food they use for him, to get you started. They should also give you a diet sheet, as puppy will like his routine to be the same. At this stage, puppy may well be on four meals a day, or at least three for a while, though diet and feeding times will change as he grows.

You will also need a suitable feeding bowl and water bowl. Puppies have an incredible knack of standing in their bowls so bear this in mind, especially with the water bowl. Many a time a puppy has stood in a water bowl and the floor has been flooded. Heavy ceramic bowls are good for water as they are usually too heavy for puppy to tip over.

Puppy may try carrying his dinner bowl around, so it is preferable to use something unbreakable; either a metal or plastic bowl is best – though if left on his own, puppy will probably have a good chew on a plastic one.

What Else will Puppy Need and What Else Needs to be Considered?

- Check exactly what will come with puppy, but you will probably need to buy him a light-weight collar and lead. It is a good idea to get a collar that can be extended as the puppy grows. Your puppy will not be used to either collar or lead, so it is best to get him used to the feel of both as soon as possible
- Get an identity disc for puppy's collar
- Puppy will want toys, just like a young child. Toys that make a noise are always fun, but when purchasing toys, as with children, ensure they are recommended for a puppy and there is nothing detachable a puppy could choke on, or are so small that he might try and swallow them. Giving your puppy toys to chew is better than having him chew your furniture, and the toys can be used with early training
- You will need a soft brush with which to groom your puppy
- Ensure you have registered puppy with your vet. He may need a second vaccination or worm treatment, but again, the breeder should advise you of what treatments he has received, and what is due. Remember, puppy should not go out in public areas until two weeks after his second vaccination; this is usually at around twelve weeks of age
- Check that puppy is microchipped, and if so, has the breeder transferred the paperwork into your name, or is this down to you?
- Get insurance quotes so you can put insurance into place when puppy comes home. Many breeders will give you four weeks free insurance through a main insurance company, the idea being that you continue the policy with that company. However, do not feel obliged to continue the policy, as there are many competitive insurance companies out there from which to choose

A safe bowl for puppy to drink from.

- Find out where your local puppy socialization and training classes are, get recommendations or visit a class, and if needed pre-book a space
- Ensure your garden is puppy proof, because although it may seem secure to you, a puppy can wriggle through some very small gaps, and get stuck or lost very easily when young. Also ensure there is nothing dangerous in the garden on which he can hurt himself, and nothing poisonous on which he can chew. You should not leave puppy in the garden unsupervised, however secure it is. If you have a back gate, ensure it is locked so it cannot be opened by a passerby
- Ensure your car is ready for puppy. Remember this may be the first time he has been in a car so he may well be sick, so wherever you are going to put him to travel, it is a good idea to put towels down. A smaller space is best for puppy at this age so he doesn't 'roll' around, say in the boot of the car, but ideally someone should hold him, as this is the most reassuring way for him to travel

BRINGING YOUR PUPPY HOME

So you have collected puppy and arrived home. How you introduce puppy to your home will depend if he is the only pet, or whether there are resident pets that he needs to meet. The most important thing when bringing puppy home is not to overwhelm him, so avoid having a welcoming committee at the front door!

If puppy is the only pet, then the best idea is to take him straight out into the garden, as by now he probably needs to go to the toilet. If successful, remember to praise him! If your garden is fully secure you can let puppy explore at his own pace, and then of course you should show him 'his' area in the house. All the new sounds and smells will tire him out quite quickly, so don't be surprised if he crashes out for a snooze.

Introducing Puppy to Resident Dog/s

If puppy is coming into a home where there is already a dog or dogs, then the garden is the safest place to do introductions. If you have more than one other dog, then it is best to introduce them one by one to start with, so puppy does not feel 'ganged up' on. Keep him on the lead and stay at his level so you are there for reassurance – but be careful when your 'resident' dog comes out not to over fuss puppy and thus put your dog's nose out of joint: he must always be allowed pride of place.

Most adult dogs accept a puppy with little fuss as they seem to have a natural understanding of its vulnerability. Puppy may be nervous to start

with, so don't force interaction; or, puppy may get far too excited and start jumping all around the resident dog, and you may need to try and calm him down. The resident dog/s should be allowed to sniff puppy and may reprimand him if he is misbehaving. This usually involves a look with a curled lip and a growl. Do not automatically think your dog is being aggressive, as nine times out of ten, this is your dog's natural instinct coming into play, of guiding puppy's behaviour; however, do not assume anything, and at this stage never leave puppy with the other dog/s unsupervised.

You should feed puppy in a separate area from the other dog/s, as he may well want to try what is in their bowl, and will get a nasty shock when the older dog/s defends its food. This is also where a crate comes in useful, as puppy is not only learning to associate the crate with nice things, but as a safe space of his own.

Introducing Puppy to the Resident Cat and Other Pets

You will need to ensure that your cat's food and water bowl is out of puppy's reach.

When introducing puppy to the cat, remember that if this is the first dog your cat has met it may be just as curious or scared as puppy will be. If

Meeting new friends can be fun.

My toy is much more interesting.

your cat is used to living with a dog it should be easier.

Puppy should be restrained, and you should allow your cat to be at a vantage point, such as on a table; it should also have an escape route. Puppy will want to sniff it and may try playing, and it is most probable he will get a 'bop' from the cat, who hopefully at this stage is surveying the situation in a relatively calm manner. Be careful if your cat seems extremely anxious, as it may well strike puppy with its claws out, which could damage a puppy's eye badly and have a detrimental effect on his future behaviour with cats.

Never force introductions in one go. With a more nervous cat it may be necessary to do gradual introductions over a period of time, so the cat can see puppy but is safely protected from him behind a gate, or is positioned on a higher vantage point.

If puppies are introduced to pets such as rab-bits and hamsters at an early age, they will see them as being part of the family unit rather than prey. Remember, German Shepherd puppies can be very boisterous, so do not allow them to have direct contact with smaller pets to start with.

PLANNING FOR THE ARRIVAL OF YOUR DOG

Planning for your new dog's arrival is basically the same as for the arrival of a puppy, but obviously a mature dog has already learnt many of the rules in a home and should by now understand the 'no' command.

Where Will Your Dog be Sleeping?

A dog should be used to sleeping in a specific place in a house, so decide where his bed is to be and set it up accordingly. There are many bed options on the market including, of course, the crate, but consider how well and how much you

31

Where will your new dog be sleeping?

know about the dog before spending lots of money on an expensive bed, at least until you are sure your new dog is settled and not likely to destroy the bedding. Some dogs may do this simply because they are stressed at a change in environment, others purely because they are naughty. Hopefully the dog's previous owner will also pass on his bedding, which even if it is in a poor state will be useful to help him settle into his new home.

Remember, crates should never be used for long-term confinement other than at bed time.

Where Will Your Dog be Allowed in the House?

As with a puppy, the boundaries should be put in place from the start, so if you do not want your new dog going upstairs, for example, make that clear with a firm 'no' – or again, consider the use of a dog gate. It will obviously depend on what your new dog has been used to in his previous home as to how quickly he picks up the new house rules; however, many a time a new dog has come into my home and has never even considered the stairs as an option. Furniture can be more difficult with a dog that has previously been allowed on it, but persistence and patience

will soon teach him that this is not acceptable behaviour in this particular house.

Many a rescued German Shepherd has established himself as the dictator when not given clear guidelines from the start.

What Will Your Dog be Eating?

The previous owner or rescue should be able to tell you what your new dog is used to eating and when he is used to being fed. If this is not the case then it is best to start with a good quality complete kibble, fed twice a day.

What Else Will Your Dog Need, and What Else Needs to be Considered?

- Collar and lead
- Identity disc
- Toys
- Grooming brush
- Registration with your vet, and what routine treatment may be required in terms of vaccinations, worm and flea treatment
- Insurance
- If your new dog is microchipped, has the previous owner given you the necessary paperwork to update the details, or will they do the change? If your new dog is not microchipped this should be one of your first duties

- Local training and/or socialization groups in your area
- Secure garden
- A dog guard or harness to ensure secure travelling in the car

BRINGING YOUR DOG HOME

As with a puppy, the most important thing is not to overwhelm your new dog. So many times we tell new owners this simple rule and they ignore it: they expect their new dog to deal with a house full of visitors, they take it for numerous walks, pay a visit to the vet and the grooming parlour – and then he bites someone. This is because he is overwhelmed and stressed, as he has not been given the opportunity to discover and take in his new environment and family. With a rescue dog we even suggest not walking him out of his new home and garden for the first couple of days while he is adjusting. Mental stimulation can be just as tiring as physical exercise for a dog.

Travelling to his new home may be daunting for your new dog, and this is when he may be nervous and try to escape. So when collecting your new dog ensure that you have the collar fairly tight. Ideally use a half check collar which cannot be 'slipped', or have an additional slip lead attached to his collar and lead. Leave the lead on the dog when travelling, and if possible connect the lead to a fixing point in the car so you can get hold of the dog safely when opening the car door on arrival home. You can leave the lead on once you are in the house so there is something to get hold of should you need to catch him, without grabbing at his collar.

Introducing Your Dog to Resident Dog/s

It is to be hoped that you were given the opportunity for your current dog/s to meet your new dog before bringing him home, in a neutral place such as a park. Resident dog/s may not be as accepting of a new dog coming straight into their home uninvited as they are of a puppy.

Assuming that both/all the dogs have met before you bring the new dog home, avoid just walking your new dog in through the front door expecting everything to go smoothly: it is a

Life can be so stressful.

completely different situation for your resident dog/s to allow the new dog into their home, as opposed to simply meeting them in a park. Ideally you would meet up with your current dog/s at the local park and walk them all home together, allowing the resident dog/s to walk into the house before the new dog.

As with a puppy, it is important that the current dog/s is allowed pride of place, and it should be allowed to sniff the new dog calmly. As with a puppy, they will probably also reprimand the new dog if it does not conform to the rules and boundaries of the house. In fact a new dog will learn much more from your current dog/s than it will learn from you. Many a foster home will tell you that the resident dogs teach the foster dog all about house etiquette and boundaries with little human intervention.

If it is not possible to introduce your new dog to the other dog/s outside the home, then ensure that your new dog does not walk through the front door and come face to face with the resident dog/s. This could overwhelm and stress them all. Personally when bringing a new foster dog into the house, I ensure my dogs are shut in a room whilst I bring the new dog into the home and out into the garden. I let the new dog off the lead to toilet and sniff around and pick up my other dogs' scents. I then let my older bitch out to meet the new dog, and can gauge from

33

this introduction how confident and socialized the new dog is. Then one by one my other dogs are allowed out to say hello.

Many a time I have been told that a foster dog is 'dog aggressive', but in fact that dog has just never been allowed to meet other dogs in a near natural way. Obviously it is also important to know your own dogs and be able to read their body language so you can intervene if the situation does become tense.

Introducing Your Dog to the Resident Cat and Other Pets

The same rules apply to your new dog as they do with a puppy. Obviously a more mature dog is faster and more accurate than a puppy, so you need to be more aware and to ensure the dog is held firmly on the lead. Again, introductions may need to be done over time, depending how much interaction your new dog has had with cats in the past, and vice versa. The use of a basket muzzle is a good way of ensuring that your cat does not get injured should your new dog pull free to get to the cat. Never take on a dog who is known to be not good with cats, as this is a sure recipe for disaster. If a dog is unknown with cats, try and find out if it has a prey drive – if he likes chasing small furry things – because if he does, he is probably not a candidate for living with a cat harmoniously.

Careful introductions make for a better relationship.

4 CARING FOR YOUR GERMAN SHEPHERD

CARING FOR YOUR PUPPY

Early Learning

Puppies need lots of time and patience. You should already have a routine in place for when and what to feed puppy, and at this age his life revolves around eating, sleeping, playing and going to the toilet, and it can be in any order. One minute he may be playing happily, and the next he may just fall asleep, or he could be playing and suddenly realizes he needs to go to the toilet and will just stop immediately and do it wherever he happens to be. At this age your main priority is teaching him the boundaries in the home, and house training him. Socialization is an important factor too, but this may be restricted to start with if he hasn't had both of his initial vaccinations.

Probably the most important training words at this stage in puppy's life are 'no' and 'good', along with his name, though remember it is not just the word but the tone used that puppy will understand the most. 'No' is a firm but fair command if, for example, he is trying to jump on to furniture or is chewing something he shouldn't. The 'no' command is usually given at the same time as he is removed from a forbidden area, or something is taken from him. 'Good', as in 'good boy' or 'good girl', should be said in a fun and rewarding tone of voice if, for example, he has done his toilet in the garden or come to you when called, and should be accompanied with a stroke or a treat.

House Training Puppy

House training is usually the most daunting task facing a new puppy owner; however, a German Shepherd puppy is likely to pick up what is wanted more quickly than some other breeds

---

POSITIVE TRAINING FOR A BALANCED DOG

Commands should be consistent, and all family members should use the same commands from day one so puppy does not get confused. Gently but firmly train him to realize what is, and what is not acceptable. Try and avoid bad behaviour by distracting him with something positive, such as playing with a toy, rather than constantly reprimanding him so he feels you are always saying no. Positive training makes for a balanced dog in the long term. However, don't expect too much, too soon, as a puppy must learn his place, and he has to learn he cannot always have his own way.

---

because of his natural urge to want to please. We have discussed the use of crates for encouraging a clean puppy overnight, and will now consider how we can help puppy the rest of the time. The important tool is predicting and recognizing the signs that indicate puppy needs to go to the toilet. This usually follows having just woken up, having eaten, or having had a play session, so after any of these events, take him outside and encourage him to go to the toilet, maybe using a command he will later relate to, such as 'quickly'. Stay with him, and when he has done his toilet, praise him. Other signs that puppy needs to go to the toilet are if he starts sniffing or circling. If you are too late and catch him in the act in the house, say 'outside' in an urgent manner and take him outside. This tactic may well leave a trail through the house, but if you can get one drop outside so you can praise him, you have turned a negative into a positive.

Many people use newspaper or puppy pads when house training. Whilst this may protect the floors and make clearing up slightly easier, it is still encouraging puppy to do his toilet in the house, which defeats the purpose of house training. Some puppies may 'leak' when meeting new people or dogs, and this is actually their way of communicating their submissiveness, so it is best to ignore this. Also, there is little point in getting angry with puppy for making a mistake, as he will not associate the act of making the mess with your anger.

Feeding Puppy

You don't want your puppy to become possessive over his food bowl, but the practice of taking his bowl away and giving it back again a bit later, in the belief that this will make him less

Yes I know, I'm cute!

possessive, is, in my opinion, nothing more than teasing. How would you feel if someone walked up to the table and took your roast dinner away from you? Always encourage puppy to sit for his food, and then just sit with him while he is eating. Sometimes I will have my hand in his bowl and hand feed some of his food; this gives him the assurance that you are not a threat.

Socializing Puppy

Puppies, like children, need to learn body language and social manners both with people, other dogs and, if possible, other livestock.

Happy being handled.

Before puppy is allowed out in the big wide world, try to have different people and children visit him in his home. Once he is allowed out, then you can start taking him for short walks to allow him to see common-day things we take for granted, such as cars and bikes.

Puppy classes are especially useful as this gives puppy the chance to interact with other youngsters of different breeds, so as they grow older they do not become dominant, and have a more balanced attitude when meeting new dogs when out and about. Puppy classes should not be a free-for-all but rather about controlled play, which should be rewarded appropriately. Some people use food, others use toys to reward their puppy. There is no fixed rule as to which is right or wrong, though you could end up with a fat

A litter broadening their horizons.

puppy if you are constantly rewarding with food! Most working dogs are rewarded with their favourite toy.

Puppy will quickly learn that barking gets attention, even if it is only to be told to be quiet. The best way to deal with barking is to ignore it, as puppy may well decide your discontented attention is better than nothing at all. Barking in a class, however, may be a sign of stress rather than being naughty, so learn to 'read' your puppy. German Shepherds are typically anxious to please and can be incredibly sensitive to their owner's mood, so if disappointment is shown in your puppy, this may well be interpreted by puppy as that particular environment being stressful.

Handling Puppy

Puppy should be handled from day one, and should allow you to touch and examine every part of his body. Daily grooming will help in this, as he will get used to the brush on his body and will learn that it can be quite an enjoyable process as well. A well handled puppy will make life a lot easier for you when taking him to the vet for a check-up, or in an emergency. So the more people who have handled puppy, the better will be his response.

Bite Inhibition

Puppy will have needle-sharp teeth and he uses biting as a process of discovery to learn about his environment and how hard he can bite (bite inhibition). This is demonstrated by a litter of puppies playing and biting each other: if bitten too hard a puppy will yelp, and the offender will withdraw, realizing that his nip was too hard. Puppy will do the same to us, so the best thing to do is to give a yelp yourself, so he learns that whatever strength his bite, it is unacceptable. Puppies will see children as playmates, so if play is getting to the stage where biting may start, it is best to call time out, or distract puppy with another game or toy.

> **TOP TIP**
>
> Puppies chew mainly when teething and during adolescence. This is why it is important to give puppy plenty of toys or treats he can chew on whilst teaching him what he is and is not allowed to chew.
>
> Remember, prevention is better than cure.

Adolescence in a puppy can be a trying time, when his behaviour may deteriorate vastly. However, this phase does pass, like a teenager's moods, so try not to worry, and continue training and working through it with your puppy. At this stage it is quite common for young German Shepherds to be brought into the rescue centre, because that cuddly puppy has become uncontrollable, as his owner did not give him the right socialization experience and training when he was young.

Never be afraid to ask for help or advice from the breeder, your vet or trainer, as problems can usually be resolved if they are dealt with sooner rather than later.

All ears, tongue and paws!

CARING FOR YOUR DOG

Early Learning

It is important not to over-fuss or spoil your new dog. You should have been told of any behavioural problems or issues that perhaps he suffered from in the past, so you are aware of what you may have to deal with. But with time, experience and consistency it is possible to transform a rescue dog from being anxious or over-excitable into a calm family member. However sorry you feel for your new dog, depending on their past experiences, what they need more than anything is routine and security.

The other mistake that is commonly made when bringing home a new dog is spending too much time with him in the first few days. Whilst he should not be left alone for long periods, many people take time off work, for example, to 'settle' their new dog in – but as this is not the normal routine it will confuse him and can cause separation anxiety when he is actually left. This can be more severe in a German Shepherd, who is a loyal breed and can over-bond. It is better to try and stay in your normal routine, though perhaps making allowances, or if you do take time off, to follow some simple guidelines. For example, when you are at home with your new dog, ensure he is not with you all the time. A German Shepherd in a new home will often 'shadow' your every move, so now and again take time out and ask him to go to his bed while you are in another room. Pop out for ten minutes and leave him, gradually building up the length of time you are away. These are all simple things that will make your new dog more balanced and settled.

Do not be lulled into a false sense of security if your new dog appears to settle into your routine and way of life immediately. To start with he may well keep his head down until he has worked out the system. This is the honeymoon period: it is when a dog feels more secure in his new home that problems may occur, so don't be surprised or anxious, just take a step back and be fair and firm until he settles back into acceptable behaviour.

A new dog should be house trained, but may well make a mistake if he has been in kennels a while, or a male may well try to 'mark' his new home. As with a puppy, the way to react is to give a stern 'no' and take him straight outside. It is rare for this to happen, however, and after a couple of times of being told off it usually stops.

Feeding Your Dog

Don't be surprised if your new dog doesn't eat or is picky with his food for the first couple of days. A German Shepherd won't starve himself, so don't try tempting him with a variety of foods, but keep to what is to be his normal diet. Do not leave food down. Feed at the normal time, and if your dog is not interested, remove the bowl until his next feeding time is due.

Always ensure there is fresh water available, as a German Shepherd tends to drink a lot, especially when stressed. You may also notice him panting heavily, but this is quite normal.

Depending on your new dog's past, he may have food possessive issues. As with a puppy, always ask your new dog to sit for his food, place the bowl on the floor and let him eat undisturbed.

TOP TIP

Never feel ashamed or too weak to ask for advice, especially if you have taken on a rescue dog, as many problems and issues will already have been encountered by the rescue and they should be able to steer you in the right direction. Your vet and trainer should also be able to give you advice on many things.

Settled for sure.

A happy family at dinner time.

If possessiveness is an issue there are methods of working with the problem, including hand feeding him little and often throughout the day, to reinforce the idea of the human being the provider and not the taker.

Don't panic if your dog doesn't go to the toilet the first day – we have seen bitches that have not relieved themselves for a couple of days. It appears that sometimes this is because they are unsure of where they are allowed to go, and at others just because they can hold it. Males tend not to be able to 'hold on' for so long.

Socializing Your Dog

German Shepherds are naturally protective and territorial, so visitors to your home must be introduced properly so your new dog accepts them being there. He may not bark for the first few days or weeks until he truly feels that this is his home, so don't assume he will just accept a stranger in. It is best to put him into another room when a visitor comes into the house. Once the visitor is seated and the new dog is calm (if he was barking), let the dog into the room with a lead on. If he is food orientated, your visitor can give him a treat to reinforce this encounter as a positive experience.

GROUP SOCIALIZATION

Training or socialization groups are a great way to introduce your new dog to other dogs and breeds once he is settled in his new environment. Whilst a breed-specific class or group means you will be socializing with people that understand the German Shepherd, you also want your dog to be social with all breeds of dog, large and small.

Handling Your Dog

Whilst we recommend that you do not over-fuss or crowd your new dog in the first couple of days, he must accept you touching and handling him all over. This is a matter of trust, and also makes vet examinations easier. This process should be built up slowly, and should start with daily grooming gently over the back. As he learns to trust you more, you can move on to other areas of his body. German Shepherds do not like having their feet grabbed, especially by a stranger, so do not attempt to dry your dog's feet with a towel, for example, until he fully trusts you. The other area they can be less keen on you brushing is their 'trousers', as you are out of their view and in a personal area that is important to dogs when they meet and greet one another. Your handling of this area could be misinterpreted as a clumsy or rude introduction.

Your new dog should allow you to take toys from him, though some may be possessive. Do not allow this to turn into a battle, but distract him with something else, such as a treat. Ask him to sit for the treat, remove the toy from his area, and then reward him.

Exercising Your Dog

German Shepherds are active dogs and require a substantial amount of exercise. Having allowed your new dog a couple of days to settle in, you should ensure he is kept on the lead for the first couple of weeks until recall has been fully established in the garden and he has fully accepted and learnt to trust you as his owner. The use of a long training lead is also helpful as you can practice recall when out whilst giving the dog more freedom to explore. If you have the time it is useful to have a little obedience training session in the garden before going out for a walk, as not only will this persuade your dog to focus on you, it will also help calm him down if he is being over-exuberant. A plastic bottle with some stones in to shake is a useful tool to carry if you need to regain your dog's focus.

INSURANCE, IDENTIFICATION AND NEUTERING

Insurance

Veterinary care in an emergency or through illness can be very expensive, especially when you

Most German Shepherds love water!

consider some of the common health issues associated with a German Shepherd, such as 'bloat' (*see* Chapter 12 'Breed Specific: Ailments and Diseases'). And suppose your dog injures somebody or damages something? This could lead to a heavy compensation claim.

SHOP AROUND FOR INSURANCE DEALS

You should insure your new dog as soon as possible, and always read the small print and understand what you are paying for. Do not choose the cheapest without checking it gives you all you require. Price comparison websites are a good place to start, also recommendations from other dog owners. The cost of a policy is governed by the dog's breed, age, where you live and what you want covered.

Just as when insuring your car, there are many options available to you on an insurance policy, but at the very least you should ensure that your dog is covered for third party liability. This can be done through some home insurance policies. The next important thing is cover for vets' fees. This will not cover the costs of routine treatments such as vaccinations, but it will pay out against accident and/or illness, depending on what level you choose. There will be a waiting period before you can make a claim, and an excess can be applied.

If a dog has a pre-existing medical condition this will be excluded. It is possible, however, although quite difficult, to transfer an existing policy for such a condition from an old owner to a new one. A number of different policies are offered for vets' fees: lifetime cover, which will cover a condition for the life of the pet up to a certain limit each year; per condition, which will cover an individual condition up to a limit over any period of time; and twelve-month cover, which will run up to a monetary limit or a twelve-month limit for each condition.

Other benefits offered by insurance policies are:

- loss from theft or straying
- advertising and reward if your dog goes missing
- death
- boarding kennel fees in the event that, for example, you are rushed to hospital
- holiday cancellation
- overseas travel
- legal fees

Very often a quote will be stacked with these options, but by asking for irrelevant ones to be removed you can bring your premium down.

Identification

The old-fashioned method of permanently identifying a dog was by tattooing it in the inside of the ear. Whilst some breeders do still use this method, the tattoos can become hard to read over time, and there have been cases of stolen dogs having their ears removed so they cannot be identified.

Microchipping your dog is the best way forwards, and will be compulsory by law from 6 April 2016. If your dog is not microchipped, then your vet or a trained implanter will be able to do this very easily. The procedure involves a quick injection that inserts a microchip the size of a grain of rice between the dog's shoulder blades. Each microchip has a unique fifteen-digit number, which must then be registered with the database company. As the owner of the dog, you are responsible for ensuring that the microchip is initially registered to the database company, and that the details are updated if you move or if ownership changes.

Should your dog ever be lost or stolen, he can be scanned for his microchip number and quickly reunited with you. Remember to report your dog lost or stolen with the relevant database company as soon as possible, along with the local police, local animal wardens, local vets and rescues.

By law, all dogs when out in a public place should wear a collar and an identity tag with your name, address and postcode on it. Many people also include a telephone number. Whilst this is perhaps seen as an old-fashioned way of identifying a dog to their owner, it does mean that if your dog has managed to get out and is found by someone just a few streets away, they can quickly contact you, rather than having to get your dog to a vet or animal warden to be scanned for a microchip.

It is also now possible to have your dog DNA profiled. Whilst not an instantaneous test of who is the keeper, should there be a dispute it is the ultimate evidence of a dog's identity.

Neutering

'Neutering' is a general term used to describe spaying a female and castrating a male, and there are many reasons as to why this should be done. The most important of these is to reduce the number of unwanted dogs in this country. A female can have up to two litters a year, and a German Shepherd can produce up to ten pups a litter. With the number of unwanted dogs and strays at an all-time high, as a responsible owner you should not leave anything to chance. German Shepherds may not be socially mature until they are three years of age, but they are sexually mature from around seven months.

There are also definite benefits to neutering your dog. Having an unneutered female can be quite stressful, as they come into season every six months, their season lasts for up to three weeks, and not only will they spot (bleed), but they must be kept on the lead and kept away from entire males. Your calm girl can turn into a veritable sex maniac, trying anything to find herself a man. Neutering a bitch can also help with temperament, as her hormones will settle down. Neuter-ing a male and thus reducing the testosterone levels can influence the temperament of a male dog, especially the younger the dog, though this is not always the case.

There are also medical benefits to neutering your dog, and it is quite common now for dogs to be neutered between the ages of six and twelve months. If a bitch is spayed before her first sea-son she is much less likely to develop mamma-ry tumours later in life. Spaying your bitch also prevents cancer of the ovaries or womb infec-tions (pyometra), which are often fatal. Castrat-ing your male dog prevents testicular cancer and reduces the risk of prostate problems. If a bitch has had a season your vet will probably suggest that she is spayed three months after she has come 'off' – thus midway between her twice yearly seasons – to reduce the risks dur-ing the operation of increased blood flow in the area.

HOME OR AWAY, AND TRAVELLING

Remember when booking your holiday to make the necessary arrangements for your dog well in advance as well, as good care can be hard to come by for your German Shepherd.

If you are planning on taking your dog with you somewhere in the UK then ensure that where you are staying allows dogs, and if you have more than one, how many, and of course the cost. It is also a good idea to check out the surrounding area for dog-friendly pubs, beaches and/or walks. For this to be a viable option your German Shepherd should be sociable with new dogs and people and should not be a constant barker. The last thing you need is to be asked to

---

WHEN TO NEUTER

There are many myths as to why and when you should or should not neuter your dog: my dog will get fat; my bitch needs to have a season before she is spayed; my bitch needs to have a litter before she is spayed; my male dog must be two years of age before being castrated otherwise he will not grow properly. However, there is no scientific evidence to support any of these statements, and yes, each dog is individual: but discuss with your vet sooner rather than later so as to give your dog a healthier life.

leave because your dog is causing a nuisance or disturbance – but this has been known.

There are many options for your dog's care nowadays, including commercial boarding kennels, dog sitters or boarding your dog in a carer's home. If you are very lucky, you will have a friend or family member who can move in with your dog(s), or take them into their home while you are away: this is much the preferred option, as your German Shepherd will be in an environment they know and with people whom they know and trust.

Road Travel

Travelling in a car can be very stressful for some dogs, and it is important to accustom your German Shepherd to the car from an early stage. Many rescue dogs that are somewhat older and wiser love the car, as they know it usually means a nice walk or a visit to friends. From day one, tra-velling in the car should be a positive experience for your dog. If your puppy or dog is not used to travelling, trips should be short to start with, and built up over a period of time. Do not assume that your six-month-old pup, which has only ever been in the car to go to the vet's, will be happy travelling for four hours to go on holiday! If your dog suffers from car sickness, remember not to feed him for twelve hours before travelling.

Your dog should be secure in the vehicle at all times, because should there be an accident, 40kg plus of German Shepherd flying through the interior of a car can cause an awful lot of damage. They also have a tendency to want to join you in the front and help you drive, which of course is very dangerous. Ideally your dog will have a good space in the boot of the car, and will be separated by a dog guard or crate. If you travel your dog on the back seat, it should be safely secured with a seatbelt harness.

A proper dog guard means safe travel.

RISK OF HEATSTROKE

Never leave your dog unattended in a car, especially in hot weather. Every year dogs die from heatstroke because their owner has left them for five minutes while they popped into a shop.

Consider the weather, because if it is very hot and sunny, even in an air-conditioned car, your dog will need shade from direct sunlight. If you do not have air conditioning, then a good flow of air should pass through the car for your dog. You should ensure you have a bowl and plenty of water available just in case. Plan for toilet breaks, and also to allow your dog to stretch his legs and have a drink. Use a cooler bag or thermos to keep his water cool. Always keep your dog on the lead when you stop, because however obedient they may be normally, a pit stop at motorway services can be quite stressful.

Boarding Kennels

As a general rule, dogs adapt to a new environment fairly quickly, especially if they have a rounded temperament and nature. German Shepherds are known to over-bond with their owners, so some can be prone to stress in kennels, which may become apparent by constant pacing and crying, or through guarding their kennel space from strangers.

The cost of a kennels is based on a twenty-four-hour charge and can vary greatly depending on where you are in the country and the services offered. Do not assume because one kennel is more expensive than another that it is the better one! The best way of finding a good boarding kennel is by word of mouth and recommendations.

You should ask to visit the kennels you intend to use so you can see where your dog will be staying and the facilities available, such as, are they able to run in an enclosure, or how many walks do they get a day and where? Chat to staff to ascertain their experience with the breed, and the feeding and exercise routines. Kennels will normally include food in the price, but should be happy to feed your dog's normal diet if it is supplied to them.

Boarding kennels must have a licence issued by their local authority, and one of the requirements for this licence is that dogs coming in are fully vaccinated to prevent the spread of disease.

A rescue volunteer experiencing a stay in kennels for a fundraising event.

Some authorities are more flexible than others, as are some kennels, but the standard requirement is that your German Shepherd's vaccination card is completely up to date. If your dog is not vaccinated, plan ahead because they will need an initial vaccination, a second vaccination two to four weeks after, depending on the vaccination type, and then some kennels will require a further two-week grace time before the dog is allowed into the kennels. In some cases a boarding kennel will also require your dog to have had the kennel cough vaccination, which again will require a period of grace before they allow him entry.

If your dog has never been into kennels before it is a good idea not to 'throw him in at the deep end'. Ideally you would leave him for twenty-four hours initially to see how he gets on, and then for maybe a few days, before you disappear for a fortnight. Always ensure the kennels know all

your German Shepherd's likes and dislikes, and give them an emergency contact telephone number, along with the details of your vet.

Dog Sitters and Boarders

This is a fast expanding industry and is not answerable to any governing body. Dog sitters will actually stay in your home with your dog, whilst dog boarders are people who take your dog into their own home while you are away.

Having a dog sitter come into your home has the distinct advantage that your dog stays in their own environment with their normal routine. It can also be quite cost effective if you have numerous pets, besides which your house is not sitting empty for a fortnight. Again, recommendation and word of mouth is the best way to get a good dog sitter. You may find an individual who offers this service, but it is worth considering such things as, for example, whether they

Compatibility is key.

hold insurance should anything go wrong. There are plenty of agencies out there offering dog sitters, and whilst they may charge a little more, you should receive a comprehensive contract and be covered by their insurance for any mishaps. As with anything nowadays, read the small print and check the details as to each party's responsibilities.

Sending your dog to a dog boarder can be more comfortable for your German Shepherd than kennels, but considerations need to be made as to how many other dogs your dog will be with, and their compatibility. Dog boarders may need a licence from their local authority, depending on the number of dogs they board at any one time – the fewer the better from your dog's point of view! Again, consider insurance and the contract.

Travelling Abroad

Rules regarding travelling abroad with your German Shepherd are subject to change, so plans should be made well in advance, and you should check the regulations for the country you are visiting. Information can be found on the DEFRA website. Your vet should be able to advise you on

---

REGULATIONS FOR TRAVELLING A DOG ABROAD

You must comply with the following regulations when travelling your dog abroad.

Your dog must be microchipped, and this must be done prior to the rabies vaccination. You can add your holiday contact details to the microchip database while you are away, so should you be parted from your dog you can be tracked down wherever you are staying.

Your dog must be vaccinated against rabies at least twenty-one days prior to travel. UK vaccinations for rabies have a validity period of two to three years, however some countries may require more frequent vaccinations.

Your dog must be issued with a pet passport by your vet, which must include:

- your pet's date of birth and age
- the microchip number, the date it was put in, and where it is on your pet's body
- vaccination date
- vaccine product name
- vaccine batch number
- the date the vaccination is valid until

The final requirement is when coming back to the UK. Your dog must be treated for tapeworm within one to five days (24 and 120 hours) before you are scheduled to enter the UK, and the vet must record the following details in the 'Echinococcus treatment' section of your dog's pet passport:

- the name and manufacturer of the product used to treat your dog
- the date and time they treated your dog
- their stamp and signature

The treatment must have praziquantel or an equivalent as its active ingredient.

health requirements, but you will need to check with your mode of transport for specific regulations for travelling by plane, train or ferry.

If travelling by Le Shuttle, your dog can stay in the car with you for the short journey.

If travelling by ferry, most companies will not allow your dog up on deck with you, and he needs to stay in the vehicle. If this is the case it is essential to ensure he has adequate ventilation and water. Some ferry companies will allow you to check on your dog during the crossing, but if not, ensure there is a member of staff on the car deck at all times to monitor him.

If travelling by plane, you will need to check the regulations with the airline, and a large factor will depend on whether you are accompanying your dog. If this is the case, most airlines will allow you to book in your dog as excess baggage rather than cargo. Dogs must travel in IATA-approved crates, so check with the airline about measuring your dog for the right crate size.

And finally, don't forget to check that your final destination is dog friendly before making any travel arrangements!

Moving House

Moving house can be stressful for all of you, including your German Shepherd: it can be disorientating, and may lead to behavioural problems, or even to him going missing. It is therefore important to try and keep his routine as normal as possible up to the move. Plan ahead, and get him a new identity tag with your new address, and register with a local vet if you are moving out of the area. Hopefully you will already have checked out your new area, so will also have a good idea where you can walk your dog, and will have sourced the amenities available to you.

When packing, try and keep your dog's living area as normal as possible until the last moment, and ensure his bed, toys and other belongings are kept readily to hand. Make sure he is kept securely in one area of the house while moving furniture out, as he may slip past a removal man.

On arrival at your new home, try to settle your dog with his belongings into a secure area while you bring furniture into the house. Think about giving him a new toy or chew so he relates his new environment with nice things, and also have something to keep him distracted while you are busy. Change his identity tag, and ensure you now update his microchip details to your new address.

To start with, keep your dog on his lead when in the garden until you have fully checked that the fencing is secure and there are no escape routes. It is at this stage that your German Shepherd will be very interested in exploring all the new smells, and may wander off without realizing he has crossed the boundary of his new property.

FIREWORKS

German Shepherds can be very sensitive to noise so can become very stressed during the firework period (which seems to last a minimum of three weeks). You can tell your dog is upset if he tries hiding, messing in the house, digging up the carpet or barking incessantly. The effects of his behaviour can be cumulative over time, resulting in an increase in seemingly irrational and uncontrolled behaviour. It can also have the effect of elevating his response to other sudden noises, such as thunder.

We cannot stop the fireworks but some simple rules will help your dog in the long term:

- Ensure you walk him in daylight before the fireworks start
- Ignore unusual behaviour such as panting, shaking or whining. If you worry and fuss over him you will only exacerb the problem
- Ensure all windows and doors are closed, and pull all the curtains closed, to lessen the noise and flashes of light
- Turn on the television to dull the noise of the fireworks
- Distract him with a new toy or chew
- Try not to leave him by himself as he will be more relaxed and confident with you around
- Do not punish him for unusual behaviour as this will only make him more uneasy
- If he is considerably stressed, then consider long-term sound desensitization, and speak to your vet to see if they can prescribe something to help calm him.

DOG LAWS

Dog legislation is constantly changing and is in great need of a major overhaul. One of the biggest problems is that the main burden of enforcing dog laws falls to the local authorities, and in these economic times of cutback, many such authorities do not have an animal warden (previously known as a dog warden) but in fact contract the work out, or have such a small budget that their staff can only cover the bare minimum of duties expected.

The normal duties and responsibilities of animal wardens can include:

- dealing with stray dogs
- enforcing dog-related legislation
- the promotion of responsible dog ownership
- dealing with dog fouling
- dealing with noise pollution caused by dogs
- education
- liaising and working alongside other agencies

Whilst the position of an animal warden is powerful, because of their low number and limited available budget, many concentrate on dealing with immediate problems such as stray dogs. They just do not have the manpower to 'police' all they are responsible for, which in April 2016 will also include compulsory microchipping.

A complete tidy-up of legislation is needed in order to achieve the following:

- Prevent back-street breeders producing so many unwanted dogs, with stronger legislation and enforcement
- Control the number of dogs coming in from abroad, exacerbating the problem of an already saturated country
- Update the Animal Welfare Act 2006, which is currently interpreted by many in a position of power as meaning that if a dog has clean water, food and shelter it is safe, which is not always the case. It needs to provide for 'the ability to exhibit normal behaviour patterns', which needs more definition and enforcement. Just because a two-year-old German Shepherd has food and water and lives in the house, if it is never exercised or given the opportunity to socialize, has its owner really provided a duty of care to it?
- Update the Dangerous Dogs (Amendment) Act 1997, which still blames specific breeds rather than the deed. This act has been responsible for the death of many a much loved family dog, just because it falls into the category of 'Pit Bull type'. Whilst the Anti-Social Behaviour, Crime and Policing Act 2014 attempts to deal with the deed, it has not given the banned breeds any form of respite. It is also surprising, in this day and age, that DNA testing is not accepted evidence of a dog not being 'type', but the decision is completely left to a particular officer's judgement

The laws below are current at the time of writing; they are given in their most basic form.

The Animal Welfare Act 2006
This act tackles acts of cruelty, neglect, mutilation, tail docking, animal fighting and the giving of pets as prizes. In addition to this, it introduces a duty of care for all pet owners to provide the following for their animals:

- a suitable environment
- a suitable diet
- the ability to exhibit normal behaviour patterns
- protection from pain, suffering, injury and disease
- consideration of the animal's needs to be housed with, or apart from, other animals

The Clean Neighbourhoods and Environment Act 2005
This act means that you could be fined up to £1,000 for breaching dog control orders. Local authorities can make orders for standard offences, such as failing to clear up after your dog, and not keeping a dog on a lead in a designated area. It also updated the law on stray dogs by transferring the responsibility for strays from the police to local authorities. Dog wardens are obliged to seize stray dogs, and they only need wait for seven days for the dog's owner to reclaim the

Microchipping your dog can ensure you are reunited quickly.

dog, and then they are allowed to put that dog to sleep. Destruction and re-homing policies will vary across local authorities.

Byelaws on Noisy Animals

If your dog's barking causes a serious nuisance to neighbours, the local authority can serve a noise abatement notice, which if unheeded can result in fines and legal expenses.

Breeding and Sale of Dogs (Welfare) Act 1999

Breeders who breed five or more litters per year must be licensed by their local authority. Breeders with fewer litters must also be licensed if they are carrying out a business of breeding dogs for sale.

Licensed breeders must:

- not mate a bitch less than twelve months old
- not whelp more than six litters from a bitch
- not whelp two litters within a twelve-month period from the same bitch
- keep accurate records
- not sell a puppy until it is at least eight weeks of age, other than to the keeper of a licensed pet shop or a Scottish rearing establishment

The sale of puppies in pet shops is currently under debate by MPs.

The Control of Dogs Order 1992

This act makes it mandatory for any dog in a public place to wear a collar with the name and address of the owner engraved or written on it, or engraved on a tag. A telephone number is optional but advisable. At the time of writing the fine for not complying is £5,000.

The Dangerous Dogs Act 1991 (section 3)

It is a criminal offence to allow a dog to be 'dangerously out of control' in a public place, in a

This dog could be perceived as dangerous.

place where it is not permitted to be, and some other areas. A 'dangerously out of control' dog can be defined as a dog that has injured someone, or a dog that a person has grounds for reasonable apprehension that it may do so.

If your dog injures a person it can be seized by the police, and your penalty may include a prison sentence and/or a ban on keeping dogs. There is also an automatic presumption that your dog will be destroyed unless you can persuade the court it is not a danger, in which case it may be subject to a control order, such as keeping it on a lead and muzzled when out.

The Dangerous Dogs (Amendment) Act 1997

The 1991 Act was amended by this act, which removed the mandatory destruction order provisions on banned breeds and re-opened the 'Index of Exempted Dogs' for dogs which the courts consider would not pose a risk to the public. The courts were given discretion on sentencing, with only courts able to direct that a dog be placed on the list of exempted dogs.

The banned breeds are:

- Pit Bull Terrier
- Fila Brasileiro
- Dogo Argentino
- Japanese Tosa

The Dangerous Dogs (Amendment) Act 2014

The key areas of change in this act are as follows:

- the extension of section three to apply to all places including private property
- the extension of section three to apply to assistance dogs
- extended rights of seizure
- increased sentencing
- courts' new assessment in deciding whether a dog is a danger to public safety
- civil proceedings

The new penalties are as follows:

- You can be fined up to £5,000 and/or sent to prison for up to six months if your dog is dangerously out of control. You may not be allowed to own a dog in the future, and your dog may be destroyed
- If you let your dog injure someone you can be sent to prison for up to five years and/or fined. If you deliberately use your dog to injure someone you could be charged with 'malicious wounding'
- If you allow your dog to kill someone you can be sent to prison for up to fourteen years and/or get an unlimited fine
- If you allow your dog to injure a guide dog you can be sent to prison for up to three years and/or fined

This makes it more important than ever to be a responsible dog owner.

Anti-Social Behaviour (ASB), Crime and Policing Act 2014

This act came into force on 20 October 2014 and gives the police, local authorities and certain others designated, the power to tackle irresponsible dog owners.

Community Protection Notice (CPN): Low level offences, such as an owner failing to control a dog and causing a nuisance to others/other animals. The owner can be required to microchip/neuter/muzzle/keep dog on a lead, attend training classes, attend behavioural classes, put up signage. The aim is that the quick intervention process allows early engagement with individuals to improve their understanding of responsible dog ownership and the training and welfare requirements of the dog, thereby improving the behaviour of both the owner and the dog. A breach can result in a £2,500 fine for owners.

Injunctions: Higher level incidents, such as attacks or incidents involving other animals. The owner can be required to microchip/neuter/muzzle/keep dog on a lead, attend training classes, attend behavioural classes, prohibited access to certain areas at certain times. The injunction can offer quick relief to victims, and nip problems in the bud before they escalate. A breach can result in an unlimited fine, or imprisonment of up to two years.

Criminal Behaviour Order (CBO): Serious and continuing ASB, such as when dogs are used to intimidate people. The owner can be required to microchip the dog, neuter it, muzzle it, keep it on a lead, undertake compulsory training; it limits the number of dogs an individual can own, and prohibits access to certain areas at certain times. The CBO can be run alongside other behaviour that can have a serious and harmful impact on victims and communities. A breach can result in a summary conviction of six months' imprisonment, and/or an unlimited fine, or both, or an indicted conviction of five years' imprisonment, and/or an unlimited fine, or both.

Public Spaces Protection Orders (PSPO): This will replace and permit similar restrictions as Dog Control Orders under the Clean Neighbourhoods and Environment Act 2005. Prohibitions or requirements can be made to exclude dogs, require faeces to be picked up, have dogs on a lead, and/or restrict the number of dogs walked by one person. The primary purpose of the PSPO is to deal with anti-social behaviour that adversely affects other people using the same public space. A breach can result in a summary conviction with a level 3 fine of £1,000, or the issue of a fixed penalty notice of up to £100 from a police constable or a local authority.

Road Traffic Act 1988

It is an offence to have a dog on a designated road without it being held on a lead. Dogs travelling in vehicles should not be a nuisance, or in any way distract the driver during a journey.

Animals Act 1971

You could be liable for damage caused by your dog under this act, if it was the result of some degree of negligence.

Dogs (Protection of Livestock) Act 1953

Your dog must not worry (chase or attack) livestock (cattle, sheep, goats, pigs, horses and poultry) on agricultural land. Farmers have the right to stop your dog even by shooting it in certain circumstances.

Dogs and livestock can mix happily.

5 HEALTHCARE AND NUTRITION

The German Shepherd's most outstanding characteristic is its loyalty, and for this reason it is important that it is not allowed to become too dependent on one member of the family – so ensure that all family members are involved in its daily care and feeding.

THE HEALTHY DOG

We should know our dogs so well that we recognize when they are not themselves without having to 'MOT' them, but some signs can be more difficult to spot than others, especially if you have a number of dogs to care for, and particularly when out exercising them.

The signs of a healthy dog are as follows:

- In behaviour he should be alert and ready to go for a walk or play
- Eyes should be bright and alert with no discharge
- Nose should be cold and wet with no discharge, although a little clear fluid is normal
- Ears should be responsive to sounds and held erect (unless of course you have a naturally floppy-eared German Shepherd). They should be free of wax and unpleasant smell, and silky in texture
- Coat should be glossy and soft to the touch. A dog's coat will smell, but this should be their normal doggy smell
- Teeth should be white and smooth; however, as a dog ages they will become dull and yellow with plaque and tartar formation, depending on how well you have cared for them
- Claws should be at ground level, but not too long or broken
- Stools should be passed at least twice a day, and should be firm and free of blood
- Urination should be regular but not excessive, and of a normal colour with very little odour

- Weight should be 'ideal' in that you can feel the dog's ribs but not see them, and he has a 'waist'
- Eating should be normal

Alert and ready to go!

NUTRITION AND YOUR DOG'S DIET

Diet has a direct and indirect effect on your dog's behaviour and physiology, so it is important to understand what you are feeding him.

There is much controversy regarding the best diet for a German Shepherd. One argument

Very thin: BCS 1.

Obese: BCS 5.

maintains that a dog is a carnivore and therefore a diet of raw meat is best; however, a dog is actually an omnivore, because when he catches a rabbit and devours it, he will eat every last scrap including the digestive system, which consists of ingested vegetable matter – and this was also true of his ancestor the wolf. In fact there is no right or wrong diet, and no scientific evidence on this subject at present. The important thing is to ensure that your dog receives all his nutritional requirements in the correct amounts.

In terms of feeding commercial dog food, it can be a case of 'you get what you pay for'. If a food is lacking in the nutrients that the body craves, the dog may well overeat to compensate, and you end up with a fat and unhealthy dog. Obesity in dogs is an increasingly common problem and can lead to other medical problems, so ensure that you feed your dog only what is necessary. German Shepherds should be lean and muscular, not fat and flabby.

Bodyweight and body condition score (BCS) should be regularly monitored. Dogs whose nutrition is well managed are alert, have an ideal BCS with a stable, optimal bodyweight and healthy coat. Stools should be firm, well formed, and medium to dark brown in colour.

There is a wide range of complete dry foods on the market, though the quality varies considerably. Premium dry foods may seem more expensive, but can in fact work out cheaper in the long run because you will have a healthy dog. Some dogs may not be accustomed to complete dry food, so to encourage them the food can be soaked in warm water to soften it, or mixed in some wet food.

As with the dry food, there is a wide range of semi-moist and wet food on the market, ranging in quality and price. However, if you intend to feed purely tinned or wet food be aware that your dog is not getting the chewing it needs to help its teeth. All German Shepherds need to chew: this helps jaw development and healthy tooth growth in puppies, and keeps the teeth clean in adults. A wide variety of dog chews is available – though never leave your dog alone

Complete dry kibble.

54

with a chew, especially rawhide chews, as these can lodge at the back of the throat and cause suffocation. Also consider that natural bones can splinter into small sharp pieces.

Whatever you choose to feed your dog, avoid changing his diet once it is established, as German Shepherds can have quite a sensitive digestive system, and any changes should be done gradually. It is recommended that you feed your dog two small meals a day, although many German Shepherds are fed just once a day with no adverse effect – and of course you should allow a good hour after eating before exercise.

Remember when feeding that water should be available at all times.

Ensure your dog's food bowl is clean, and do not refill half-empty bowls but ensure the food is fresh at each mealtime. Store your dog's food in a cool, dry place, and if a tin is opened, cover it and put it into the fridge until the next meal, when it should be allowed to reach room temperature before feeding it.

Semi-moist food.

Whatever you choose to feed your dog, ensure you follow the recommended guide on the packaging. Adjustments to these guides may be matched to the individual animal and its response to feeding. Some dogs appear to be sensitive or intolerant to certain ingredients and additives, which can lead to a variety of problems including lethargy, aggressive or hyperactive behaviour, skin and ear problems, loose stools or diarrhoea, and bloating. In extreme cases the dog can get colitis: if this happens you should consult your vet immediately.

As with children, the most common food intolerances appear to be colourings, sugars, wheat, milk and soya. If you suspect intolerance to a certain food, try excluding it from your dog's diet; however, always consult your vet in case there is something of deeper concern to account for, such as IBD (*see* Chapter 12 'Breed-Specific Ailments and Diseases').

Nutrition and Health

Dogs exhibit omnivorous feeding behaviour and so their diet should be composed of proteins, carbohydrates, fats, vitamins, minerals and water, in the correct proportions. A dog food that meets all these requirements is called a 'complete' or 'balanced' diet. Dogs need a careful balance of calcium/phosphorus, and sufficient vitamin D for strong bones and healthy teeth. Fats and oils are a source of energy, which is important for active and large breed dogs. Protein is required to maintain the body muscles.

Proteins: Consist of twenty-three different amino acids, known as the 'building blocks' of the tissues. The dog's body can manufacture thirteen of these amino acids, but the other ten must be supplied in their diet and are known as 'essential amino acids'. In general, animal proteins (meat) have a higher biological value than vegetable proteins (corn).

Fats: Supply energy and essential fatty acids, and transport the fat-soluble vitamins A, D, E and K. Fats also make a diet more palatable to a dog. If the fat becomes rancid, the vitamins A and E are destroyed; this is why many dog foods contain natural or synthetic additives called 'antioxidants', because these prevent fat rancidity and prolong shelf life.

Carbohydrates: Provide energy, and are made up primarily of sugars, starches and cellulose (fibre). They are supplied in the diet from plant sources such as grains and vegetables. The sugars are 100 per cent digestible; however the starches, which are the largest part of most plant carbohydrates, need to be cooked before they can be digested by a dog and are therefore of any nutritional use. Fibre is not digestible, but can help prevent constipation and diarrhoea, and maintains gastro-intestinal health.

Vitamins: Are necessary for many of the body's chemical reactions. Vitamins A, D, E and K need fat in the diet to be absorbed by the body, but the B-complex vitamins dissolve in water so are readily absorbed by the body. Vitamin C is not needed in the diet of a healthy dog as they make it themselves through a process known as 'de-novo synthesis'.

Minerals: Are needed by the body for structural building and chemical reactions. They must be given in the correct proportions, as damage can be done by over-supplementation; this is particularly true of calcium and phosphorus.

Water: The most important nutrient for all animals. Healthy dogs regulate their intake as long as clean, fresh water is always available. A dog can lose all its body fat and half of its protein and survive, but if it loses only one tenth of its body water it may die.

Feeding a complete balanced diet formulated for the given life stage, together with a supply of fresh water, is all that most dogs need to stay nutritionally healthy.

Types of Dog Food

Complete and balanced dog foods most commonly come in three forms: dry, semi-moist and wet (tinned). Whilst all may contain the essential nutrients the dog needs, the primary difference is the amount of water in a product. Tinned foods are sometimes more palatable, while dry foods may be more economical.

If a product is marked as 'complementary', then it needs to be fed alongside another product to ensure the dog receives all the nutrition it requires. For example, there are many tinned products on the market which should be fed with a complementary dry mixer.

Special diets: Are scientifically formulated for dogs with specific conditions or diseases. They should only be used under the advice of your vet.

Homemade diets: Should be prepared from recipes that are nutritionally complete and balanced by experienced nutritionists. Feeding single food items or diets consisting of an indiscriminate mixture of human foods often results in dietary-induced disease.

Raw Diets

As with all other options of diet, it is important to ensure that the dog receives all its nutritional requirements from a raw diet. There is a growing trend within the German Shepherd community to feed a raw diet, and if this is the route you choose, you should research the subject as there are many sources of advice to be found. A good raw diet could include:

ABNORMAL SYMPTOMS

You should ask for advice if any of the following symptoms are displayed by your dog:

- Frequent upset stomach
- Wind
- Allergic reactions to external factors
- Stools very smelly or very frequent, or large motions
- Underweight
- Over-active or under-active
- Eating plants, grass, tissues or sticks
- Eating own or another dog's faeces
- Nibbling, chewing or scratching at the base of the tail, feet or abdomen

---

OPPOSITE: *Raw diet feeding plan.*

FOOD PLAN to GET GOING - 6 weeks

	BREAKFAST	DINNER		BREAKFAST	DINNER
WEEK 1			**WEEK 4**		
MONDAY	Minced lamb tripe	Chunky lamb tripe		Half a rabbit	Half a rabbit
TUESDAY	RMB – lamb ribs	Minced lamb tripe		Lamb tripe with egg	Chunky lamb tripe
WEDNESDAY	Minced lamb tripe	Chunky lamb tripe		RMB lamb neck	Minced lamb + liver
THURSDAY	Minced lamb tripe	Chunky lamb tripe		Chicken back + liver	Chicken mince (no more bone)
FRIDAY	RMB – lamb ribs	Minced lamb tripe		Ox tripe with egg	Chunky ox tripe
SATURDAY	Minced lamb tripe	Chunky lamb tripe		Lamb shoulder bone with kidney	Lamb heart, lung
SUNDAY	Lamb neck	Chunky lamb tripe		Chicken wings /necks	Chicken gizzards with egg
WEEK 2			**WEEK 5**		
MONDAY	RMB lamb ribs	Minced lamb		RMB veal	Veal muscle meat with liver / trachea
TUESDAY	Chunky lamb tripe	Minced lamb tripe		Ox or lamb tripe with egg	Chunky ox or lamb tripe
WEDNESDAY	Minced lamb	Minced lamb + lung		RMB lamb ribs	Lamb mince mix
THURSDAY	Minced lamb tripe	Chunky tripe		Chicken back with egg	Minced chicken mix (no more bone)
FRIDAY	RMB lamb ribs	Minced lamb + heart		Half a rabbit	Half a rabbit
SATURDAY	Minced ox tripe	Chunky tripe		Ox or lamb tripe	Ox or lamb tripe with egg
SUNDAY	RMB lamb neck	Minced lamb + liver (20 gms only)		RMB veal ribs	Minced veal muscle meat with liver
WEEK 3			**WEEK 6**		
MONDAY	Chicken mince (no bone)	Chicken wings /hearts, egg		Duck necks /wings	Lamb tripe with egg
TUESDAY	Lamb tripe	Chunky lamb tripe		Half a rabbit	Rabbit minced mix
WEDNESDAY	RMB lamb ribs	Minced lamb /liver		Lamb neck	Lamb mince with liver & egg
THURSDAY	Chicken mince (no bone)	Chicken neck /gizzards		Ox or lamb tripe	Ox or lamb tripe
FRIDAY	Ox tripe	Chunky ox tripe		Chicken necks, hearts, liver	Chicken mince (no bone) with egg
SATURDAY	Lamb neck	Minced lamb + heart		Ox or lamb trachea and tripe	Ox or lamb tripe
SUNDAY	Chicken wings /hearts	Minced chicken (no more bone) with egg		RMB Veal neck	Veal with liver, heart.

By Angie Roberts.

Muscle meat: Contains 20–25 per cent protein, providing all the essential amino acids. It is also a source of vitamins A, B, D, E and K, phosphorous, and omega 3.

Fat: Mother Nature provides the correct proportion of fat to muscle meat, and experts say that 11–12 per cent fat is the ideal balance for dogs.

Offal: The diet should contain 10–15 per cent of offal as it is highly nutritious and provides enzyme-rich protein, vitamins, minerals and essential fatty acids.

Oily fish: Feed once or twice a week as it contains essential fatty acids, valuable trace minerals, vitamins and amino acids.

Eggs: A valuable source of vitamins, minerals, fat and protein. Raw eggs with shells provide a good ratio of phosphorus to calcium, and other minerals.

Vegetables: Phytonutrients are considered to be beneficial, but not all raw diet feeders believe vegetables are necessary.

However, feeding a raw diet is less convenient than feeding commercial foods, and a freezer for raw dog food is a must – but it will take up space

Tripe and minced chicken.

(and cost money), and strict hygiene should be practised.

There are also certain risks in feeding non-commercial (raw diet) foods, as described below:
Raw meat: Is a potential source of parasites and pathogenic bacteria for the dog and the owner.

Eggs: Although eggs are an excellent source of protein, raw eggs contain an enzyme called avidin which decreases the absorption of biotin (a B vitamin): this can lead to skin and coat problems. Raw eggs can also contain salmonella.

Milk/yoghurt: Some dogs cannot tolerate dairy products because they contain high lactose levels.

Liver: Although liver contains protein, fats, carbohydrates, minerals and vitamins of high biological value, it is also a potential source of parasites and pathogenic bacteria, and overfeeding may cause vitamin A toxicity.

Bones: Although bones can help to keep tartar from building up on the teeth, the dangers of bone chewing are digestive upsets, intestinal blockages and perforations. Cooked bones should never be fed to your dog as they are more likely to splinter.

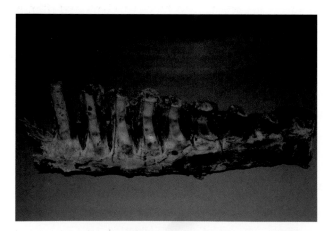

Rack of ribs.

Potatoes: Feeding potatoes is not advised as they promote yeast production, which can lead to ear and skin infections, and digestive issues. If they are fed they should always be cooked.

Chocolate, coffee, tea: Contain caffeine, theobromine or theophylline, which can be toxic and affect the heart and nervous systems. Chocolate should never be fed to dogs.

Onions, garlic, raisins and grapes: Are potential toxins in a dog's diet.

Table scraps: Are not nutritionally balanced, and should never comprise more than 10 per cent of the diet.

The Truth about Pet Foods

Statutory labelling is required on pet food, but even with recent guidance as to how to interpret the regulations, manufacturers are still allowed to be vague about the contents, using words such as 'cereals' or 'meat and animal derivatives'. Explanations for some of these terms are given below. Some manufacturers do choose to list all the ingredients separately, and manufacturers must now give the exact level of an ingredient rather than a minimum level, starting with the largest to the smallest.

The following terms are used by manufacturers to describe certain contents in a pet food:

'Meat and animal derivatives' or **'animal by-products':** Usually made up of heads, feet, entrails, lungs, feathers, hair.

'Cereals': Can be an alternative to more expensive ingredients, and are used to bulk up food.

'Derivatives of vegetable origin': Anything not classed as a cereal, and usually a by-product from human food preparation; usually contains no nutritional value, and again is used to bulk up a food.

'Bakery by-product' or **'bakery derivative':** Waste material from the human food preparation process, such as stale goods and pre-frozen goods.

'Chemicals': Necessary in lower grade foods, because without them, because of the poor quality of the ingredients, the pet food would rapidly deteriorate.

'Added sugar': Animals should not need added sugar, and this is only added to make the food more palatable for your pet.

If a manufacturer states that their food is a 'premium food', many people will assume, and are usually right, that it is more expensive, while the manufacturer is trying to indicate it is of a higher quality. But is it more expensive in the long run? If you are feeding your dog a cheaper brand with bulking agents he will need to eat more to get the necessary nutrients than if he were eating a premium brand. And where do all the ingredients that his body cannot digest end up? In your garden, as expelled rubbish. Premium foods should also have a higher protein quality, which helps to reduce hyperactivity.

EXERCISING YOUR DOG

Like most working breeds, mental stimulation is as important for a German Shepherd as physical exercise, otherwise they can quickly become bored, and boredom can lead to them being vocal and destructive. Training is a constructive and fun way to give your dog mental stimulation, and many German Shepherds enjoy obedience work, agility and tracking. Toys and games can also help, as they can learn to play with them when left alone.

High-drive dogs need an outlet for their energy in addition to mental stimulation. Whilst walks on the lead are a convenient form of exercise, it is much more advantageous for your German Shepherd to run off lead. Of course recall must be established first, and we do not recommend letting your new dog off lead for the first couple of weeks, but a good session of fetch in the park will burn off a lot more energy than a trot round the block on the lead.

How much exercise you should give your German Shepherd depends on his age and level of fitness. There are no fixed rules as to how

Off-lead exercise is great for your German Shepherd.

much exercise a puppy should get, but be aware that too much exercise can cause a strain on its skeletal structure, which can be irreversible. Lead walks should be kept short until your puppy is about six months of age. Off-lead exercise is much better for him, because if he is tired he will just stop and rest, rather than having to keep following you on the lead.

Once your German Shepherd has fully matured, the amount of exercise he has will normally depend on how much you can give him! I've yet to meet the owner who can wear their dog out if it is fit and healthy. Some people will advise you that your adult German Shepherd will need two hours of exercise a day, and if all you can give him is lead exercise, then this is probably

PANOSTEITIS

Panosteitis is found to affect predominantly German Shepherd youngsters from five to eighteen months. It is characterized by inflammation of the bone marrow, especially that of the limb bones, with episodes of bone pain, which can be severe, and lameness. It is thought to have a genetic basis, but the genes involved have not been determined. The cause of panosteitis is still a matter of theory and investigation: no one really knows what causes it. There is no cure, but restricted exercise and pain relief will help a youngster until it has grown out of it. Most dogs make a full recovery with no lasting side effects true. Dogs that are allowed to run off lead, however, will cover a lot of ground in a short space of time, so gauge the time you exercise your dog with the form of exercise you are able to give him.

As your dog gets older, he will slow down and be happy with shorter walks, and not necessarily at such high speeds. He will let you know in his own way when he wants to slow down and when he has done enough for one day.

Swimming

Most German Shepherds love water, and swimming is a great way to keep your dog trim whilst not putting excessive strain on his joints. If you have access to a clean lake or nearby pond, this can be a cheap form of exercise in the warmer times of the year – whereas using a hydrotherapy pool can be costly. In this case initially the staff will need to have authorization from your vet that your dog is medically fit to swim, and then

they may want to assist in the first few sessions until they are sure your dog is comfortable with the swimming process.

It should also be remembered that a short swim can be equivalent to ten minutes running off lead. This is why hydrotherapy pools are so useful in the rehabilitation of a dog after some forms of surgery, or in preventing muscle wastage in a dog with a condition such as CDRM (*see* Chapter 12 'Breed-Specific Ailments and Diseases').

Toys and Play

German Shepherds tend to love toys, but due to their intelligence, some toys can lose their novelty within a couple of days, and others will be destroyed very quickly. Interactive toys are ideal to relieve frustration or boredom, for example when a dog is left alone. Hollow rubber toys filled with treats can keep them occupied for quite a while.

Swimming is a great form of exercise.

A good game of retrieve.

Retrieving a ball is another game that most dogs love, and is a great form of off-lead exercise. Always make sure that the ball you use is of a suitable size, because if it is too small it could choke your dog. Avoid throwing sticks for your dog, as a stick could become impaled into his mouth or throat, and splinters could damage the gut lining.

Just as you would check that a toy is child-safe, ensure that your German Shepherd's toys are dog-safe!

REGULAR CARE OF YOUR DOG

Grooming

Grooming is important whatever length of coat your German Shepherd has: they have a naturally thick coat, and grooming helps to stimulate the skin's natural oils and removes dead hair. Some people say you should groom your dog every day, and whilst this may be the most ideal, it is not always practical when it comes to the time you might have available. Short-coated German Shepherds do not need as much grooming as the long-coated variety, whose hair can mat very quickly if it is not groomed regularly.

There are many grooming products on the market, and if you have a German Shepherd you tend to try them all, as they may seem to moult 365 days of the year. For those dogs with a short coat and not so much undercoat, a soft brush may suffice; however, for those short-coated dogs with a thick undercoat a sturdier brush or comb will be required to help remove the dead hair. Combs are very useful for long coats when grooming behind their ears and their 'trousers', but be more careful of upsetting your dog by stabbing him or tugging at a tangle too hard.

Grooming will not take long the more regularly it is done. Start by brushing the head and neck, especially behind the ears, comb the fur at the side of the head and then the chest, brush the body, and brush through the longer fur on the trousers and tail.

German Shepherds should not be bathed more than necessary, as bathing can wash out the natural oils in the coat. If a bath is needed, use a mild shampoo and rinse thoroughly. It is quite common for owners of long-coated German Shepherds to shave their underside during the winter to prevent mud accumulating and tangling the coat – besides which, a wet undercarriage on a long-haired dog can take forever to dry.

Grooming sessions should be a pleasant experience for both of you, and grooming is another way of maintaining good handling skills and co-operation with your dog. It is also a good opportunity to check for cuts, lumps and bumps.

Ears and Teeth

You should regularly check your dog's ears and teeth. German Shepherds can be prone to ear infections, so any signs of discharge or smell should be dealt with by a vet immediately. We have seen many cases where an owner has ignored an infection and the outcome has been major surgery to save the ear canals. A baby wipe is very useful for giving the insides a quick clean from general dirt, but never poke your fingers too far down the ear or you could damage the ear drum.

Dogs build up tartar on their teeth in just the same way as we do, and those on a soft diet are much more susceptible as they are not using the chewing action required to keep their teeth clean. You can brush your dog's teeth with a soft brush and special toothpaste, but this is something you will probably have to get your dog used to from day one, or your vet may advise a supplement to their food which helps remove plaque. Ultimately your vet may recommend a dental under anaesthetic if tartar build-up looks to be leading to tooth decay, which can result in bad breath along with discomfort and eating problems.

Nails

The majority of dogs will never need their nails trimmed as they are kept short naturally by exercise on a hard surface; however, if your dog is only ever exercised on grass it may well need a nail trim.

Handling the feet and nails should be started when the dog is a puppy. With many adult dogs, especially those you may have adopted through a rescue, it may take a lot of time and patience before they will allow you to touch their feet.

Trimming nails is best done by your vet or professional groomer.

Many a mistake has been made where a new owner has decided to dry a new dog's feet or clip their nails and has ended up being bitten. Trust must first be established, because all the dog knows is that you are grabbing a part of his body that is rarely interfered with, and in doing so you are restraining him and preventing him from being mobile. The fear factor results in him biting you.

Clipping is best done by a vet or professional groomer, because if you accidentally cut into the blood supply to the nail, the quick, which runs through each claw, will bleed profusely – and I doubt your dog will allow you near his nails again!

Keep an eye on dew claws, which are found on the inside of some dogs' 'wrists', because they can grow curved and therefore back towards the skin. If you think your dog's dew claws are a problem it is worth discussing their removal with your vet. Not all dogs have these.

HEALTH CARE REQUIREMENTS DURING A TYPICAL YEAR

Vaccinations

A number of dangerous diseases can still affect dogs in the UK, and some of these can even be transmitted to humans. Vaccination is the only safe way to provide immunity against these diseases, and if carried out regularly according to set guidelines, it can protect your dog for life.

Immunity and vaccination: Immunity is the body's natural ability to fight infection. Vaccination confers immunity by exposing the body to a small but entirely harmless dose of the disease in question. Antibodies are produced when an antigen (such as a virus or bacteria) provokes a response from the immune system.

Immunity in puppies: Puppies are usually protected during their first weeks of life thanks to immunity passed through their mother's first milk, known as 'colostrum'. This immunity fades rapidly, however, leaving the puppy susceptible to disease. At this point vaccination can take over from the mother in providing protection.

Initial vaccination: This is probably the first time a puppy is vaccinated, or it may be a question of starting again for an adult dog with no vaccination record or where boosters are out of date. An initial vaccination is a course of two injections separated by two or more weeks, depending on the vaccine being used. The primary course can be started as early as six weeks of age, but seven weeks is the norm.

Socializing with other dogs: Your vet will advise as to the earliest time it would be safe for your dog to socialize with others, especially a puppy, as vaccinations do not work immediately: it takes a week or so for immunity to develop.

Boosters: Immunity to disease may fade, leaving your dog at risk. For some diseases, a booster may be needed every three or four years, but for others it is needed annually. An annual visit to your vet will allow for a general health check and for necessary boosters to be given.

Vaccination card: You will be given a certificate that contains a record of the vaccination and tells you when the next booster is due. Boarding kennels, training classes and your vet will need to see this certificate, so keep it safe.

Diseases that are Vaccinated Against

Canine parvovirus: This is a hardy virus that can survive for long periods in the environment; it is more common in puppies and older dogs. It caused major epidemics in the 1970s, and remains widespread in pockets throughout the UK. It is usually fatal.

Canine distemper: Another severe, usually fatal disease, mercifully rare in the UK in recent years due to vaccination. However, major outbreaks have occurred in Europe.

Infectious hepatitis: This disease still exists in the UK, although it is now rare due to vaccination. It is often fatal.

Leptospirosis: Contracted from the urine of rats and/or other dogs. Canals and rivers can be contaminated, and the bacteria that cause this disease are widespread in the UK. It can also cause severe disease in humans (Weil's disease).

Kennel cough: An extremely unpleasant whooping cough-like infection, usually transmitted in places where dogs gather (not just kennels). The disease may occasionally be life-threatening, typically in young puppies, older dogs and other dogs with poor immunity.

Rabies: A fatal disease not found in dogs in the UK. Vaccination is required if your dog is travelling abroad.

Core vaccinations should not be given more frequently than every three years because the duration of immunity is many years, and may be up to the lifetime of a pet. The core diseases are canine parvovirus, canine distemper and infectious hepatitis. It is suggested that vaccinating against leptospirosis is only necessary in geographical areas where there is a significant risk. It is also suggested that kennel cough cannot be vaccinated against as there are different strains;

however, some boarding kennels may insist your dog has had the vaccination before allowing them to stay.

To Vaccinate or Not to Vaccinate?

The jury is out on vaccinations, as there are people who believe we over-vaccinate our animals and cause more harm than good. There are cases where a dog may have an adverse reaction to a vaccination, although this can be true whether it is a person or an animal, vaccination or drug. It is also said that a healthy puppy will continue to build on the immunity passed on to him by his mother. Many people suggest that there are homoeopathic and holistic alternatives. However, one thing on which both these groups and the manufacturers of the vaccines are agreed, and that is only to vaccinate healthy animals.

A titre test can be carried out on your dog: this is a laboratory test measuring the existence of, and the level of antibodies to, disease in his blood. The most recommended test examines antibodies for parvovirus and distemper, the most dangerous viruses. The test is to enable you to decide if your dog requires additional vaccination, especially with an animal whose vaccination history is unknown, or for determining if puppies have received immunity after their initial set of vaccinations. The test cannot be carried out until fourteen days after vaccination. As yet there is no strict guideline as to how often to test. The titre test results will not be accepted in place of a vaccination certificate.

Vaccinations have to be a personal choice, but consider the limitations that not vaccinating may incur. Your dog will not be allowed into a commercial boarding kennel, may not be allowed into a training class or activity such as agility, and it should also be noted that some insurance policies insist that your dog is vaccinated in the conventional way by your vet otherwise you may risk voiding your policy.

Control of Parasites

There are two categories of parasite that can affect your dog: endoparasites – worms; and ectoparasites – fleas, ticks and ear mites.

Endoparasites

Endoparasites live inside your dog and include roundworms, tapeworms, hookworms and whipworms.

This is something you do not want to see in your dog's poo.

Roundworms: Puppies can have roundworms (*Toxocara canis*) from as young as two weeks of age, as this worm can be spread to the pup from its mother's milk. It can also infect children, so it is vital to worm your puppy every two to three weeks from two weeks of age.

Tapeworm: The most common tapeworm in dogs is *Dipylidium*: it is transmitted by fleas, and any dog that has had exposure to fleas will be infected. Other tapeworm species can infect dogs as a result of scavenging, hunting or eating raw meat.

Whipworms and hookworms: Can cause diarrhoea, anaemia and skin irritation in dogs, and can infect humans, leading to skin disease.

It is almost impossible to stop your dog from coming into contact with worms throughout its lifetime, and worms can live inside your dog without your knowledge. Different worms can also pose risks to humans. A regular worming regime tailored to your dog's need and lifestyle will help protect the health of both the dog and your family, and will reduce any contamination of the environment.

The British Small Animals Veterinary Association (BSAVA) recommends that your dog is wormed at least every three months; however, young animals, pregnant bitches and those in a higher risk environment may require worming more regularly or with a specific regime. Your vet can give you advice as to which products are suitable for your dog, and how often they should be given to be effective and safe.

Ectoparasites

Ectoparasites live on your dog's skin, and include fleas, ticks and ear mites.

Fleas: Transmit one of the dog tapeworms, as well as causing intense irritation and scratching. Some dogs will become sensitized or allergic to flea saliva, leading to a syndrome called 'flea allergic dermatitis'. High flea burdens on puppies can lead to anaemia and in severe cases death. One flea can lay a vast number of eggs, which can survive in the household for up to two years. A few fleas can become a huge infestation.

Ticks: Parasites that can live on or off the host. They generally attach to the ears, face or abdomen to feed on the dog's blood. They are common in woodland, moorland and rough grazing, and can transmit Lyme disease, which can be fatal to both dogs and humans.

Ear mites: Commonly affect young puppies. They are transmitted from one animal to another via close contact, and live on the skin of the outer ear canal. They cause irritation to the ear canal, leading to excessive wax, scratching and head shaking. Treat immediately at the advice of your vet, as effective and easy-to-use treatments are available.

Regular ectoparasite treatment can prevent infestations developing, and reduce the risk to your dog from other diseases.

Treatment must always include both the animal and the environment, and a prevention programme must also be maintained. There are products you can apply directly to the dog and some that can be taken orally, and they are usually administered monthly. Your vet will be able to give you the best advice.

The effectiveness of feeding natural supplements to repel the effects of fleas has not been proven. Also, some plants such as garlic can cause adverse effects, and long-term feeding has been shown to cause anaemia in dogs by breaking down red blood cells.

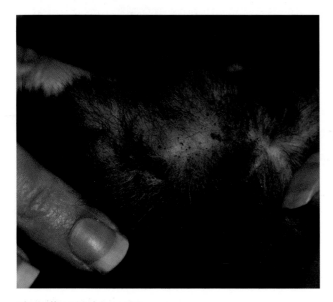

Flea allergic dermatitis.

Hot Spots

Any of the parasites that cause itching may increase the possibility of a hot spot developing. This appears suddenly as a bald patch of skin that is wet and sore, and is a moist eczema or summer sore.

Normal canine skin has millions of superficial, non-pathogenic bacteria living quietly on its surface. For a hot spot to occur something has to upset the normal balance, allowing the usual non-pathogenic bacteria to reproduce, invade the skin, spread deep into the hair follicles and give off toxins that cause further damage. The dog will lick and bite the spot to try and get some relief.

The most common causes of hot spots include moisture on the skin that does not get a chance to evaporate; bee stings; tick, fly or other insect bites; contact allergens such as tree and weed pollens settling through the coat on to the skin; and scratches or abrasions.

Treatment consists of drying the area, and often antibiotics are given either by injection or orally. Occasionally corticosteroids are helpful, to reduce swelling and itching. In some cases your dog may need to wear a buster collar to prevent it scratching or biting at the affected area.

CARING FOR THE OLDER DOG

As long as your German Shepherd is well cared for during its life you may never notice it getting older, and so you should just keep up its usual care. However, it is common for the older dog to start slowing down, just like older people, as physical changes such as arthritis may occur, along with deafness and blindness.

Health

As your dog gets older you should be more vigilant towards him, looking out for any problems, and make sure health checks are done regularly. Something he may have shrugged off as a youngster he may find more difficult to deal with in his later years.

Obesity is common in older dogs as they slow down, and at this stage of his life it is more important than ever to keep your dog at his ideal weight. Perhaps you have not reduced his food intake accordingly, but as with any ageing creature, the heart and circulation, lungs, muscles and joints will not be as efficient as they were when he was younger, and could suddenly fail if he is carrying excess weight.

Remember, too, an older dog may be irritable and less patient, especially if his senses are failing, so although your German Shepherd may have been a saint with young children in the past, he might not be so tolerant now. Let him have his own space and comfort.

Feeding

There is a belief that an older dog needs less protein, but there is no evidence to back this up. There are many commercial foods designed for the older dog, which contain increased amounts of nutrients such as fatty acids, which will benefit them. Also your older dog may require more palatable food, which can easily be digested, and consider also old teeth, which may not be as strong as before. However, remember to change your dog's food gradually, so as not to upset his digestive system.

Exercise

Your older German Shepherd will not require as much exercise as before, but it is important to ensure they still get enough to keep them 'young'. And while the pace and length of walks will slow down, fill the gap with some mental stimulation to keep their mind active; they actually have a longer attention span as they get older.

Older dogs may need to relieve themselves more often, so ensure they have outdoor access regularly, and do not leave them alone for long periods of time. An older German Shepherd that has been clean in the house can be mortified if they have to 'go' because they could not get into the garden.

Also consider that your older dog will need help to be dried and kept warm in the winter, and cooled in the summer as their circulation slows. A coat is not a bad thing for winter months, and there are 'cooling ' products on the market for your dog to wear or lie on in the summer, and of course you can always use a damp towel.

If you habitually take your German Shepherd out in the car, you may find that he starts to find it a struggle to jump in, and it would be worth considering a ramp to assist him. There are also harnesses and slings available. Ensure that any products you buy are suitable for your dog's size and weight.

Goodbye

You must also be able to recognize when it is time to say goodbye to your faithful old companion, and this is the last act of love you can give him. It is very hard to see things clearly when emotions are running high, so listen to your vet's advice. The number of dogs we have taken into rescue from pounds with only a few weeks to live is shocking. If the most that we can do is give this wonderful breed a few

As your dog gets older he will need considered care.

weeks of care and love, and be there holding them at the end, then that is what we must do.

People deal with the grief of losing their dog in different ways, and the one thing we dog lovers hate the most is when somebody says, 'It was only a dog'. There is no wrong or right way to deal with your loss. Some people need time to adjust before considering having another dog, whilst others need to fill the gap in their home as quickly as possible. We have helped many people through this difficult time by suggesting they foster a rescue dog so the home is not empty, and they do not feel as if they are replacing their faithful friend.

The one thing we have found is that it can help other dogs in your home to see their friend, brother or sister at the end, because whilst they also will grieve in their own way, they understand death and can move on. Sometimes when an older dog leaves the home and does not return, the other dogs don't understand and may continually look for them. So remember to think of how your other animals are feeling as well as yourself.

DEALING WITH BASIC FIRST AID, ACCIDENTS AND EMERGENCIES

First aid should only be carried out in an emergency for the following three reasons: to keep your dog alive; to reduce pain and suffering; to prevent further injury and promote recovery. It should be given to your dog following an accident or sudden illness, and should be carried out to stabilize him so you can take him to the vet, whose surgery will be better equipped to diagnose and treat him. It is much better to take your dog to the vet, rather than calling the vet out to you, as they may not have the equipment they need with them to help your dog.

You should ensure you always have your vet's phone number to hand, including any out of surgery hours contact details.

The Rules of First Aid
The basic rules of first aid are as follows:

- Keep calm, because if you panic you will not be effective in helping your dog
- Contact the vet as soon as possible, to let them know what you are dealing with and how long it will take you to get to their surgery, so they are prepared for your arrival and can give you any advice you may need before travelling
- Avoid injury to yourself or others. A distressed dog can very easily bite in his panic and shock, so it is sensible to put a muzzle on him unless he is suffering from an airway obstruction, has lost consciousness, or has compromised breathing or a severe chest injury
- Control haemorrhaging, as excessive blood loss will result in severe shock and death
- Maintain an airway: if the dog cannot breathe or obtain enough oxygen, brain damage or death can follow within minutes

Common Accidents and Emergencies
Whilst advice is given below on what to do immediately at the scene of an injury or illness, it is always best to seek the advice of your vet.

Shock
The shock syndrome can follow an accident, burns, extreme heat, poisoning or insect sting, to name just a few examples.

Signs of shock are as follows:

- Weakness or collapse

BASIC FIRST AID KIT

- Saline wash – to wash away dirt and debris
- Medium dressing with ties – to cover any injury
- Large dressing with ties – to cover any larger injuries
- Foil blanket – to retain body warmth and help combat shock
- Gauze swabs – used with saline wash or for cleaning up fluid
- Microporous tape – for holding dressings or bandages in place
- Conforming bandage – use around a limb if a sprain is suspected, or apply over a dressing for security
- Vinyl gloves – to avoid cross contamination
- Plastic pouches – to cover foot injuries and help keep them clean
- Alcohol-free cleansing wipes – to clean wounds prior to applying any dressing
- Scissors – for cutting tape and bandages
- Tweezers – to remove any foreign objects

- Pale gums
- Cold extremities, feet and ears
- Weak pulse and rapid heart rate
- Rapid, shallow breathing

Your dog may need cardiac massage and/or artificial respiration. Remember to check the airway for any obstruction prior to giving artificial respiration.

   You should keep him flat and warm.

Road Accident

In the event of a road accident, you should proceed as follows:

- Assess the situation and move your dog to a safe place using a blanket as a stretcher and keeping the dog flat
- If your dog is breathing and has a heartbeat, treat for shock
- If your dog shows no sign of life try cardiac massage and artificial respiration
- Control any external bleeding

It is important to keep your dog flat, warm and calm at all times, as it is the unseen internal injuries that can be fatal.

Obstruction of the Airway

The obstruction may be a foreign body such as a ball caught in the throat. Proceed as follows:

- Do not try to pull the object out, but push it up and forwards from behind to dislodge it
- Remove the object from the mouth

Following an accident the victim may be convulsing, and there may be blood, saliva or vomit in the throat. In this case proceed as follows:

- Pull the tongue forwards and clear the obstruction with your fingers
- Extend the head and neck forwards to maintain a clear airway

Drowning

- Lay your dog on his side with his head lower than his body.

- With your hands, apply downward pressure on his chest at five-second intervals.

First Aid Treatment

Cardiac Massage

Massage is required if your dog's heart fails:

- Lay your dog on his right side and feel for a heartbeat with your fingers on the chest wall behind the elbows on his left side
- If you cannot feel a beat, squeeze rhythmically with your palms, placing one hand on top of the other, at two-second intervals, pressing down hard

Artificial Respiration

Artificial respiration is required if your dog is not breathing:

- Use mouth-to-mouth resuscitation by cupping your hands over your dog's nose and mouth and blowing into his nostrils every five seconds.

Haemorrhage

- For surface wounds you should locate the wound and apply pressure with either your thumb, pressure bandage or a tourniquet. Tourniquets should never be applied for more than fifteen minutes or tissue death may result
- For internal bleeding it is vital to keep the animal quiet and warm whilst minimizing movement: seek veterinary advice immediately

Wounds

A sharp stone, broken glass or a dog fight can result in wounds, and the size and depth of a wound will decide whether your dog needs to see their vet.

- A small wound can be bathed in warm salt water and have antiseptic cream applied
- Cut feet or pads should be bandaged to prevent further blood loss
- Be sure there are no foreign objects in the wound

- Larger wounds may need suturing by a vet
- Deep wounds, especially caused by a fight, may need antibiotic treatment

Fractures and Breaks

Be careful lifting and transporting your dog. You will need to be very gentle and take great care.

- Broken lower limbs can sometimes be gently straightened and can be splinted
- In all cases support the area of the break and try to prevent any movement

Other Accidents and Emergencies

Convulsions

Convulsions (fits or seizures) can be very alarming for an owner; they can be caused by a head trauma, brain tumour, meningitis or epilepsy. Dogs will lose consciousness, may involuntarily urinate whilst suffering uncontrolled spasms. These spasms may only last a few minutes and after the dog is very often dazed and confused.

It is best not to touch your dog whilst he is convulsing as he will have no control over his muscles, and any intervention could result in a nasty and unintended bite. Also move away any objects in close proximity to the dog to prevent injury, and dim the lights, pull the curtains and turn off the television or radio: this will reduce stimulation to the brain. Give your dog time to come out of a convulsion, and keep his environment quiet and calm.

Veterinary treatment should always be sought.

Heat Stroke

Dogs left in cars on hot days can suffer heat stroke within minutes, and this is an acute emergency as the dog will become very distressed and can die very quickly.

The dog should be moved into a cool, shady area as quickly as possible. Do not place your dog in a cold bath as this can cause shock. Cold, wet towels should be placed over the dog but must be changed regularly as the dog's body will warm them up rapidly.

GIVING BLOOD

If your dog was in an accident and needed blood, have you ever wondered where that blood came from?

Pet Blood Bank (PBB) is a charity that provides a national canine blood bank open to all UK veterinary practitioners. Just like human blood services, PBB collects blood from donors at organized collection sessions; the blood is then processed into red blood cells and plasma, and supplied to vets across the UK.

You could allow your dog to donate a pint of blood and help save the lives of up to four other dogs. Donors need to fulfil the following criteria:

* Be aged between one and eight years old
* Weigh more than 25kg
* Have a good temperament
* Have never travelled abroad
* Be up to date on all vaccinations
* Not be on any medication
* Be fit and healthy

Throughout the donation experience the donors are given lots of attention and treats, so it is as stress free as possible.

Try to encourage your dog to drink small amounts of chilled water.

Burns and Scalds

Immediately apply running cold water and then cold compresses, using an ice pack or a pack of frozen vegetables. Seek advice from your vet.

Electrocution

Electrocution can occur from a bored dog chewing through a cable. It could kill him immediately or lead to delayed shock.

Turn off the power source before checking your dog for signs of life.

Snake Bite or Poisoning

Seek veterinary advice immediately.

In the event of your dog ingesting a poisonous substance, have its packaging with you as this might assist the vet.

Trying to make your dog vomit is not always the best course of action unless your vet decides this is necessary, in which case it will need to be done as soon as possible as this can reduce the risk of the toxin being absorbed.

Bloat/Gastric Dilation Volvulous (GDV)

A GDV can occur without warning, and if left untreated can be rapidly fatal due to circulatory failure and shock. The stomach becomes distended due to trapped gases, and then twists on itself, cutting off the blood supply.

This is a real emergency and your dog must be rushed to the vet immediately. Symptoms of bloat include gagging and trying to vomit, a distended abdomen that is tight and hard to the touch, drooling and heavy panting, severe restlessness, collapse, and pale mucous membranes.

(*See* Chapter 12 'Breed-Specific Ailments and Diseases'.)

6 TRAINING

TEMPERAMENT: BORN OR MADE?

Many owners and enthusiasts will argue that if a dog grows up in a sound environment then you can dictate his temperament – but they would be wrong! You can encourage his naturally good traits and discourage his less desirable ones, but the bottom line is that temperament is genetic: it is inherited, not developed. Thus a dog with a naturally difficult temperament will remain this way no matter what its environment, and the same goes for a dog with a sound temperament: it will stay this way in spite of its home life.

However hard you try, you will never change a high-drive dog and turn him into a couch potato.

A dog's temperament is made up of a collection of drives, traits and instincts inherited from his parents. It is true that with the correct training you can modify many of your dog's behaviours, but his core temperament will remain the same. Thus the old saying 'It's how you bring them up' is not true, because it's actually all down to the dog's DNA from both parents – which is why breeding should be a science and not a shot in the dark.

Now you can see why, when buying a puppy, you should ask to see mum and, if possible, dad – or at least be told who dad is, because the DNA will be there for all to see.

Early handling, training and socializing will all help to bring out the good traits in your dog, provided they are present to start with, for example ball drive.

Ball drive is used in many areas with German Shepherds in work and play. Some dogs will have such a strong drive it is to the point of obsession, whereas others will have little to no interest at all. With time and training a dog can be taught to be more interested, but if the initial drive is not present this will remain minimal – unlike a computer where you can install drives to suit.

Other drives your dog may have are prey drive, which is normally aimed at smaller animals such as cats, rabbits and so on; and defence drive – a natural trait that all German Shepherds should possess, and a must for the working dog, but a trait that will not need encouraging in the family dog.

THE FAMILY PACK

The first rule to remember is that, much as we all love our dogs, that is exactly what they are: dogs. Many behaviour

Mum and pup.

72

My chair or yours?

problems arise when owners forget this and start to treat their beloved pet like a child. But believe it or not, dogs are much happier being treated like a dog, with rules and boundaries dictating their lives, because without these the ground rules become unclear for both dog and owner.

For instance, if you allow your dog on the furniture, this should be done with your permission, and if and when you say 'down', he should oblige immediately – and if he doesn't, then you need to take a firm stand and insist, and maybe restrict this privilege until he understands the basic rules. The same applies if we allow our dog to sleep on or next to our bed at night.

For the whole family to enjoy your dog, basic rules are essential. If everyone knows their place in the family, everyone will be happier, and family life will roll along a lot more smoothly.

I am not a huge fan of the expression 'pack leader', as it conjures up all kinds of pictures in my head, but I do believe, without any doubt, that there needs to be some kind of structure in every family or team so we all know where we stand. The easiest way to decide this would be to have Mum and Dad at the top, any children ranked by age, and then family pets. This is relatively simple to remember, and if executed in

the right way will be a resounding success for all involved – and also if things start to go wrong it should be fairly easy to trace back to see where the problem lies.

As a family, partaking in your dog's basic training is a great way for everyone to be working towards the same goals and having fun at the same time. Find a local training class to join, or a group walk where all the family can go to socialize their dog and practise his obedience and lead work.

Even if you are wary of a large number of dogs off lead, and are apprehensive as to how your dog will react, speak to the person who runs the group and I am sure they will give advice and reassurance: this is a fantastic family activity as well as a treat for your dog.

I do not believe, and never have, that if my dog eats before me he will assume some kind of dominance over me – or if he walks through the door first he immediately rises up the pecking order in the family. What is important is that he waits when you ask him to, that he doesn't mind if his dinner is not at exactly the same time every day, and that if you eat and he doesn't, he doesn't make a fuss about it – and if he does, a positive 'no' or 'bed' should suffice until it is his turn.

Knowing the difference between work and play.

73

Group walks, a fantastic way to socialize your dog.

While I am a firm believer in respect, it does work both ways, and when you have reached this point you will have a happy unit and the full enjoyment of dog ownership.

BASIC TRAINING

To my mind, basic training comes in three separate and essential disciplines: walking to heel, sit and stay, and recall.

This is something that every owner should endeavour to teach their dog at some stage in his life, preferably as early as you can, but in the case of a rescue dog, better late than never – and you can teach an older dog new tricks.

When we say 'basic', that is just what it is: nothing too regimental, but fun to do for both of you. Find a local training class to go to, which will also socialize your dog and help him to learn at the same time. If there doesn't seem to be anything in your area, don't worry, because you can do all the basic commands on your own on walks; or you could form your own group with a few friends, and ask a freelance dog trainer to come along to help you.

Walking to Heel

Start by teaching your dog to walk calmly on the lead without pulling: every time he pulls, stand still and wait until the lead goes slack again, and only then walk on. This may be repetitive, but it will be worth it in the end.

You can start your lead work at home in the garden, a secure environment that will give you both confidence. Always walk your dog on your left side with the slack of the lead passing in front of you, into your right hand. Your dog's age and how bad he is at walking on the lead will help determine your choice of collar or one of the many headcollars in use today. Training leads are very popular and easy to handle and are available in fabric as well as leather. Put your dog on to your left side with the slack of the lead in your right hand, and walk forwards positively whilst saying 'walk on' to your dog. If he surges forwards, stop, wait, and try again until he realizes that pulling doesn't actually get him very far, and by staying close to you he is rewarded – this will soon transmit to him as a good plan.

Some people use the method whereby when the dog starts to pull they will quickly turn in the opposite direction, which not only disorientates him, but the rapid change of direction will break the pulling cycle and you can resume the exercise. As teaching your dog to walk to heel is no quick or easy feat, I would have plenty of reward treats on you – but only give them when you feel

A PULLER MAKES A PULLER

One important thing to remember is that a puller makes a puller, so when your dog is straining forwards on the lead you pulling him back will only turn into a game, with no successful end.

he has understood and completed what you have asked for, as over-treating will not work at all and may cause further confusion.

Once you feel that you have made good progress at home with this exercise, then you could do the same on your daily walk, bearing in mind that there will be a lot more distractions for your dog; therefore initially keep stopping and getting him to look at you to gain his attention, and then reward him.

There is a large variety of collars, headcollars, harnesses and leads on offer to today's dog owner – in fact so many it's hard to decide which one is for you. If your dog is not a great puller but you would still like a little more confidence in your control, then a half check collar is sufficient for this, and you can make small corrections with big results. For a more seasoned puller you may want to try one of the many headcollars that will break the cycle in that when you check the dog his head will be turned to the side; these have been proven to work well with many a hard-core puller. For a dog that walks well on the lead you

may want to invest in a harness, though in my own opinion, with large dogs such as a German Shepherd, I would always prefer to use a collar of some kind, and not have to rely solely on a harness.

Sit and Stay

Some people say that the sit and stay should be taught before walking to heel, but for me, by gaining some degree of control on the lead you will already have your dog's attention – therefore when you do your regular stops he will be focused on you, so asking him to sit at this moment should fall into place more easily. Never force your dog to sit, though by all means gently push his bum to the floor while saying the word 'sit' so he can associate the two actions together; then praise him. Once you have taught your dog to sit you can use it in so many of your everyday chores, such as making him sit for his dinner and wait until you put it on the floor, sit while you open the door and wait while you go through it, sit at the side of the road before you cross –

Sit and stay.

Down and stay.

Obedience pairs.

With a slightly older dog, recall will come in varying degrees of acceptance. Start the same way as you would with a puppy, in the garden after he has done the necessary: so shout his name and clap your hands, and see what reaction you get – how much notice does he take, do you need to call him again, does he make steps towards you, or does he completely ignore you and disappear in the opposite direction?

At home any reaction is workable, but until you have 100 per cent recall from your dog, letting him off lead in a public place is definitely not a good idea.

If you want to allow your dog some running time whilst out on your daily walks, but can't risk letting him run free, then get yourself a training line: these come in varying lengths and will allow your dog some freedom, but you still have the control to recall your dog back to you should he decide he doesn't want to listen.

This is a great training aid for you and your dog. Now you can practise sit and stay with him, because you and the training line can move a certain distance away from him, getting him to wait until you instruct him to come to you, all in perfect safety while teaching him the third discipline in your basic training.

You will be pleasantly surprised how often you will use this basic training in everyday life, which is why every owner should invest a little time in establishing these three basic elements of training.

you can use it in almost everything that you and your dog do together, and it will become second nature to do so.

RELEASE WORD

When you have asked your dog to sit and wait, it is important to have a word or phrase that releases him from the sit, so he knows to wait until he hears this word.

The Recall

The recall is definitely something to start practising at home first where it is safe and secure, so if it all goes wrong it has no lasting effects. Right from the beginning with your puppy you will start recall without even thinking or knowing you are doing it: for example, when he goes out into the garden for a wee, once he has done what he needs to do you will call his name and maybe clap your hands to reinforce your voice command, and he will run back towards you. That is your first recall.

Here, boy!

TRAINING OUT PROBLEMS

Separation Anxiety

Separation anxiety can be quite stressful for both owner and dog alike, and is not an uncommon problem in many rescue dogs due to the instability of their lives, moving from one home to another or into kennels for longer periods; or maybe you were off work for a period of time, but have now returned.

Does your dog follow you everywhere to the point of becoming stressed when you go to the toilet without him? Does he get anxious when you put on your coat and shoes and pick up the car keys, as he knows you are preparing to go out without him? When you go to bed at night and he is left to sleep downstairs in his bed or a cage, does he whine and bark, scratching at doors until you go down to him? When you do go out, does he behave in an inappropriate way, by soiling or urinating in the house, barking excessively, and maybe destroying things belonging to both him and you?

If the answer is 'yes' to any of the above, then your dog may well be suffering some degree of separation anxiety.

Helpful Hints
The initial cause of the separation anxiety, and the severity of it, will dictate the treatment that will be necessary.

- **Please be warned there is no quick fix for separation anxiety**

The first thing you need to establish with your dog is that sometimes you will need to be apart from each other, and this is something best sorted out at the start of your relationship; here are some suggestions as to how this might be done:

- Always make sure your dog has access to fresh water and his own bed, maybe with an item of your clothing with your scent on – something you won't mind being ripped up
- Before you go out, give your dog a good walk or run so he uses up some of his excess energy and to give him some stimulation
- Leave him with a toy stuffed with his favourite food or treats: this will help to keep him busy for a short time
- Make a habit of putting the radio on even when you are at home, so that when you do go out the radio is a constant comfort, and not something you put on only when you go out
- Introduce your dog to a crate in everyday life, but leave the door open and allow him to go in and out as he pleases; try feeding him in it, let him feel that it is a safe and comfy place for him to be. Try giving him a toy stuffed with treats in the cage while you are at home, and when he is busy with the toy, leave the room for short periods, gradually increasing the

THE CAUSE OF SEPARATION ANXIETY

Many people think that separation anxiety only happens to a dog that is the only dog in the family – but it doesn't. The dog's anxiety is based around you, and not other dogs.

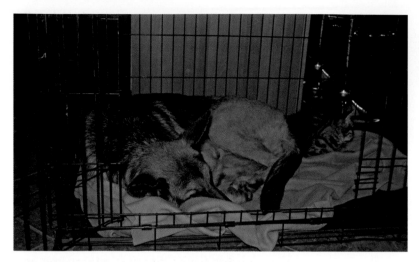

A safe haven for your dog and his friends.

length of these periods, and see how long it is before he comes to look for you. In my experience, if introduced in a sympathetic way, and not abused, crates can become a very good friend to your dog

- When you are at home with your dog, try to distance yourself from him, and do not give in to his demands to be with you, or keep petting him when he asks. Try ignoring him so that he has to go and amuse himself more with his own toys, or tell him to go and lie on his bed and make him stay there for a short period of time to start with. If your dog reacts well to this, reward him – though remember not to go overboard with the praise or you may ruin what you have just achieved

When you are getting ready to go out, start to ignore your dog fifteen to twenty minutes before you actually go, and when you are going out the door do not make any grand gestures that will create an adverse reaction from your dog, but just go calmly. On returning, do the same, and if your dog is very excited, jumping up and crying, try ignoring him until he has calmed down, and only then give him a short fuss – otherwise if you reward his excitement as you walk through the door he may think that his behaviour has contributed to you coming back.

Excessive Barking

Barking excessively can be a very annoying habit and one that can take time to break, depending on the reason your dog does it.

Firstly, you don't want to stop your dog from barking, but just try to control the excessive way he is doing it. Dogs love to bark, German Shepherds especially – it is the most natural thing in the world for them, just as talking is to us, and there are many situations when we want our dogs to bark.

The first thing to do is to identify why our dog is barking, then we can implement the correct training solution.

Why do Dogs Bark?

There are several reasons why a dog might bark:

- Some breeds naturally bark more than others, the German Shepherd being one of them
- To tell the rest of the pack (family) that there is an intruder nearby
- Territorial barking
- Being left alone or separated from other pack members
- Attention barking – this can be behaviour that is learnt from, or taught by an owner, sometimes inadvertently: if the dog has been given treats to try to stop the barking, in reality it has worked the opposite way
- Expressing dominance
- Feeling insecure or threatened by something or someone
- Boredom, lack of exercise and stimulation
- Long periods spent alone (a common reason that many dogs come into rescue)

Home Alone Barking

Being left alone in the home is probably the most common cause of barking, and possibly the hardest to eliminate, as you are not there – probably you have been made aware of the problem by neighbours who are annoyed by it – double

How many times have you told your dog to be quiet, telling him there is nothing to bark at? But remember, a dog's hearing is far more acute than ours, so they will often hear things we could never hope to hear.

Can you all hear me?

trouble. This could also be closely related to separation anxiety mentioned previously.

Firstly check that all the dog's basic needs are being met: that he has fresh water, food, and toys to alleviate boredom, and most importantly that he is getting enough exercise and stimulation.

If he is standing on furniture looking out of the window, and this is fuelling his barking, then remove him from that room as this is unacceptable behaviour whether he is barking or not.

When you return and suspect your dog has been barking, do not make a fuss of him, but ignore him and go

Confidence over dominance.

about your business as normal until he is calmer; only then say hello.

Try making short trips away, or even leave the house and hide round the side of the house, letting him think you have gone, and wait to see how long it is before he starts to bark. If there is no barking after ten to fifteen minutes, go back in and calmly make a fuss of him; however, if he barks almost immediately he thinks you are out of earshot, then return as before and sternly tell him 'no', and then proceed to ignore him. Although this may well be a very time-consuming exercise, it will eventually start to have some effect. There are also a number of cameras on the market these days that can be set up so you can see your dog from wherever you are and also talk to him, which for some dogs, as well as their owners, may work very well.

Some people say that spraying water or having a bottle with stones in and shaking it at the dog has some effect, but this may or may not work when you are present. Personally I think reinforcing your training is the long-term way forwards.

Lacking in Confidence

Some dogs are just like some people and are naturally lacking in confidence and are more sensitive than others, and this will manifest itself in many different ways. The first thing to remember and consider when training these dogs is that the way you chastise them will matter greatly, as you

do not want to lower their confidence any further.

Sensitive dogs may show their total lack of confidence by submissive urination, so as previously mentioned, punishment would only be counterproductive as in the dog's mind he is being 100 per cent submissive to you – so to be punished further will only encourage more of the same behaviour.

Confidence is the key with a sensitive dog, therefore positive reinforcement is paramount so as not to compound the problem.

A dog with no confidence can conversely become nervous/fear aggressive. Again, your confident and positive handling will be the key to success. In this scenario, instead of the dog submitting, he chooses to attack, and as a result of his lack of confidence will more than likely snap and then run to a safe distance and bark to warn you to stay away. For a confident German Shepherd owner this is fairly straightforward to deal with, but a novice *should not* attempt to train this out by himself.

Firstly, do not force your presence on to the dog and constantly invade his space; rather, ignore him and carry on with your normal day-to-day routine, occasionally stopping to maybe pass him a treat, but only in a non-confrontational way, and then ignore him again. Do not make a big issue of this problem as this will only make it ten times worse. Almost act as if he is not there, as pressure will only inflame the situation: the dog needs confidence, and not bullying tactics.

- **Always remember confidence breeds confidence**

If you have other confident dogs, this will be your secret weapon as they will let him see that actually you are not something he needs to fear, nor should he feel the need to attack: you are, in fact, OK. Your resident dog's confidence will very soon transfer to the sensitive dog, who will start to mimic your resident dog's behaviour around you, and relax. This is when you can reward him – and thus he has been given his first dose of confidence. His age and the reason he felt it necessary to display this sensitivity will govern how long it

will take you to turn this behaviour round. In my experience 99 per cent of cases are successful in the long term, provided you keep up with the confidence building, and never weaken and tell him that it's OK to be ultra sensitive, because it is not.

- **Never mistake or mix up nervous/fear aggression with dominant aggression – they are very different**

Aggression and its Different Guises

Food Aggression

Food aggression can be brought on by many different events in a dog's life. It happens if a dog has been starved of food or has been on limited rations for long periods, or has had to fight for food with other dogs where the stronger ones get fed, and the others get what's left. In most cases food aggression is relatively simple to deal with, and in a lot of cases, to live with, unless it is very severe, as feeding time is only a matter of ten minutes out of your day, once or twice a day. Always make sure the dog sits and waits for you to put the food down, *and* until you have moved your hand out of the way before he proceeds to eat.

Stand close by him while he eats, don't give him any direct eye contact, and don't speak to him: just be present. And don't try to take his bowl away while he is eating: how would you feel if your food was taken away and returned several times during a meal? This wouldn't help the issue, but could actually inflame it further.

Try feeding several smaller meals so you get to spend more time together while he is eating, staying close by to show him that you are no threat to him or his dinner. Once the dog realizes he gets fed on a regular basis and that there is no competition for what is his, hopefully he will calm down and become less obsessive about it. However, a small minority of dogs are seriously obsessive about their food, and very little can be done to change this. But knowing about it is half the battle, and if this is your dog's only vice, then make him sit to be given the food, then leave him alone to eat, and remove the bowl when he

Close contact during feeding.

has finished. If the food aggression extends to other dogs being around when he is fed you can either feed him in a crate or in another room, or you can stand next to him and make him sit once he has finished his food until the other dogs have done the same.

Remember also that dogs that are food aggressive will quite possibly be the same with treats, so be careful if you are doing this as a group, because to a dog, food is food.

Many dogs with this issue tend to bolt their food to make sure no one else gets it; however, this is easily sorted by buying your dog an anti-gulp feeder, which is a bowl with raised lumps inside it – the food falls between the lumps, and the dog has to work hard to get it out, which slows him down considerably. There are plenty of different bowls on the market, and they seem to have the desired effect. Feed time can go from twenty seconds to five minutes, which with a greedy feeder is a vast improvement.

If your dog is a rescue case and he suffers with food aggression, remember you probably don't know his full history, so you are working with a jigsaw which has many pieces missing. This will no doubt be something he has learnt to do for many different reasons and changes in his life – so be patient.

Toy Possession

Toy possession is a quite common problem that many people face with their dogs – and some people don't know their dog is toy possessive until a new dog arrives in the home and takes an interest in the resident toy box. Nevertheless it is not a difficult problem to solve if you are realistic about the situation.

First, remove all toys for an interim period until all the dogs have settled down and found their place in the family hierarchy; then try introducing them again. If there are enough toys to go round there is generally no issue, but in certain cases one toy will become the favourite and cause an argument. In a lot of cases dogs will sort out their own pecking order in the toy department, but if this doesn't happen then toys may have to be banned when all dogs are together, and only brought out as a treat for when you and your dog have some 'one to one' time.

Dog Aggression

Being aggressive with other dogs is a serious issue and will manifest itself in varying degrees of severity. If you think this is definitely your dog, before you despair too much, in many cases the dog is not so much dog aggressive, but has a lack of socialization skills around other dogs, which increases massively when he is on the lead. Here are a few basic tips that you should put into place when you are out with your dog.

Always put a Baskerville muzzle on your dog and then everyone will feel and be safe, and any training you do with him will be more productive because you can do it with confidence. Never use the smaller nylon muzzles as they will prevent him from barking (a natural communication, remember), panting and drinking, and his breathing will be compromised, all causing the situation to become even more stressful.

My toy. No, my toy.

Basic obedience will be a key starting point. At the first sign of anxiety or aggression, if another dog comes into view, get your dog's attention with a command such as 'Look at me', and make him sit and focus all his attention on you and away from the other dog. If this goes to plan, reward him with a positive 'Good boy!', followed by a treat. Use this as your signature move every time he sees another dog, so that he gets to know the routine and starts to find you more interesting.

Try not to tense up yourself when another dog approaches, and gather up the lead, as this will create more tension, which will instantly transfer to your dog and mentally tell him that other dogs *are*, in fact, something of which to be afraid and fearful.

Another excellent way of socializing your dog at any age is to join a group walk like the ones our rescue volunteers organize. These are specifically geared towards the German Shepherd, so whatever your behaviour problem, it will not be anything that the group has not encountered before, and you will be given all the help you need week after week to help you and, more importantly, your dog to overcome any fear.

These walks have been found to be invaluable to some of the rescue dogs, who arrive with the 'does not get on with other dogs' label attached, when really he just hasn't had the correct introduction to dogs away from home. Once out on a group walk, with your dog wearing his muzzle, and you putting your obedience training to the test, you will visibly see your dog improve and grow in confidence around other dogs. This really is a great feeling.

Other Types of Aggression

There are other types of aggression that can also be dealt with relatively simply.

Nervous/fear aggression: This has already been discussed earlier in the chapter.

Territorial aggression: Where the natural guarding instinct in the German Shepherd is misplaced, and the dog has been allowed to guard and protect the house and the family. This is something not needed in a family pet, and can very quickly get out of hand, creating a huge problem for both the owner and the dog. It very often results in the dog being given up for rehoming because owners cannot deal with it, or correct it, by themselves.

Learned aggression: Can occur when a number of dogs live together or within a sibling group. If one dog is nervous and barks at everything and everybody, this behaviour will soon pass on to other members of the pack, making double the trouble and a problem which is much harder to deal with. For long-term success it is advisable to split siblings, and to look at the structure and stability of your pack with regard to why this happened in the first place.

Dominance/sexual aggression: If you have entire dogs of either or both sexes in the home at certain times of the year, this type of aggression may rear its head. If a bitch comes into season, even if a male is neutered, he may still try to mount her, perhaps causing a fight between them. If there is an entire male he may get very wound up and fight with other males in the home even if they have shown no interest in her. This kind of dominance can also occur in bitches.

Correct use of a muzzle.

Everyone feels safe and relaxed.

HOW DOGS COMMUNICATE

The last section of training with our canine soulmates is learning to communicate with them, as this can make such a difference to your relationship with your dog; it is also something children should be taught in their early years.

A dog's need to communicate goes back to their

On your marks, get set, go.

ancestors' need to develop the necessary skills to hunt and protect shared resources of food and shelter. A dog communicates with other dogs with vocal signals, body language, touch and smell. Vocal communication enables dogs to talk over long distances, which is why wolves howl: it is a way to maintain contact. A bark can be for defence, play or attention, and you should be able to recognize which is which. A growling dog is giving a warning or threat. Whimpering and whining is used to deflect social challenges, or can be an excitable greeting.

Communicating via scent is something we leave to the dogs, as their sense of smell is so acute – we cannot imagine how acute. Each dog has an indi-

vidual odour signature, which is why dogs 'mark': they are leaving pheromones, which are chemical messages to another dog. Marking is most common with males, but many bitches will mark as well. If you see your dog scratching the ground with their back feet, it is to spread the scent or possibly to deposit further scent secreted from glands on the sides of their footpads.

Dogs have a language all of their own, and all owners should try and learn the basics of this language to be able to communicate with their dogs. Although at times dogs will use vocal language, most of their talking is done through their bodies and facial expressions. Studies have shown that dogs are more than capable of reading our body and facial expressions, so we owe it to them to be more in tune with them and to learn to read their language. This will also help you to help your dog by knowing when he is scared, nervous, on edge, playful, submissive, alert or aggressive.

Relaxed

When your dog is in a relaxed, happy state of mind he will be carrying his weight evenly over all four legs with his head up; his ears may be pricked but are not necessarily forward, or they may be relaxed slightly out to the side; his mouth may be slightly open and relaxed with his tongue lolling out; and his tail will be either hanging down or will be wagging, depending on the moment. A dog demonstrating this posture is telling us that he is happy in the environment he is in, and will normally be approachable.

Alert

An alert dog will appear stiffer in his stance and taller, and he may lean slightly more forward, his eyes will be wide, his ears pricked up and forward, and possibly twitching if he is trying to focus on a particular sound. His tail will be carried higher than in the relaxed state, but not rigid and high, his mouth is normally closed. Your dog may adopt this position if he has detected something of interest or unknown to him, and he will be trying to take in as many factors as he can to decide whether there is a threat and what action he may need to take.

Dominant/Aggressive

A dominant/aggressive dog will appear very confident in himself, and this will show itself in his posture: he may lean slightly forward, his ears will be up and forward, his forehead and nose may show signs of wrinkling, his lips will be curled and his teeth visible, depending on the severity of his mood. His tail will be carried very high, and his hackles may be standing up on his back. If your dog shows this behaviour he may not only be expressing his social dominance, but might also be telling you that he will become aggressive if he is challenged.

Fear Aggressive

Fear aggressive is the opposite to dominant/aggressive. The dog's posture will be somewhat of a crouch, with more of his weight on his hind legs, his ears will be pinned back and his pupils will be dilated, his lips may be curled and his teeth may well be showing. His tail will be tucked between his hind legs and well under his body, and his hackles will be raised. The dog is frightened but not submissive, and may attack if he feels under threat.

Stressed or Scared

Do not confuse being stressed or scared with fear aggression. The dog will adopt a low posture with his tail carried down and often under his body, with his ears back, and again his pupils may well be dilated and he will very often be seen to pant. He will often try to flee the situation that is making him feel this way, which may be the environment he is in, or the company.

Submissive

This depends on the dog and the situation in which he is displaying this emotion, and can dictate the severity of it. If your dog is just being submissive to you in play and he rolls on his back for a belly rub he will show the same signs as the relaxed dog – but if he is being submissive out of fear you may also see him avert any eye contact away from you, his ears will be flat and back, his mouth closed and his tail tucked underneath him, and he may even urinate involuntary out of fear. If the action is of the latter, then what your dog is saying is that he accepts his lower status and he is showing this with his actions in the hope that he can avoid any confrontation with higher-ranking members.

Learn Your Dog's Language!

Please try and take time to learn your dog's first language, and I guarantee you will enjoy each other's company even more than before.

Look into my eyes.

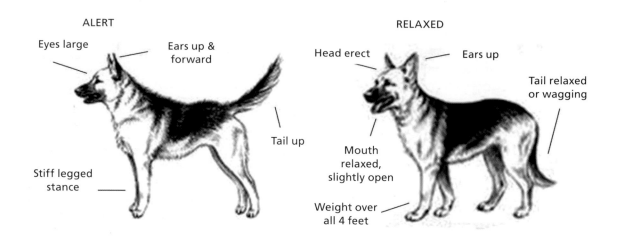

ALERT

Eyes large

Ears up & forward

Tail up

Stiff legged stance

RELAXED

Head erect

Ears up

Tail relaxed or wagging

Mouth relaxed, slightly open

Weight over all 4 feet

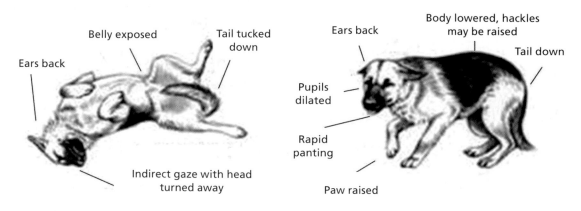

SUBMISSIVE

Belly exposed

Tail tucked down

Ears back

Indirect gaze with head turned away

SCARED/STRESSED

Ears back

Body lowered, hackles may be raised

Tail down

Pupils dilated

Rapid panting

Paw raised

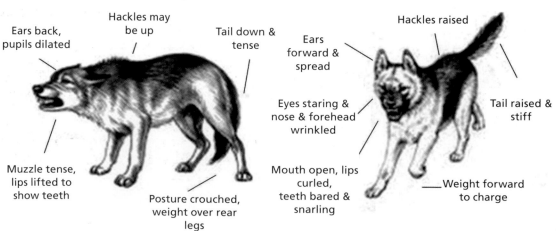

FEAR AGGRESSIVE

Ears back, pupils dilated

Hackles may be up

Tail down & tense

Muzzle tense, lips lifted to show teeth

Posture crouched, weight over rear legs

DOMINANT/AGGRESSIVE

Hackles raised

Ears forward & spread

Eyes staring & nose & forehead wrinkled

Tail raised & stiff

Mouth open, lips curled, teeth bared & snarling

Weight forward to charge

Know your body language.

7 ACTIVITIES AND COMPETITIONS

The following chapter is to give all owners and enthusiasts a small insight into different activities you can enjoy with your four-legged friend. I have spoken to so many people who say they would love to do something with their dog but are stuck for ideas, so I hope what is included here will inspire you to get out there and have a go.

THE KENNEL CLUB 'GOOD CITIZEN DOG SCHEME' (GCDS)

There are four levels to the GCDS scheme, increasing in difficulty from: Foundation Puppy, Bronze, Silver and Gold levels, each requiring the combination to pass a series of tests.

Puppy playtime.

Puppy Foundation Award

The first level is for your puppy, and is a fantastic introduction to socializing and meeting with new people and dogs while starting his training in an enjoyable way. The minimum age is at the discretion of each individual club, but will not be younger than ten weeks, as both vaccinations will need to be in place and effective. You can enrol up to the age of twelve months, but then must move on to the Bronze level.

The first section covers basic care for owning a puppy and includes a discussion and questions, hopefully among owners:

- Cleanliness and identification
- Recognition of basic health problems
- Health protection for the puppy
- Teething, chewing and daily routine
- House training and separation anxiety
- Socialization with people and other dogs

Other sections will cover the following:

- Always making sure you have something to remove poop with, as puppies always manage to produce some
- Using pup's name and getting a good response with little effort
- Showing the examiner how puppy plays with you and his toys
- Socializing with a placid, friendly dog not previously known to the puppy: being wary, unsure or even omitting a low grumble is OK if followed by making friends
- Introducing puppy to a person unknown to them: no grand gestures, just gently make contact

- Your puppy should show little interest or stress once he has heard and understood everyday noises
- Puppy should be handled by the owner and another person so that if, for example, he visits the vet, there should be no problems if this is done in the correct way
- This is where your recall starts: taking a few paces away from pup and calling him back to you, followed by lots of praise
- Basic commands such as sit, stay, stand and down should be introduced and encouraged
- Walking on the lead with minimum distractions for a short period of time to begin with
- Asking your pup to stay while you back away a few paces; if he moves position this is fine, but encourage him to stay put for a few seconds
- Take things away from pup when you decide; this should be done with little to no fuss, but if you need help, this is the right place to be
- Teaching manners where food is concerned, taking a treat gently, and waiting until told to take food

The Bronze Award

The Kennel Club Good Citizen Dog Scheme Bronze Award aims to produce a dog that will walk and behave in a controlled manner on the lead, will stay in one position on command, and will allow his owner to clean, groom and inspect him. He must also allow himself to be presented by his handler for inspection – to stand, sit or lie down on either side or on his back, all on the lead – and he must come to his handler when called. The Bronze Award aims to provide handlers with a basic knowledge of understanding and training their dog

The scheme is aimed at all dogs, whether Kennel Club registered or not, and there is no age limit. Handlers must show that they have a means of cleaning up after their dog, and that he has proper identification. It is a legal requirement to inscribe the name and the address of the owner on the dog's collar or on a plate or disc attached to it.

The test is not a competition, but examiners should be satisfied that dogs are worthy of passing. Examiners should also observe the spirit of the scheme, which is to produce happy, contented dogs that are well behaved, and under the control of handlers who fully understand their responsibilities to their dogs and other members of the public. A certificate will be awarded when the required standard has been achieved. Any uncontrolled behaviour, mouthing, barking, growling or other threatening behaviour is not acceptable and further training will be required before the dog can be passed. Emphasis must be placed upon the ability of the handler to handle, care for, and generally be responsible for their dog.

Dogs may be tested either on their own or in groups; those passing all parts of the test will receive a Good Citizen Dog Scheme Bronze Certificate. The examiner will enter the comment 'Passed' or 'Not Ready' against each exercise. In order to receive a certificate, dogs must receive the comment 'Passed' for each exercise during one testing session.

The Test
Exercise 1: Cleanliness and identification
Each handler must carry with them some form of 'poop scoop', and all dogs must wear a collar and identification tag complying with the law. The owner should always remove any fouling caused by their dog. It is a legal requirement to inscribe the name and the address of the owner on the collar or on a plate or disc attached to it. Furthermore it is a legal requirement to clean up after your dog in public areas and dispose of the bag in an appropriate bin.

Exercise 2: Collar and lead
The object of this exercise is that the handler learns how to put on and take off the collar and lead safely. It is important that the collar and lead are suitable for the type of dog, and that the handler is able to fit them correctly.

Exercise 3: Walk on a lead
The object of this exercise is for the dog to walk on a lead without distractions. The handler and dog should walk for approximately thirty paces, including some turns, and should demonstrate

that this can be done without issue or the dog pulling forwards or back unnecessarily.

Exercise 4: Control at the door/gate

The object of this exercise is for a handler and dog to walk through a gate/doorway with the dog under control and on a lead. The dog should not pull or be pulled through the gate/doorway. When this exercise commences the dog can be in any position and should wait while the handler opens the gate/door and then proceeds to go through. The handler should then recall the dog through the gate/doorway. While the handler secures the gate, the dog should remain settled.

Exercise 5: Controlled walk amongst people and dogs

The object is for the handler to remain in control of their dog whilst walking amongst people, dogs and distractions. The handler should walk for approximately thirty paces and include some turns. They should demonstrate that this can be done without any problem and without the dog pulling forwards or back. The dog should behave in a quiet, relaxed and controlled manner whilst the handler holds a conversation for one minute. The dog may adopt a stand, sit or down position at this time. This is not a stay exercise.

Exercise 6: Stay on lead for one minute

The object of this exercise is that the dog will stay on the spot while the handler moves away for one minute. The handler should remain in sight. The handler should place the dog on lead in any position – stand, sit or down. Upon instruction, having quietly dropped the lead, the handler will move a distance of five paces away for a period of one minute. The dog will be required to stay in this position throughout the exercise.

Exercise 7: Grooming

The object of this exercise is to test the handler's ability to groom the dog without a struggle. The grooming performed should be relevant to the individual dog, it should be conducted on a lead, and should include all parts of the dog's body. Handlers are required to provide their own grooming equipment. If the dog shows any signs of aggression or dislike during this exercise he will be deemed not ready and will not get a pass for this section.

Exercise 8: Examination of the dog

The object of this exercise is to demonstrate that the dog will allow inspection of its body by its handler. This exercise will be carried out on a lead. The examiner will be shown how a handler can examine their own dog. The dog should be placed for inspection of its mouth, teeth, throat, eyes, ears, stomach, tail and feet when standing, sitting or lying down as required. Other than mild avoidance, the dog should allow inspection without concern. Again, if the dog objects to any of the elements in this section he will require further training before he gains a pass.

Exercise 9: Return to handler

The object of this exercise is for a dog to return to his handler when instructed to do so. The handler will unclip the lead and play with the dog with or without a toy, or in some other way distance themselves ten paces away from the dog. When directed to do so, the handler should call the dog. Having returned to the handler, the dog should stay close in any position and the lead should be replaced.

Exercise 10: Responsibility and care

The object of this exercise is to test the knowledge of the handler on specific subjects relating to owning a dog. The examiner should construct questions based on Section One of the *Responsibility and Care* leaflet. Topics include a dog's needs, illness, and the responsibilities of ownership. The questions should be put to the handler in a way to encourage understanding of dog ownership and what is required. At the start of each training course, in addition to the description, handlers should be given a copy of the *Canine Code and Responsibility and Care* leaflet. There should be a discussion period during which the importance of correct socialization can be explained, problems discussed, and advice given on choosing a suitable collar, identity disc and lead.

Sit and stay.

Note: Only one numbered item may constitute a question. The handler should be able to give three out of six correct answers from Section One of the Responsibility and Care leaflet.

The Silver Award

The Test

Exercise 1: Play with the dog

The object of this exercise is to demonstrate that the dog will play with his handler. Play adds pleasure to a dog's life and can be used to make training fun. When instructed to do so the handler should commence to play with the dog. Play should be under the handler's control, and if it involves toys or training aids the dog should readily give them up when asked. Play fighting of any description will not be accepted in this exercise.

Exercise 2: Road walk

The object of this exercise is to test the ability of the dog to walk on a lead under control on a public highway. This exercise should be carried out at a suitable outdoor location and an occasional tight lead is acceptable if needed to make the situation safe. The handler and dog should walk along a pavement, execute a turn, and then stop at the kerb, where the dog should remain under control. Having observed the Highway Code, they should proceed to the other side, turn and continue walking. Distractions should be incorporated, such as passing vehicles or bicycles, people, wheelchairs, prams, pushchairs.

Exercise 3: Re-join the handler

This exercise is for the dog to remain steady, off lead, while the handler moves away; the dog will then return to the handler when instructed to do so. Having left the dog and moved approximately ten paces away, the handler should call the dog when directed to do so. Having returned, the dog should stay close to the handler in any position; the lead shall then be put back on. The dog should not return to the handler if not told to, although a slight anticipation will be overlooked.

Exercise 4: Stay in one place for two minutes

During this exercise the idea is that the dog will stay on the spot while the handler moves away for two minutes. The handler should remain in sight. The handler should place the dog with the lead attached in any position of their choice, be this stand, sit or down. Upon instruction, having quietly dropped the lead, the handler will move a distance of five paces away for a period of two minutes.

Exercise 5: Vehicle control

This exercise is to test whether the handler can get the dog in and out of a vehicle in a controlled manner. The dog should remain quiet, relaxed and under control during this exercise. Without pulling, the dog should be taken on lead towards a vehicle, and should wait while the handler opens the door. The dog should not attempt to get in until told, but should then enter willingly and the door should be closed. The handler, examiner and, if necessary, a driver will get into the vehicle. The engine should be started and run for a short time to enable the examiner to assess how the dog reacts: the dog at all times should remain quiet, relaxed and under control. The dog will then be asked to get out of the car in an orderly manner. The handler should then close the door with the dog calmly under control.

Exercise 6: Come away from distractions

This test is to see that the handler remains in control of their dog when there are distractions. The handler should take the dog, on lead, to a gathering of people with dogs also on leads. When told to do so, the lead should be removed and the handler should walk or run away calling the dog, which should return without delay and be placed on the lead.

Exercise 7: Controlled greeting

This exercise is to demonstrate that the dog will not jump up. Should this happen, the handler must be able to successfully instruct the dog to stop and get down. The examiner will greet the dog as they may do when entering a house. A dog that does not jump up will pass.

Exercise 8: Food manners

This exercise is to show that your dog has good manners when around food. Food should be picked up and eaten while the dog, on a loose lead, is close to the handler. The dog should not show too much interest in the food – that is, not beg for food or steal. The examiner will determine how close the dog needs to be to show this off in full.

Exercise 9: Examination of the dog

This exercise is to demonstrate that the dog will allow inspection of its body by a stranger – that is, the veterinary surgeon. The dog on lead will be asked to stand for inspection of his mouth, teeth, throat, eyes, ears and feet whilst standing, sitting or lying down as asked. Other than mild avoidance, the dog should allow inspection without concern.

Exercise 10: Responsibility and care

This exercise is to test the knowledge of the handler on specific subjects relating to owning a dog. The examiner should ask questions based

Remote stay.

on sections one and two of the *Responsibility and Care* leaflet. Topics include a dog's needs, illness, the responsibilities of ownership, other responsibilities, children, barking, dogs and stationary vehicles and vehicle travel. At the start of each training course, in addition to the description, handlers should be given a copy of the *Canine Code and Responsibility and Care* leaflet. There should be a session during which the importance of these topics in everyday life situations is discussed.

Note: Only one numbered item may constitute a question. The handler should be able to give six out of eight correct answers from Sections One and Two of the Responsibility and Care leaflet.

The Gold Award

The Test
Exercise 1: Road walk
This exercise is to test the ability of the dog to walk on a lead under control on a public highway beside the handler, and for the handler to determine the speed of the walk. This exercise should be carried out at a suitable outdoor location, and an occasional tight lead is acceptable. The handler and dog should walk along a pavement, execute a turn, and then stop at the kerb, where the dog should remain focused on his handler. On command they should proceed, observing the *Highway Code*. When reaching the other side they should turn and continue walking, making a few changes of pace from normal to slow or fast walking pace. The handler and dog will return across the road to the starting point of the exercise. Distractions should be incorporated such as passing vehicles or bicycles, people, wheelchairs, prams, pushchairs and so on. This is much the same as in the Silver award, but with greater detail.

Exercise 2: Return to the handler's side
This exercise is to show that you are able to bring the dog back under close control during a lead free walk. With the dog off lead and not less than ten paces away, the dog will be called back to the walking handler's side, and both should

continue together for approximately ten paces. A dog that stays relatively close to the handler's side is fine, and no halt or sit is required to complete this exercise.

Exercise 3: Walk free beside handler
The object of this exercise is for the dog to be kept close to the handler's side, as may be necessary on a walk in the park. It is to show control whilst walking with a dog off lead beside his handler for approximately forty paces. Competition heelwork is not compulsory, but is acceptable; therefore it is only necessary for the dog to be kept relatively close beside the handler. Two changes of direction are required, and there will be the distraction of another handler passing with a dog on a lead. Upon completion of the task the handler will attach the lead to finish the test.

Exercise 4: Stay down in one place
In this exercise the dog will stay down on the spot while the handler moves away for two minutes both in and out of sight. This stay will be tested off lead, and handlers should place their dogs in the down position. During the test the handler will be asked to move out of sight for approximately half a minute. While in sight handlers will be approximately ten paces away from their dog.

Exercise 5: Send the dog to bed
The handler may provide the dog's bed, blanket, mat, or an article of clothing, and should place this in a position as requested by the examiner. The handler will stand approximately ten paces from the bed. Upon instruction, the handler will send the dog to bed, where he will remain until the examiner is satisfied he is settled. No toys or treats can be used to entice him into the bed, neither should he be told to go to his bed in a harsh tone.

Exercise 6: Stop the dog
This exercise is to show that the handler can stop the dog at a distance, off lead in an emergency situation, not less than approximately ten paces away. The handler will be instructed to stop the dog on the spot in any position. This will be exe-

cuted with the dog moving, and he must stop immediately unless he is running, when he will be allowed a degree of time to stop safely.

Exercise 7: Relaxed isolation

This is a test for when your dog is left alone. During this exercise the dog should not become agitated, stressed or defensive. It will be attached to a line approximately two metres long, and then the handler will move out of sight for between two to five minutes. Alternatively the dog may be left in a room on his own, where he can be watched, but without him knowing. The right venue will be needed to perform this test. Any number of dogs may be tested at the same time, provided they are isolated at different locations. It is acceptable for the dog to move around during isolation, however should the dog whine, howl, bark or indulge in any disruptive activities, he should not pass this exercise. The handler will be allowed to settle him down before leaving him, but no toys or blankets can be used.

Exercise 8: Food manners

The handler will offer food to the dog either by hand or in a bowl. He must wait for permission to eat. After a three- to five-second pause, the handler will be asked to give him a command to eat. If the dog tries to eat the food before he is told to, the handler may tell the dog 'no' but not touch it.

Exercise 9: Examination of the dog

This exercise is to demonstrate that the dog will allow inspection of his body by a stranger as might be undertaken by a vet. The dog on lead will be required to be placed such as to allow the inspection of his mouth, teeth, throat, eyes, ears, stomach, tail and feet whilst standing, sitting or lying down. Other than mild avoidance, the dog should allow inspection without concern. This is as in the Silver award.

Exercise 10: Responsibility and care

This exercise is exactly the same as in the Silver and Bronze awards.

Note: Only one numbered item may constitute a question. The handler should be able to give eight out of ten correct answers from Sections Two and Three of the Responsibility and Care leaflet.

The GCDS is now a well established dog training programme that has been in operation since 1992. The scheme is open to all dogs, young or old, pedigree or crossbreed, whether Kennel Club registered or not. It provides a quality standard of training for dogs and owners, and incorporates many domestic obedience exercises. On passing at each level, combinations will be presented with a certificate, which they can display with pride.

Basic agility.

COMPETITIVE OBEDIENCE TRAINING

We should all teach our dogs basic obedience: whether this is by you at home or by joining a local training club, basic manners on and off the lead are a must. As described above, the Kennel Club 'Good Citizen Dog Scheme' is an excellent place to start, and there are clubs all over the country running them. A full list can be found on the Kennel Club website.

Competitive obedience is exactly what you would imagine: obedient and well trained dogs having their abilities tested at different levels. The first step to having an obedient dog is to take it to training, and there is no better place to start than at a Kennel Club registered dog-training club or listed status club.

After attending a basic dog obedience course such as the Good Citizen Dog Scheme, you may want to try your hand at more competitive obedience training, and in due course test your progress by entering your dog in an obedience competition at one of the hundreds of obedience shows held across the UK throughout the year.

Obedience has been likened to the equine discipline dressage, for its precision and harmonious partnership with the human partner.

There are six 'classes' (levels of competitive obedience) available for entry at obedience shows. Newcomers will start in the basic pre-beginners and beginners classes; as you become more experienced you can move on to the higher classes, right up to what is known as Class C (the highest and most difficult). Each class contains a set of exercises that the judge will ask you and your dog to perform.

Introductory Class

The Introductory class is to introduce and support newcomers to obedience competition. Incentives in the form of a toy or rewards may be carried by the handler in the competition ring, and given to the dog at the end of an exercise or in between exercises. Handler and dog may compete in the introductory class and must win three Introductory classes to be eligible to compete in Pre-Beginners.

Pre-Beginners Class

To compete in Pre-Beginners a handler or dog must not have won a first place in either Pre-Beginners or Beginners, or gained a third place or above in any other obedience class, apart from Introductory classes.

Beginners Class

To be eligible to compete in Beginners, a handler or dog must not have won a total of two or more first places in Beginners class or one first place in any other obedience class, apart from Introductory and Pre-Beginner classes.

Novice

More experienced handlers will start with a young dog in Novice classes. The dog must not have won two first places in obedi-

Obedience has been likened to the equine discipline dressage.

ence classes apart from Introductory, Pre-Beginners or Beginners classes.

Class A
Class A is for dogs that have not won three first prizes in Classes A, B and Open Class C in total.

Class B
Class B is for dogs that have not won three first prizes in Class B and Open Class C in total.

Class C
There are three different types of competition at this level:

Championship Class C at Championship Shows: Dogs must be out of Novice, Class A and Class B, and have won an Open Class C on one occasion and have been placed no lower than third on three further occasions; all Open Class C places and wins must have been won under different judges at Kennel Club licensed shows.

Class C for Open Shows and Open C Classes held at Championship Shows: Open to all dogs.

Limited Shows: Open to all dogs except Obedience Certificate winners and dogs that have obtained any award that counts towards the title of Obedience Champion or the equivalent thereof under the rules of any governing body recognized by the Kennel Club.

Getting Started in Competitive Obedience
We now know there are six levels at competitive obedience, and at each level competitors will be asked to perform a number of set exercises.

The exercises range from heelwork (on and off the lead), to a recall and control exercises such as a one-minute sit and a two-minute down stay. As you progress through the classes the exercises obviously become more difficult. When you reach Class C your dog will have to perform additional exercises such as a scent exercise and also a send away and distant control exercise. If you think back to the GCDS section, a lot of this was covered in there.

Each exercise is given a maximum number of points, and judges will judge each combination against their personal view of the execution of the test. Dogs are expected to work in a happy and natural manner, with the handler responding smartly and quickly to the steward's commands.

Down and stay.

Competing at Your First Show
The requirements for competing at a Kennel Club show are relatively simple and are as follows:

- Your dog must be registered with the Kennel Club, either on the Breed Register or on the Activity Register
- Competitors must familiarize themselves with the Kennel Club rules and regulations and know what the Obedience Regulations are. All of this can be readily found on the Kennel Club website
- Dogs can only compete in any obedience event from the age of six months and above, not before

The Activity Register
For many of you, myself included, who did not know about the Activity Register, here are the facts:

- If your dog is not registered on the Breed Register but you still wish to compete in Kennel Club-run competitions, then the Activity Register is for you

- This register is open to cross breeds as well as pedigrees
- The dog must be registered in their owner's name
- This register does not allow you to compete in gundog working tests, bloodhound trials, field trials or breed shows
- It is very easy to join – just visit the Kennel Club website and fill out the form. Once your application has been approved, your dog's details will be uploaded to the register and you will be sent a certificate

FLYBALL

Flyball first became popular in America, and made its debut as a competitive sport at Crufts in 1990. It is a team sport run on a knockout basis.

Two teams of four dogs race down parallel lanes jumping over four hurdles to a peddle, which they must tread on to release a tennis ball, which the dog must catch: he then goes back down the racing lane, clearing the hurdles to tag the next team member being held by their handler, who will be ready to send their dog down the lane to repeat the exercise.

The first team to have its fourth dog across the finish line, with any part of the dog's body, wins the race. Each dog must cross the finish line before the next dog can start, and handlers aim to launch their dog so that it will cross with a returning dog just at the line.

If a run is not completed correctly the dog must re-run at the end of the line – for instance, if the dog drops the ball, misses out a hurdle or starts too early, if the ball-loader assists the dog, or if the handler crosses the start line while their dog is running. Usually the best of three runs decides which team proceeds to the next heat, but five runs are also sometimes used. Each team consists of four handlers plus a 'box loader' and some reserves. Teams may also provide stewards.

The area needed for a flyball race needs to be fairly large, as dogs can run at terrific speeds and therefore require a good distance at the end of the race in which to slow down. A wide area at the end of the hurdles is also necessary to allow dogs enough room to pick up the ball and turn

around safely. Any design of commercially produced flat-fronted flyball box may be used provided it is of the correct safety standard.

There are four things you will need to set yourself up for flyball:

Hurdles: These should be 30.9cm (12in) high for all classes and all sizes of dog, and must be painted white. For safety, the top rail must be flexible or padded.

Flyball box: Any flat-fronted commercial flyball box may be used, provided the safety of the competing dogs is not at risk.

Backstop board: There has to be a backstop board in place as dogs can really hurtle over the course and there must be something there to slow them down.

Tennis balls: Only unpunctured balls should be used and nothing smaller, or the dog may choke on them.

WORKING TRIALS

Working trials date back to 1924 when the Associated Sheep, Police and Army Dog Society (ASPADS) held the first event. In May 1927, the first Championship Working Trial to be recognized by the Kennel Club was held by the Alsatian League and Club of Great Britain at Castle Bromwich. The format of working trials was changed in 1961, and since then only very minor amendments have been made to the discipline – which bears testimony to the standard that was set all those years ago.

Working trials incorporate many of the disciplines mentioned in this chapter. It is also said that working trials emulate police dog type work, so they can be very demanding on both man and dog but also very rewarding.

Working trials are divided into three main sections: nose or scent work, agility and control.

Nose or Scent Work

The dog follows a track laid by a 'tracklayer' (who is a stranger to the dog) walking a set route set by the judge and identical for each dog. The track is approximately half a mile long and laid on grassland, arable fields or heathland with each competitor working on similar terrain to others in the stake, making the competition as fair as possible.

As the dog follows the track it also has to sniff out and recover items placed along the track by the tracklayer. The track is laid at different times before the dog's work begins, depending on the level of the competition. The other component of nose/scent work is 'search' where the dog has to search for and retrieve items placed in a marked area.

Agility

This is to assess how agile each dog is. They must attempt three different obstacles; a three foot hurdle, a six foot high wooden scale and a nine foot long jump. Two attempts may be permitted for each obstacle.

Control

There are six separate tests in this section:

Heelwork: The dog must walk to heel with his shoulder reasonably close to the handler while the handler makes their way around people and obstacles at different speeds.

The sendaway: The handler sends the dog away across a minimum distance of fifty yards. The handler will then instruct the dog through a series of commands.

Retrieving a dumbbell: The dog must retrieve a dumbbell, which has been thrown by the handler.

The down stay: The dog must stay in the down position while the handler is out of sight for a period of time set by the examiner.

Steadiness to gunshot: The dog is tested on its reactions to gunshot. It will be penalized if it shows any signs of fear or aggression; this is very important in a working trial dog.

Speak: The dog is ordered to 'speak' and 'cease

speaking' on command by the handler with a minimum of commands and/or signals. In other words, the handler will use the word 'speak', and the dog will bark on hearing this word. Often showing the dog the palm of your hand will act as the command to stop.

Training for Working Trials

There are many clubs and societies all over the country that offer training for this discipline, so have a look on the internet.

Previous experience in obedience and agility training will benefit the establishment of a basic rapport between you and your dog, especially in preparation for particular exercises such as heelwork, retrieve and stay. It is essential that your dog is fully socialized and that you have effective control at all times, especially as he will be competing off lead.

Some elements such as 'search' and 'nose/scent work' might need specific preparation and training for working trials, and you may find it useful to attend one or two of the training weekends or longer courses that are available, as well as undertaking regular training with a club before competing in a trial. You might also find it helpful to attend a trial as a spectator where you can watch the tests for yourself and chat to competitors.

Working trials require perseverance and some hard work, but at all levels they are a rewarding

Learning to stay with the owner out of sight.

and fulfilling activity for handlers and their dogs alike. Preparing your dog so he can compete successfully will require considerable time and training – but anything worth doing is most definitely worth doing well.

Your dog must be eighteen months old or over on the closing date for entries to a working trial.

Competing in Your First Trial

Training your dog for working trials is rewarding in itself, and competing against a set standard rather than each other is very beneficial. It is at a trial that you discover how well your training is progressing. The atmosphere at a trial is always supportive and encouraging.

Always make sure you are dressed appropriately, as the trial may well be held high on a hill and in inclement weather – so warm waterproof clothing is a must, and perhaps a change of clothing would be useful. It may be a good idea not to feed your dog in the morning but to make sure you have a meal for after the trial has finished. Ensure fresh water is available when needed. He may also appreciate a cage in the back of your car as somewhere private and quiet to sit during any break times.

Book in once you arrive at the base. Take note of the briefing you will receive as to where you will be working and how to get there, and heed any advice on parking so as not to obstruct the work of farmers and landowners. Working trials are vitally dependent on the goodwill and generosity of landowners, farmers and their workers, so always treat the countryside with respect and be courteous to all those who live and work there. You should obey this rule at all times whatever you are doing.

Keep your dog under control, and be aware that this is a strange place for him, too, so give him time to adjust to being at the trial – and if he seems affected by the proximity of other competitors, give him some space and reassurance. If you feel he should not continue working, ask the judge's permission before withdrawing from that exercise. This applies at all times throughout the trial.

At the end of the trial, join the other competitors at the base for the judge's summing up and the prize giving. It is courteous and expected that you will attend the prize giving, whatever your personal results.

Advanced agility.

DOG AGILITY

Agility is probably one of the most popular of all the disciplines we have discussed in this chapter. It is essential that your dog is fully socialized, and that you have sufficient control of him at all times, especially as he will be competing off lead.

For safety's sake it is recommended that dogs do not start training on equipment until they are at least one year old.

There are, of course, many small clubs and associations around the country offering help to get your dog safely around an agility course for you and your dog's enjoyment, but if you wish to compete in Kennel Club agility competitions then there are a few things you need to do first.

As mentioned previously, your dog will need to be registered on either the Breed or Activity Register. All dogs must be measured by official agility measurers before they compete at their first agility show, as there are shows for all sizes of dog:

- Large dogs, measuring over 430mm (1ft 5in) at the withers
- Medium dogs, measuring over 350mm (1ft 1.75in) and measuring 430mm (1ft 5in) or under at the withers
- Small dogs, measuring 350mm (1ft 1.75in) or under at the withers

You will need to have an official Kennel Club Agility Record Book: copies can be bought on line from the Kennel Club, or the person who measures your dog may sell them. It is highly recommended that your dog is either microchipped or tattooed, details of which should be added to your Agility Record Book. If your dog has neither of these means of identity, then a passport-size photo is needed as identification. The dog must be over fifteen months of age for their first measurement. There will be a small fee of £4.00 (correct at the time of publishing), which should be paid to the measurer.

A second measurement must be carried out not less than twelve months and not more than twenty-four months after the date of the first measurement. If the height on the second measurement is different from the first, a third and final measurement must be arranged within two months of the second measurement, and both the measurers must be different from the meas-

Just say when, Mum!

urers who conducted the first and second measurements.

An agility show will have a series of obstacles laid out in a large ring. The Kennel Club allows a combination of sixteen obstacles to be used on an agility course. Here is a list of some of the most common ones that are used:

The A-frame: Two planks that are hinged at the apex from the ground. A section of 3ft 6in at the bottom of both planks should be painted a different colour, indicating that the dog must touch this area when going up and coming down. The ramp should be made of an anti-slip material and should have slats at intervals all the way along it.

Dog walk: A walk plank of around 4ft 6in high with ramps going down to the floor at both sides. Again, a section at the bottom should be a different colour, indicating where the dog must touch when getting on and off.

See-saw: A plank mounted on a central bracket. Again, a section at the bottom should be a different colour, indicating where the dog must touch when getting on and off.

Weaving poles: There should be a minimum of five and a maximum of twelve poles, in a continuous and straight line with equal spacing of around 1ft between each pole.

Tunnel: Two different types of tunnel may be used: one is known as a 'pipe' and is rigid, and the other is collapsible.

Long jump: An ascending jump starting at 5in and up to 15in on the backboard.

The dog walk.

Weaving poles.

Long jump.

Table or pause box: About 3ft in height and preferably square, made of sturdy material with a non-slip top.

Hurdles and spread fences: A single hurdle or two hurdles put together to form the spread fence may be used.

Other obstacles: Such as brush fences, a hoop or tyre, a water jump, a wishing well, as well as variations of all others mentioned.

Hurdles and spread fences.

Competing in Agility

All dogs must be eighteen months of age or over, and fit to take part when entering a competition. As agility is such a physical sport, make sure you have prepared both yourself and your dog thoroughly.

Agility classes can feature 'jumping' courses or 'agility' courses, each course featuring a variety of agility obstacles. Jumping courses do not require the dogs to undertake the see-saw, dog walk or 'A' ramp obstacles.

An agility competitor and their dog advance through Grades 1–7, with Grade 1 being the lowest level, and Grade 7 the highest. There are two ways a competitor/dog can progress from one grade to the next, and these are as follows:

Progression on Wins

Progression through Grades 1–5 can be achieved by winning one agility class or three jumping classes at the relevant grade. Progression from Grade 5 will require a minimum of three wins at Grade 5, one of which must be an agility class. Progression from Grade 6 will require four wins at Grade 6, two of which must be agility

101

classes. Results from combined classes (where there could be up to seven grades in one class) will only count towards progression from the dog's current grade.

A first prize or other prize win are those gained in standard classes at any Kennel Club licensed championship agility, premier agility, open agility or limited agility shows (that is, special classes and invitational events are accepted). Only a first place with a clear round completed within the course time set by the judge will count towards grade progression.

If you progress on a win you remain at the same grade for twenty-five days after the win. Following this period you will automatically be put up to the next grade. For any shows after the twenty-five days it is the competitor's responsibility to notify the show secretary of a change in grade, in writing, a minimum of fourteen days before the event.

Points Progression

At the handler's discretion a dog may progress up to Grade 4 by winning 100 points at each grade. If this method of progression is selected, the handler must ensure the show secretary signs the dog's *Agility Record Book* at the first show entered at the higher grade. There is no time limit on this progression, however: once a dog has progressed, it cannot return to a previous grade.

HEELWORK TO MUSIC

Heelwork to music is still relatively new to the competition circuit. Combinations are required to perform a choreographed routine of approximately four minutes to music of their choice to suit them and their dog – this again reminds me of the equine discipline dressage, which has been holding freestyle to music competitions for many years now. Heelwork is an extension of your obedience training but to music.

Competitors are judged over three sections: programme content, accuracy and execution of movement, and musical interpretation, each section being allocated a maximum of ten marks. Events are held around the country, usually start-

ing with classes for beginners and progressing up to advanced. Heelwork to music is broken down into two official categories: 'Heelwork to music' and 'freestyle'. Each category has equal status, and the following class structure applies to both categories:

Heelwork to Music

The principal element of the heelwork to music category is the dog working off lead in the heelwork position, on the left or right-hand side of the handler, facing forwards or backwards, across the front or back of the handler, moving in any direction, at any pace. The dog's shoulder should be approximately level with, and reasonably close to, the handler's leg. All other positions are defined as 'freestyle'. A minimum of two-thirds of the routine should consist of heelwork.

Freestyle

A freestyle routine will be the dog working off lead and holding movements in any position. Heelwork as described above is acceptable, although such movements must not exceed one third of the routine.

You can, of course, practise all your movements and routine at home, no special apparatus being needed, but by joining a club you will be able to work as a group and get ideas from each other, and share your experiences.

Your first task is to teach your dog some movements that you would like to use in what will later be the floor plan to which you will eventually put your chosen music. Repetition is the key to training movements and lots of praise, and a few treats won't go amiss either, especially in the early days.

Your dog must be twelve calendar months old or over on the day of the competition for heelwork to music classes, and he must be eighteen calendar months old or over on the day of the competition for freestyle classes.

When you think you are well practised with your routine and feel ready to present yourselves for competition, here is a guide as to what the judges will be looking for, to help you on your way:

Programme Content – ten marks

The programme content should conform to the definitions for heelwork to music or freestyle, and should be varied, with no excessive repetition of movement, and the content being appropriate to the routine.

- Movement should be appropriate to the structure and conformation of the dog
- The movements of the dog should have a greater impact than those of the handler
- The degree of difficulty of the movements should be taken into account

Accuracy and Execution of Movements – ten marks

- Movements including heelwork should be accurately and smoothly executed
- The dog should work in a natural and willing manner
- The dog should respond promptly and appropriately to the cues given (including the use of props)

- The bearing and deportment of the handler should be appropriate to the routine; dog and handler should work as a team

Musical Interpretation – ten marks

- Interpretation of the rhythm, phrasing and timing should be apparent; the choice of music should suit the team
- Choreography should be apparent, flowing and not a series of disjointed moves. The routine should include balance, structure and making the best use of available space
- Primary emphasis of musical interpretation should be on the dog's movements, although the handler should/may be expressive
- Handlers' dress and any props used should be suitable and applicable to the interpretation of the routine

Source: The Kennel Club Limited.

Note: For the latest rules and regulation please refer to the Kennel Club website.

Perfect choreography – or choredography!

8 SHOWING YOUR GERMAN SHEPHERD

In this chapter we aim to give an insight into, and a friendly introduction to showing your German Shepherd.

Showing – or 'exhibiting' as it is also known – is now the most popular activity to take part in with your dog in this country. For many, showing is a hobby, for some it becomes a consuming passion, and for others it is an important part of the business of getting their dogs recognized and thus of being able to increase stud fees.

A judge will compare all the dogs in the class against the breed standard for that breed as set down by the Kennel Club (*see* Chapter 1 'A Brief History of the Breed and Breed Standards'), and the dog matching the best characteristics, including health and temperament, will gain the highest place. A judge should always look to see that the dog is, and looks, fit for purpose, and is fit and well in himself.

Dogs must be full pedigree and be registered with the Kennel Club. There are many different types of show, and to start with perhaps attending a few low-key ones would be good practice. It would also be useful to find some ringcraft training classes so you can both learn what will be expected of you when you go to your first show. But as long as your dog is over six months of age – you are ready to go.

Learning from Mum.

LEVELS FOR DOG SHOWS

Limited shows: This type of show is limited either geographically or by membership, and may be a good starting point for you to practise your skills.

Open shows: These shows are open to all levels of dog as long as they are pedigree. They are great shows to try your hand at before moving up to the big league of a championship show.

Premier shows: These shows are also open to all levels of pedigree dog exhibitors. A premier show is a larger version of an open show, but exhibitors can also qualify at these shows for Crufts.

Championship shows: This is a much higher level of competition because at these types of show not only can a competitor qualify for Crufts, he can also win a Challenge Certificate (also known as a 'CC' or a 'ticket') – and once a dog has won three CCs he will become a show champion, which is one of the highest achievements in the showing world. There are many ways that a combination can qualify for Crufts: please see the Kennel Club website for full details and current rules and regulations.

Challenge Certificate, or CC.

TYPES OF SHOW

Single breed show: Open to a single breed only; normally held over one day only.

Group show: This show is open to one group of dogs – for example, the Pastoral group, of which the German Shepherd is a member.

General show: This type of show is the biggest in the sense that the show will take place over a number of days and will hold classes for all dog groups.

Companion dog show: This type of show is run on a much less competitive level compared to the others: if you want to have some fun with your dog, this type of show is for you. They are often held alongside fêtes, charity open days and charitable events to raise money for certain causes. These shows are more relaxed, and are a great opportunity for you to practise your ringcraft training and to gain confidence in the ring with your dog.

Companion dog show competition.

Classes
- Puppy classes are for dogs up to the age of one year.
- Junior classes are for dogs up to the age of eighteen months.
- Open classes are for dogs of any age.

Eligibility for classes may be different at different shows, so do check.

TRAINING FOR THE RING

Many people say it is never too early to start the basics of ringcraft. This includes walking correctly on the lead and staying close to their human, learning to accept the collar and lead confidently, and not being scared to walk forwards in a positive way. Sessions should be kept short, and puppy rewarded with praise and/or treats; you can use small pieces of his everyday kibble so as not to over-use treats. If done in the right way, puppy will enjoy what you are doing, and lead training can be fun instead of it being a chore.

Once puppy is walking well on the lead and is happy to stay close to you, and can walk either slightly more quickly or slowly as you ask, you can now teach him to trot or gait on the lead. This can also be done in a very easy and friendly way by asking a friend to stand at a set distance and call puppy to them, and/or to entice him with a favourite toy, encouraging him to find his own way to the end of the lead as he trots forwards. If he grasps this, make sure to reward him. It is better to make the sessions short and regular.

The show stance/posture is known as 'stacking', and this will be covered in more depth later on. It is something that German Shepherds do naturally, and again can be practised at home: encourage pup to

Handsome – or what?

Puppy ringcraft training.

Increasing fitness by play.

focus on you by holding a toy or treat and slowly moving backwards, and get him to pose himself naturally. You may need to correct his stance as necessary, though only make small corrections at this early age. Reward him when he holds the pose for even a short period.

As your dog gets older you can build on what you have started with him as a puppy.

A dog's physical fitness and condition is a large factor as well as his ringcraft. A puppy or adolescent does not need too much exercise, but needs to be fit enough to be able to complete the tasks asked of him, and needs to start the process of muscle building and toning. This can be achieved through play with you or other dogs. Having a game of tug, fetching balls and catching frisbees will all start the muscle-building process without any excess strain being put on his joints. If you have ever watched puppies playing you will understand how this can build up their stamina and body shape without them even thinking about it.

Puppies and dogs under the age of two should not be over-exercised, and training should be varied and not repetitive, as this could easily cause stress injuries and joint damage.

Once your dog reaches adulthood and is well matured, you can look at increasing your conditioning programme and fine tuning his condition. To show off your dog to his full potential in the show ring he must be in the best condition possible, and have enough stamina to keep him going throughout the show: if you do not prepare him, prepare to fail.

There are many different exercises you can do to build up your adult dog's stamina. You might design a jogging schedule, slowly building up to several miles – though you may want to introduce the use of a bike if you are not very fit yourself! A more therapeutic form of exercise is water based, perhaps hydrotherapy or an underwater treadmill. Exercise in water is easier on your dog's joints and avoids stress injury. If you do not have access to a pool it may be possible to find a local stream or reservoir, and to use that. Throwing in toys for him to retrieve will be fun for both of you and a great muscle builder for your dog. Some people may enlist the help of a treadmill for building up stamina if time and location are not suitable for jogging, but remember to warm up and cool down correctly. Do not see this as a quick fix to your dog's fitness – it is not!

Agility work is a great way to build up muscle and gain condition whilst having fun. Teaching your dog to jump is an excellent means to make him use the maximum amount of muscles in the correct way, because when he jumps he will need to really sit down on his haunches and push, and this will build up a firm rear end for pushing his trot out and forwards.

Agility helps to build muscle and stamina.

I am sure many people didn't give this section a lot of thought before, as most people consider showing to be relatively sedate and quite 'arty', but if you are serious and want to show your dog off to his utmost, then his fitness and condition will need to be 100 per cent. A show dog is more of an athlete than you think.

As mentioned previously, play can be a big part of your dog's fitness programme. For example, when you or two dogs play tug of war, they will dig their front paws into the ground to gain grip, while they throw themselves back on to their hindquarters to try to win: this uses many groups of muscles. Many other things, such as playing fetch, in or out of water, or playing catch, all work the muscles. The next time you are watching your dog play, have a look and you will start to see play in a different way. Also you will notice that dogs will play for anything from fifteen minutes up to half an hour or more, depending on their age – which is quite tiring!

Ringcraft Classes

Many training clubs will often hold ringcraft classes or something very similar. You can also visit the Kennel Club website where there is a section called 'Find a Dog Club' which you may find helpful.

Ringcraft classes are usually very sociable groups of people who will meet up on a weekly or fortnightly basis to train their dogs. They can offer help and advice to each other and also encouragement to both handlers and dogs. At a well run club they will normally have different sections, starting at puppy through to the more experienced combinations. These classes can also be used for socialization, especially for the puppies, and they can start learning ringcraft at the same time.

A SHOW-OFF

Getting your dog to become a 'show-off', if this is not their natural way, can be a lot harder than it often looks. Hopefully the club or group you have joined will be run by people who have served their time in the show ring and can pass on all their tips to make your dog the star of the show. If, however, your dog has no desire to show off in the ring, and would rather hide in the corner, or just enjoys an amble round, then maybe competitive showing is not for him.

Draycore Seren at Shellmead.

Gaiting

Gaiting is another word for the trot the German Shepherd exhibits in the ring. A German Shepherd is a natural trotting dog, and the way he is put together allows him to show the pace off to its full potential. The gait or trot should be outreaching, elastic, rhythmical and with very little effort from the dog: he should be covering the maximum amount of ground with the minimum number of strides. The walk should also cover a good amount of ground, with long low strides from both hind and fore limbs. At the trot the dog moves with power and balance so the gait, although covering the ground, does so without any sway or unsteadiness. The feet stay close to the ground on both front reach and hind push.

When you watch a dog performing a perfect trot/gait you then realize and appreciate why they need to be in peak condition and fitness. As mentioned in Chapter 7, 'Activities and Competitions', watching a German Shepherd gait correctly is like watching a well trained dressage horse lower his quarters, and propel his whole body forwards with sufficient engagement of the hindquarters to slightly lift the front end up and forward. Very often the hind leg will overtrack the front leg, having to step inside or outside the track of the foreleg. This action is acceptable as long as the dog maintains his forward movement and does not start to crab sideways, which is a fault.

If the dog is viewed from the front, the feet track closely but should never cross over each other or overreach (when the hind limbs strike the forelimbs). The forelegs should move from the point of the shoulder joint to the pad in a straight line. From the rear, the hindquarters move from the hip joint to the pad in a straight line. Whether from the front, the rear or the side, any faults with the gait are considered very serious.

When dogs start to compete at the higher level shows a different handler to the owner will often exhibit the dog. The thinking behind this is that since they have more ring experience it will help to show your dog off to his best, as being in the ring is second nature to the handler.

Stacking

Stacking is the technical term for putting your German Shepherd into the traditional show stance that we all know and have seen. Stacking is by no means an easy feat to learn or perfect with your dog, so lots of practice in short sessions will be needed. The German Shepherd has its own unique way of stacking in the show ring.

First, put a collar and lead on your dog to aid with control during the exercise. Never try to stack on a slippery surface as this will not help your dog to balance, but find a flat field with short grass, as this will be more comfortable for him. Always start with his front end. Some people advise lifting the dog off the floor slightly and then gently lowering him back down, which should make the front legs drop to the floor evenly and more or less in the perfect place under the body. Other people say start by placing one front leg down squarely under the shoulder. The leg should be straight to the ground with the foot flat to the floor and with the toes pointing forwards. Once you are happy with the front leg position you can start work on the hind end.

Remember that a lot of Shepherds do not like their feet being touched, so reward your dog when he allows you to handle his feet for any length of time.

Starting with the inside hind leg first, take hold of the leg and move it underneath his body. The hock should be close to the floor and the majority of the metatarsal bone should lie close to the ground. Place the outside leg back until the hock is straight to the floor, and then slide the leg back gently, making sure the dog's foot is flat to the floor at all times. The dog should not be so stretched that he gives the impression of standing on his tip toes. With the leg now in place, reward your dog. Remember, this stance is all new to him, so do not expect him to hold this position for too long when starting out.

You will need to keep practising until your dog can hold the stacking position for up to three to five minutes, because when you are in the show ring, the judge may take his time looking at your dog, and the better he stands, the better he shows himself off. This will hopefully gain him a good placing in the show.

GSD in a natural, relaxed stance.

gered position, as described previously in this section. German Shepherds are the only dogs to be shown like this, as opposed to the four square position where front and hind legs are together, because this is the natural position for this breed.

PREPARING YOUR DOG FOR A SHOW

The German Shepherd is known as a 'double-coated' dog because they have a thick dense undercoat for insulation and waterproofing, and a shiny sleeker overcoat. German Shepherds either have a short coat, which is the easiest to manage, or a mid/semi/medium-length coat, or a long coat. The German Shepherd only moults once a year, but it seems like 365 days! It is a good idea to brush your dog once to twice a week to keep the shedding to a minimum. It will also keep the coat healthy, as removing the dead hairs will release the coat's natural oils, helping to restore a good appearance and shine.

A good stacking pose.

The picture above shows a family pet which is adopting the typical German Shepherd stance, with front legs together and hind legs in the stag-

Dogs should not be bathed too often as this will destroy the coat and skin's natural oils. If you groom on a regular basis, this should be sufficient to keep your dog's coat healthy and in good condition. Most people will bath their

Bath-time blues.

dogs at home, but if you do not have facilities large enough, you can always use a mobile dog groomer who will come to your house and pamper your pooch. Groomers should have all the required equipment including a blaster dryer, which is excellent for removing all the dead hair from the undercoat. Once all the hard work is done, you can then get to work with the final touches, such as trimming the nails, cleaning inside the ears, and trimming the toes if the hair has become a little long and straggly.

There are many different types of brush, comb, or rake to choose from, and trying out different types will help you to decide which you feel works best for you and your dog.

A pin brush is good for using on the undercoat as it can get right down to the skin, and the pins have soft rounded edges that will not damage, hurt or irritate the skin. A bristle brush is also kind to the skin, and helpful in removing dead hair and stimulating the coat's natural oils. Slicker brushes are good for removing shedding hair, but care needs to be taken as they can cut or break the overcoat. Shedding rakes are very popular these days for use on the undercoat, but be careful of the effect that rakes with flat teeth have on the overcoat.

Checking in your dog's ears should be something you do on a regular basis. As we all know, in most cases the German Shepherd has large upright ears to allow for ventilation and avoid heat build-up, and protect against infections which are often found in dogs with closed ear flaps. To help maintain healthy and clean ears, use a cleaning solution from your vet: you squirt it in, give it a good rub in from the base of the ear, and then wipe out with cotton wool. For good measure you can apply a few drops of a

Finishing touches at the groomers.

recommended ear treatment, but this should not be necessary in most cases.

The dog groomer will, if asked, trim your dog's nails for you, as will your vet if you don't want to do it yourself. If you do want to try, just be very careful not to take off too much and cause bleeding, which can be excessive. Most dogs do not relish this part of their makeover, and you will not be easily forgiven if you cause them pain.

ENTERING AND ATTENDING A SHOW

You may already know of shows that are happening in and around your area, but if you are ready to have a go but are not sure where to go, visit the Kennel Club website to find a listing of shows close to you.

Once you are decided on the show that you wish to attend, give the secretary a call and ask for a schedule to be posted out to you. These are normally free of charge. When it arrives there will be an entry form inside, and once you have decided on which class/classes you want to enter, complete the form and return it to the address given, along with the correct entry money, ensuring you do so before the closing date. The closing date is normally two to four weeks before the show, so you will need to be organized so as not to miss out, as entries received after the closing date will more often than not be refused, unless the classes are undersubscribed and spaces are still available. Do not use this as your entry plan because sooner or later it will let you down.

The Day Before

Having finished your preparation leading up to your show day, give your dog his final good groom, and tweak any little areas you feel need attention.

Have a checklist of all the things you will need on the day, and then tick them off as you pack them, to be sure that nothing has been forgotten. Include things such as the grooming kit, water bowls, food bowls, spare lead and collar, towels, poop scooper and bags. Depending on how much space you have, a crate or cage is always pleasant for your dog to relax in, out of the way of everyone else, especially if it is all new to them.

Check if you need any passes or tickets to the show you are attending. Always take your schedule with you as this may have a mobile number to contact on the day should you get lost or need help. Directions will also be helpful if you have not been to a show site before – it cuts down the stress levels if you know where you are going!

At the Show

Always give yourself plenty of time to get to the show so you can arrive, park up, find out where you need to be, and let your dog stretch his legs and go to the toilet. Declare that you have arrived to the relevant people, and then set up camp for the day so you can all stay as relaxed as possible.

If time allows, try to have a look at the other classes happening on that day, and watch how the other entrants perform in the ring. We can learn something from everyone we watch, either how to do it or how not to. This can be of immense help!

Check that all classes are running to time, find your ring, and see if your judge is judging any other classes on that day so you can watch him in action.

As you near the time to go into the ring, finish off last minute grooming and trimming, and keep an eye on the class before yours so you don't miss it – and lastly, enjoy!

In the Ring

The steward will tell you where to stand in the ring.

When it is your turn, the judge will call you forward to stand.

The judge will examine your dog from a distance and then more closely, checking his eyes, teeth, structure and musculature, along with overall conformation.

The judge will then ask you to move your dog. Different judges may require dogs to move in different ways, so do watch and listen carefully to their instructions.

Best in show.

SUCCESSFUL SHOWING

If you win, there is little in the way of prize money – winning at a show should be done for the fun and the actual thrill of winning.

The key to being successful in anything you do is to make sure you prepare and that your attention to detail is second to none. Remember the saying 'Fail to prepare – prepare to fail'.

Having the ability or belief that you can win starts with the conditioning, fitness and training of your dog. A winning combination does not happen overnight, and it won't happen at all if you are slack and lazy in your preparation.

Always start at the bottom so as not to put undue pressure on yourself or your dog. If your expectations are unrealistic then this will only lead to disappointment, making you feel despondent. Many people give up before they have started as they gave themselves unreachable goals too soon.

When you go to a show, or even during training sessions, get a friend to take a video of it for you. It is amazing how much can be learnt from reviewing your performance, as you will see exactly what you did or did not do, so you can then endeavour to change and improve. Study the videos for the finer details, as it is these that

LEARNING IS A LIFELONG HOBBY

Spend time watching others and learning from their performances, keep training, and don't ever think you know it all, because you don't. Learning is a lifelong hobby, so never close your mind to learning as you will be the only loser.

may make the difference between first or second in a hotly contested class.

Be patient and consistent. Losing your temper will set you back weeks in training and ruin trust with your partner. If you run into an issue that you are not sure how to fix, call a friend or have a glass of wine and think about a solution. The problem will still be there the next time you go out to train, but you will be better prepared to correct it.

Always stay positive towards your dog and you will have a partnership of which others will be envious. Nobody wants to work with or for a bully: remember you are a team, and teams always work better when they are working together.

Remember, success does not happen overnight, and it will take several years to climb the ladder to claiming big prizes and rewards. Try to make it a positive and enjoyable event for you and your dog, and tell yourself often that 'Rome was not built in a day'.

That winning feeling for Champion Draycore Chilli.

9 BREEDING AND PREGNANCY

Breeding is a controversial subject for rescues. If dogs were not bred at such a rate, then not as many would end up in rescue. On the other side of the coin is the fact that we still need good breeders to keep the good breed lines in existence. Ultimately, as with other aspects of dog legislation, there should be a way of monitoring breeders and only allowing those who adhere to legislated standards to be allowed to breed. The Breeding and Sale of Dogs (Welfare) Act 1999 does not go far enough to stop the 'back street' breeders churning out puppies for profit.

It is mainly unscrupulous breeders who flout the current laws, and this will continue until there is harsher 'policing' and enforcement by the authorities. Some local authorities have attempted to reduce the problem within their tenancy agreements, giving them greater powers of punishment by ultimately evicting tenants if their terms are broken. The terms will restrict the number of dogs allowed in the property, and will insist on the dogs being microchipped and neutered. This is a positive way forward, but is restricted by local authority budgets in many cases.

We need to prevent overbreeding and breeding from poor lines whilst ensuring that any pups bred are only sold to suitable homes, if only to prevent the constant flow of unwanted and abandoned dogs going into pounds every day.

Overpopulation is the number one cause of cruelty to dogs and is not just applicable in third world countries. Here in Britain we have far too many dogs for far too few good homes, with almost every dog rescue working to capacity. Each year in Britain, thousands of dogs are destroyed, mostly because they are not in good health, either physically or mentally, or simply because they have done their seven days in a pound and there is nowhere else for them to go. The cause of this is simple – overpopulation, and dogs being treated as a disposable commodity.

The breeding of dogs is far too easy and is often seen as lucrative to the semi-professional and hobbyist. Many people breed simply because they thought it would be good for their bitch to have a litter, a belief which has no medical founding, or because they wanted another dog from their favourite pet. The web and media is crammed with adverts of puppies for sale, and many people are drawn into breeding pups because of these types of advert, not realizing that many of these dogs don't get sold and end up in rescue centres across Britain.

- **Breeding should be taken very responsibly with full consideration of all the facts**
- **Breeding is not a lucrative money maker and should not be entered into purely for profit**

PLANNING AHEAD

If you are planning to breed from your bitch a number of key considerations should be made, as described below.

Is there Space in Your Home?
The whelping area should be set up in a quiet, heated room of your house, large enough for a whelping box. Mum and pups will spend their first three weeks here, as you will too, whilst monitoring their progress. Consideration must also be given with regard to mum and pups getting too hot if the puppies are born in the summer months, so a conservatory would not be a good idea, nor would a room that receives a lot of sun during the day.

Mum should be familiar and comfortable with whichever room you use, so if she is not normally allowed in the spare bedroom, for example, and that is to be used as your whelping room, allow her access prior to whelping so she does not have the additional stress factor of a strange room. Of course the room should not be accessible to other animals in the home, and should not receive a lot of 'through traffic' and noise.

After their initial first weeks, mum and pups will need to be in a completely different environment where they can start seeing the world around them and can begin their socialization with people and domestic life. A playpen is useful for this, but consider its sturdiness with regard to when the pups are about six weeks old and much stronger and more boisterous; and be sure it will be big enough – a litter of ten pups can take up a lot of space! They should also have a bed in the playpen for 'quiet time', and mum should be allowed a bed in the same room but away from the pups so she can get some precious time to herself.

Weather permitting, it is also beneficial for pups to be able to encounter the great outdoors in the safety of the garden. Again, playpens are ideal for this, and there are specially designed ones for such use, which can be moved around as required. Remember, if the pups are to be left outside for any period of time they must have some form of shelter, and mum will still want to come and go to them.

Finally, consider having your home invaded when buyers come to visit the pups. They will want to see the pups with their mum, and will probably come as a family group during an evening or at a weekend. Buyers will probably be with you for a couple of hours, and ideally will visit twice or more. Think about accommodating these extra bodies without disrupting the calm in the rest of your home.

Is there Time in Your Life?

Do you have the time to devote to breeding from your bitch? The whole process of whelping and rearing pups will require about three months of constant work. Mum will need observing full time coming up to when she is due to whelp, especially if she is a first-time mum. Many people use CCTV for these purposes, as it allows full observation without disturbing her.

Once born, you will need to be on hand during the first week almost constantly whilst you ensure mum is able to care for all the pups. If she struggles to feed them, for example, you might have to hand feed them every few hours throughout the day and night. This could be a full-time job if she produces a large litter.

Once pups are weaned, the immense task begins of socializing them, feeding them up to five times a day, and of course clearing and clean-

Room to play.

Cute and cuddly, but a major time investment.

ing up after them! Be prepared, as this task can take up all your waking hours.

Finally, consider that not all the pups may sell as quickly as expected, and you must be able to give the necessary time to any remaining youngsters in their development and training to give them the solid start to life they deserve. Having decided to breed, you are responsible for ensuring these pups have the best possible start to life.

Do You Have the Predisposition?

Certainly there is a lot of joy and happiness cuddling a young pup and being part of its life, but are you able to deal with the heartache and emotions that can come with it? It may well be that one or two pups are born dead; that pups are born with deformities; that a weak pup dies later on.

Also you need to consider your tolerance levels: a lot of patience is needed when a litter of pups is constantly chewing anything they can get hold of and messing continually – and what if you have to care for weak or sick pups?

Finally, do you have the strength and resolve to let the pups go off to new homes? It is no good breeding a litter and then deciding to keep them all because you cannot bear to part with them, because none of them will get the attention or time they are entitled to.

Can You Afford to Breed?

You will require a substantial amount of money to get mum and pups to an age where the pups can leave home, and there is never a guarantee that the money from selling them will cover your costs, assuming they all survive.

Not only do you have the cost of using a stud dog, you will also have the cost of having your bitch checked regularly by a vet, and the cost of the provision of the whelping area, and this is before the pups are even born. Consider insurance and its costs. Mum may well need a vet in attendance, which could become costly, and in the worst case may require a Caesarean. You will then have the ongoing costs of vet checks, wormers, vaccinations, microchipping, food for mum and pups, and of course general wear and tear on your home.

Will People Want Your Pups?

What makes your pups special? You need to consider the number of breeders in your area and the time of year. If this is your first litter, buyers will tend towards the established breeder with the established reputation.

Also consider the time of year. If the pups are ready to go during the summer holidays, it may well be that families have booked time away so you may not have the market, or you may be expected to keep pup for a longer period of time than originally planned.

Never sell pups just before Christmas. This is a recipe for disaster, and rescues see so many youngsters come into them in the New Year from people who made that hasty decision for a cuddly Christmas present.

Of course you may have the advantage of an exceptional stud dog or bitch with a pedigree line that is in high demand, but pedigree means fairly little to your average family looking to buy a family pet. Their bigger concern will be the health and temperament of mum and the pups.

As puppies pass the age of eight weeks, you may well have to drop your price and encourage buyers by ensuring your pups are getting socialized and trained as they would be in a home of their own.

- **Never give away pups! If people cannot afford to pay a reasonable fee for them, do they have the finances to care for them in the long term?**

A real bundle of trouble!

CONSIDERATIONS FOR BREEDERS

A responsible breeder's ultimate aim should be to breed the healthiest puppies possible, thereby increasing their lifespan and happiness. It is therefore necessary to take into consideration the general health, temperament and predisposition of the sire and dam.

Temperament: The temperament of the potential parents will be a good guide to predicting the temperament of any potential puppies. If a dog shows any suspect tendency in its temperament, it should not be used for breeding purposes.

Breed type and characteristics: Many breeders will wish to participate in some kind of activity once their new puppies are mature, such as field trials or showing, so predicting how they will turn out with regard to desired qualities will be important. There is no substitute for experience when breeding puppies of the correct type and characteristics. If you do not have such experience it is wise to contact, or even join, an appropriate breed club that can help you.

Health test results: Inherited disease is an area that dog breeders must take into account when selecting two dogs to mate together. Over the years a number of health screening schemes have been developed, initially based on the clinical screening of individual dogs but more recently on a growing number of DNA tests for the mutations known to cause inherited diseases in the dog, and it is important for breeders to use the available breed-specific health programmes on their breeding dogs. The results of these screens gives the breeder a better understanding of the genes that a dog carries, and therefore the genes that he is likely to pass to his progeny if he were to be bred from.

Genetic diversity: Research demonstrates that for many breeds of dog, genetic diversity is being lost generation after generation, and in future dog breeders will need to manage these losses in genetic diversity in order to minimize the potentially serious associated risks.

Genetics and Pedigree

There are three forms of breeding: in-breeding, line breeding and out-breeding.

In-breeding: The bitch is mated with a close relative such as a half-brother or grandfather. This can be a successful method to fix good characteristics quickly, but it also doubles up on unwanted features such as hip dysplasia, and overall can produce a decrease in fitness and health, and may reduce litter sizes and fertility.

Line breeding: The bitch is mated to a dog of the same family, having common ancestors four or five generations back. It can be a valuable policy as long as the ancestors are fully evaluated.

Out-breeding: The bitch is mated to a totally unrelated dog, which increases genetic diversity.

A pedigree dog typically refers to a dog of a modern dog breed with a documented pedigree in a stud book; he may be registered with a breed club that may also be part of a national kennel club. In the United Kingdom it is the Kennel Club that holds the database (stud book) for pure-bred dogs. The pedigree is your dog's family tree.

Genetics is a study of genes, and every animal has a unique individual pattern carried in their cells. Genes are carried within the body on strings known as chromosomes. Dogs have thirty-nine pairs of chromosomes, each pair taking one chromosome from the dam and one from the sire. The way in which the chromosomes combine in a fertilized embryo is totally random and therefore individual.

A simple inherited disorder occurs from the mutation of a single gene and represents 70 to 75 per cent of known inherited diseases. This type of disorder can be established by DNA testing through a blood sample or buccal (cheek) swab. Some testing schemes have evolved to the degree that there are now DNA control schemes in place for some breeds.

Not all genes are equal, and are either dominant or recessive. A dominant gene shows in your dog, whilst a recessive gene is hidden and may

An example of a Kennel Club Pedigree Certificate.

only surface when your dog is mated with a partner who also carries the recessive gene.

With a recessive gene the dog inherits two copies of the abnormal gene from both parents. The results can be:

- Clear – the dog does not have the abnormal gene and will not pass it on to any progeny
- Carrier – the dog will not be affected by the abnormal gene but may pass on one copy of the normal gene or one copy of the abnormal gene to its progeny
- Affected – the dog has two copies of the abnormal gene and will be affected by the disorder, and will pass one copy of the abnormal gene on to its progeny

With a dominant gene the dog need inherit only one copy of the abnormal gene to be affected. The results can be:

- Clear – the dog will not be affected and will not pass it on to its progeny
- Heterozygous affected – the dog has one copy of the normal gene and one copy of the abnormal gene; it will be affected by the disorder, and may pass on one copy of the abnormal gene to its progeny
- Homozygous affected – the dog has two copies of the abnormal gene and will be affected by the disorder and will pass on one copy of the abnormal gene to its progeny

	Clear Sire	Carrier Sire	Affected Sire
Clear Dam	Litter will be clear	50% chance of each pup being clear	Litter will be carriers
		50% chance of each pup being a carrier	
Carrier Dam	50% chance of each pup being clear	25% chance of each pup being clear	50% chance of each pup being a carrier
	50% chance of each pup being a carrier	25% chance of each pup being affected	50% chance of each pup being affected
		50% chance of each pup being a carrier	
Affected Dam	Litter will be carriers	50% chance of each pup being a carrier	Litter will be affected
		50% chance of each pup being affected	

The recessive gene and its outcome.

	Clear Sire	Heterozygous Affected Sire	Homozygous Affected Sire
Clear Dam	Litter will be clear	50% chance of each pup being clear	Litter will be heterozygous affected
		50% chance of each pup being heterozygous affected	
Carrier Dam	50% chance of each pup being clear	25% chance of each pup being clear	50% chance of each pup being heterozygous affected
	50% chance of each pup being a carrier	25% chance of each pup being homozygous affected	50% chance of each pup being homozygous affected
		50% chance of each pup being heterozygous affected	
Affected Dam	Litter will be carriers	50% chance of each pup being heterozygous affected	Litter will be homozygous affected
		50% chance of each pup being homozygous affected	

The dominant gene and its outcome.

Health Testing

Clinical screening schemes are available for complex inherited diseases. Not all inherited conditions are congenital (present at birth), so some of these schemes are required to be repeated at stages in a dog's life.

A complex inherited disorder is often caused by a number of different genes and can also be influenced by environmental factors. Conditions are tested through a grading system. Unfortunately technology is not yet advanced enough to be able to test for these conditions through DNA.

The German Shepherd falls into the category of the Pastoral Breed Group under the Kennel Club in the UK. This group consists of herding dogs, most of whom have a weatherproof double coat to protect them from the elements in severe conditions.

It is strongly recommended by the UK Kennel Club that breeding German Shepherd dogs are screened under the following schemes:

BVA/KC Hip Dysplasia Scheme: Hips are x-rayed and evaluated by two experts who score nine anatomical features of the hip. Each is scored out of fifty-three, so a score can be anywhere between 0 and 106 – the lower the better.

BVA/KC Elbow Dysplasia Scheme: Elbows are x-rayed and evaluated by two specialists who give a score between 0 and 3. The higher of the two scores will be recorded. Again, the lower the better.

BVA/KC/ISDS (International Sheep Dog Society) Eye Scheme:

Schedule A – known inherited eye diseases and the breeds known to be affected.

Schedule B – breeds and conditions where further investigation is required.

A specialist panel is available to examine a dog on a yearly basis.

Breed club schemes: Breed clubs provide haemophilia testing for males; and health screening tests, which may be collated and shared with the Kennel Club.

The Kennel Club currently records the results for the hip dysplasia, elbow dysplasia and eye schemes.

The Kennel Club
The Kennel Club is the UK's largest organization providing a voluntary register for pedigree dogs and crossbreed dogs. It promotes health and welfare, and offers many resources in the attempt to advance breeding standards and responsible breeding.

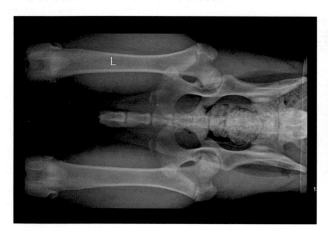

A hip x-ray taken for a stud dog.

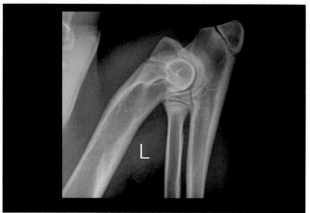

A lateral x-ray of a stud dog's elbow.

LOWERING THE ODDS

There is no formula for producing a perfect litter, but the odds of disaster can be lowered by examining the pedigree, by DNA testing, and by health screening the parents. In this way, deformities and diseases can be reduced in future generations and eventually eradicated.

The Kennel Club was founded in 1873, and in 1874 the first Kennel Club Stud Book was published. This extensive database, which is available online, is a valuable resource to aid decision making when breeding.

Your German Shepherd does not have to be registered with the Kennel Club, but he will not be allowed to participate in certain activities if he has not been registered (*see* Chapter 7, 'Activities and Competitions'). More importantly, if your dog is not Kennel Club registered, then you will not be able to register his progeny, and this will put off many a sensible buyer, who will be expecting to receive Kennel Club papers with their pup.

The Assured Breeder Scheme

The Kennel Club Assured Breeder Scheme logo.

The Kennel Club further endorses responsible breeding with their Assured Breeder Scheme, which is easy for both breeders and puppy buyers to understand. Breeders are able to register under the scheme as long as they meet the requirements necessary, and will be inspected by the Kennel Club, which is a UKAS-accredited certification body, at regular intervals. Breeders can also be recognized by achieving certain accolades, described as follows:

- Breeding Experience Accolade
- Breed Club Accolade
- Stud Book Accolade
- Accolade of Excellence

The Assured Breeder Scheme includes the following principles:

- Ensures that all animals, including puppies, are kept and reared in good conditions. This includes allowing prospective puppy buyers to see a puppy with its mother and any litter mates at the place the puppy was born and reared
- Takes all reasonable steps to breed happy, healthy dogs that are 'fit for function', making use of all relevant health-screening schemes and DNA tests
- Ensures written advice is provided on:
  - ➢ tendencies or potential traits in the breed and/or puppy
  - ➢ socialization, exercise and training
  - ➢ feeding
  - ➢ worming and immunization programmes
  - ➢ grooming
- Provides new puppy owners with reasonable after-sales service, offering support and advice where possible, and deals with any issues that may arise in good faith
- Provides all relevant information at the time of sale including the registration certificate (or if not immediately available, as soon as possible). This should include details of any breeding restrictions or endorsements
- Assists with the rehoming of a puppy throughout its lifetime should this be necessary
- Ensures the parents of each litter are readily identifiable by microchip, tattoo or DNA profile. In April 2016 it will also be compulsory for breeders to microchip pups before they leave. DNA profiling will also become compulsory in the future
- Adheres to all Kennel Club rules and regulations, particularly those relating to the minimum and maximum ages for breeding, and the frequency of litters
- Provides a contract of sale, and stud service arrangement

If registered with the Kennel Club as an Assured Breeder, the BVA/KC Hip Dysplasia Scheme is mandatory, while the other schemes are strongly recommended.

Factors that would prevent the Kennel Club registration of a litter include the following:

- The dam has already whelped four litters
- The dam has reached eight years of age
- The dam is under one year of age
- The litter is the result of a liaison between father and daughter, mother and son, or brother and sister
- The dam has already had two litters by Caesarean
- The dam was not resident in the UK at the time of whelping

Kennel Club Endorsements
The Kennel Club permits two endorsements on the registration of puppies:

- Progeny not eligible for registration – beneficial to breeders to help protect stock and ensure pups are carefully and responsibly bred from
- Export pedigree not allowed – there may be concerns regarding the welfare standards in certain overseas countries, for example.

Whilst the endorsements do not prevent breeding, they prevent the litter from being registered with the UK Kennel Club and any overseas kennel clubs.

As the endorsement is placed by the breeder, it is only the breeder who can agree to remove an endorsement. Any endorsements should be stated in a written agreement and it is helpful to state the reason for it and the conditions under which it may be removed.

Additional Kennel Club Resources
Additional kennel club resources include the Health Test Result Finder, which searches any registered dog for the results of its health screening; and estimated breeding values (EBVs), which measure the individual's genetic risk for specific complex conditions by using the individual's score and those of its relatives.

There is also the inbreeding coefficient calculator, which uses pedigree information on the Kennel Club database to show the degree of inbreeding based on a hypothetical mating.

BITCH MANAGEMENT BEFORE MATING

A bitch should be fully fit and healthy before she is mated, so ensure she has been well exercised and has received a balanced diet.

Bitches that are fed on a bulky complete diet may struggle to consume the volume of food needed later in a pregnancy, so it may be worth gradually changing her to a more compact form of feeding whilst ensuring she is getting all the nutrients she will need for herself and the pups. There are many commercial diets available for the pregnant bitch. Also consider that her diet will be continued throughout lactation as well, so the pups will in effect be on the same diet.

Your bitch should be examined by your vet to ensure she is clear of any health problems, especially with her eyes and skin; and most important

PUPPY FARMING

A puppy farmer is defined as a high volume breeder who breeds puppies with little or no regard for the health and welfare of the puppies or their parents. A puppy farmer's main intent is profit. As a result he typically separates puppies from their mothers too early, ignores guidelines about the maximum frequency of litters, provides inadequate socialization of puppies, sells puppies through third parties, keeps puppies in poor conditions, and fails to follow breed-specific health schemes or to apply basic, routine health measures such as immunization and worming. The puppies bred by puppy farmers are therefore more likely to suffer from common, preventable, infectious diseases, and painful or chronic inherited conditions, and to have behavioural issues and a shorter life span.

is a dental check, as any dental or oral disease may be passed on to the pups when she is licking them, especially around the umbilical cord.

She should be up to date with her vaccinations, but vets do not like to give boosters just before mating or during pregnancy, so plan ahead. And of course she should be kept up to date with her worming and parasite programmes.

If she is registered with the Kennel Club and you intend to register the litter you should also have considered the recommended DNA tests and health screens.

Bitches should not be mated until they are fully mature themselves, and eighteen months to two years is the earliest you should consider mating your bitch. Apart from anything else it will take this long for you to establish her season history (breeding cycle), so that you know when the opportune period for mating will be. The average age of puberty is six to seven months.

Bitches come into season (heat) approximately every six months for about three weeks at a time. A significant clue is that most bitches will lick their vulva more frequently to keep themselves clean. Other signs are displaying their vulva to other dogs, and of course other dogs showing more of an interest in the bitch! Her vulva will swell and bleeding will start. Initially the discharge will be fairly runny, but it will become darker and thicker as she approaches ovula-

tion. A bitch is most fertile ten to twelve days into her season on average. Her breeding cycle is described as follows:

- Pro-oestrus: the stage at the beginning of heat when the vulva is swollen, and a blood-stained discharge can be seen
- Oestrus: the vulva is enlarged and turgid, and the discharge is thicker. Ovulation occurs spontaneously about two days after the start of oestrus
- Metoestrus: occurs in the unmated bitch, and hormones equivalent to those in pregnancy are present. During this period the bitch may show signs of false pregnancy
- Anoestrus: the period of sexual inactivity between cycles

False Pregnancy

Also known as pseudo pregnancy, this can occur during the oestrus period when the bitch would be lactating if she were pregnant. Signs include:

- Poor appetite
- Lethargy
- Milk production
- Nest building
- Aggressiveness
- Attachment to a substitute puppy such as a soft toy

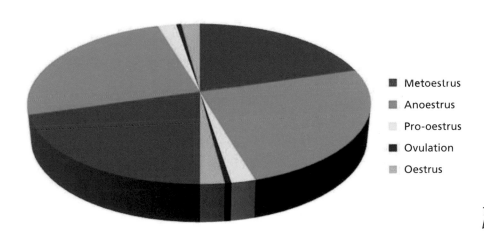

- Metoestrus
- Anoestrus
- Pro-oestrus
- Ovulation
- Oestrus

The breeding cycle of the bitch.

125

Treatment, if needed, is by hormones, and prevention is by a hormone injection. Once a bitch has had a false pregnancy it is fairly common for it to occur after each season, unless of course she has been mated.

THE STUD DOG

If you are planning on becoming a serious breeder you may consider having your own stud dog – or of course you may be the owner of a stud dog.

Just as with the bitch, the stud dog should be fit and healthy at the time of mating. Most breeders will only consider a stud dog registered with the Kennel Club, and will expect to see that relevant DNA tests and health screenings have been completed.

If you are planning on having a stud dog alongside breeding bitches, there are a few advantages and disadvantages to consider.

The advantages include the following:

- You will have complete information on character, pedigree and health
- Your bitch may be easier to mate having lived around the male dog, and it can encourage some bitches into season
- You may be able to offer your stud dog for outside work, thus broadening your breeding line

The disadvantages are as follows:

- Your stud dog will be limited in his use as you do not want to in-breed

A stud dog.

- Handling a stud dog in the same environment as bitches can be difficult when bitches are in season but are not to be mated
- Using an outside stud dog will probably cost you a lot less than keeping your own

Stud dogs usually stay at home, and the bitch has to visit to mate at the appropriate time. It is usual for a second visit forty-eight hours later, when the bitch will be more relaxed. It is rare for a stud dog to visit the bitch, as they do not always perform as well, and the owner will probably also charge travelling expenses along with the stud fee.

- **A stud dog should not be mated under the age of eighteen months**

Of course there is no way of knowing if a stud dog is fertile unless there is a very recent sperm analysis. The first timer may be keen but may not have the sperm power, either due to not having enough quantity of sperm, enough motility (power to reach the uterine tube) in the sperm, or the sperm may be deformed. In the first timer's case the owner of the stud dog may offer a reduced stud fee. A proven stud dog will therefore be most costly.

THE MATING PROCESS

So you have chosen a stud dog to use, or you have a bitch visiting your stud dog. Prior to any visits a written agreement should be made including the stud fee, the service provided (the number of visits) and of course any concessions. Concessions could include a free mating at the bitch's next season if she does not take the first time.

There can be variables in payment depending on the age and experience of a stud dog. Whilst it is normal practice to pay the stud fee in full after the mating, the owner of a young and inexperienced dog may not require payment until the litter is born. Think carefully if a stud dog owner requests the pick of the litter as payment, as it is fairly common for the pups to be sold at double the stud fee!

It is normal practice for the bitch to travel to the dog. It is a good policy to encourage your bitch to urinate before arriving at the stud dog's home, and of course she should have on a collar and lead. A head collar can be useful to control her during mating, but of course ensure your bitch is used to wearing one before the day.

The dogs should be allowed some socialization, and when the bitch is ready she will stand with her tail raised to one side to let the male know. The male will mount her, penetrate and clasp her around the waist. Your job at this stage is to keep your bitch steady, especially if she is a novice, and of course keep her standing so that the male can mount her.

The sperm should be in the uterine tubes before the eggs are ripe for fertilization.

At this stage the dogs will 'tie', where the dog's penis becomes expanded and bulbous and remains in the vagina. This can last from five minutes up to one hour; an average tie is around twenty minutes. This is the male's way of giving his sperm the best possible chance of completing the mating. A fertile mating is possible without a tie, but a twenty-minute tie is more satisfactory.

The male dog will ejaculate in three stages:

- The first, it is believed, is to clear any residual urine from the penis
- The second, which is normally within a minute or so of penetration, contains the sperm
- The third is a considerable amount of fluid ejaculated intermittently from the prostate gland during the tie to help transport the sperm to the oviduct

During the tie the male's owner will turn him so he is no longer resting on your bitch's back. This is another time you may need to keep your bitch steady as some get very irked at this stage. The tie will break spontaneously and some prostate fluid may drain from the bitch.

Two visits to mate with forty-eight hours between is the minimum you should expect for your stud fee, but of course this should all have been discussed and agreed prior to the mating.

On completion of the mating the owner of the stud dog should give the bitch owner a signed

Kennel Club pedigree of the male, along with a signed Kennel Club form certifying the mating took place. This will be required to register the litter with the Kennel Club. Some stud dog owners will only release this form on the birth of the litter, as it has been known for a bitch that has not fallen pregnant, to then be mated with a different male, but the original male's pedigree is used for registering the pups.

- **Remember that the mated bitch is still in season and could still mate with another male and will probably be quite a willing participant now, so precaution must still be taken to ensure she is not off lead in public spaces**

Should a mistake occur, parental analysis can be verified by DNA, so any pedigree pups in the litter can still be registered with the Kennel Club. DNA analysis is also a good safeguard to prevent the substitution of one dog for another! Your vet or the Kennel Club can give you full advice on DNA services available.

Mating Problems

The Bitch
Mismating: Your vet can give your bitch a hormone injection within three days of mating to prevent fertilization from taking place.

The bitch will not mate: Misdiagnosis of her 'heat' can happen. Your vet can ascertain the correct stage with a blood sample or vaginal swab. She should also be checked to ensure her vaginal structure is normal, and that there are no other unrelated problems such as pain in her hips.

No pregnancy: Try mating on the bitch's next heat. You may wish to consider a different stud dog, because although both dogs may be perfectly healthy as individuals, they could just be incompatible.

The Stud Dog
Paraphimosis: This is a prolonged erection of the penis, which is unable to retract back into the sheath after mating. The penis becomes very swollen due to the sheath constricting it. The penis should be bathed in cool, sterile water to help reduce its size, and lubrication such as petroleum jelly should make it possible to pull the sheath forward over the penis.

PREGNANCY

Pregnancy Diagnosis
Pregnant bitches do not tend to show any signs until about day thirty-five after mating. At this stage the following signs will become apparent:

- The teats will become a deeper pink as there is an increased blood supply to them, and they will become enlarged and erect. The teats between the hind legs will show most prominently
- The mammary glands will begin to enlarge as they develop more functional tissue ready for milk production
- There will be a vaginal discharge, which should be opaque or white in colour. If the discharge is blood-stained or any other colour your vet should be consulted
- The bitch will suffer morning sickness, in the form of frothy liquid. She may refuse food in the morning. This is caused by hormonal changes and pressure from the stretched uterus
- There will be abdominal enlargement, which can be hard to see in the larger breeds until forty to forty-two days after mating, and can appear overnight. This is due to the uterine horns becoming full of the developing foetuses so there is no longer room for them to lie parallel. They fold back on themselves and drop lower into the abdomen, thus changing the bitch's outline. The drop in the uterus pulls down on the spine, making the vertebrae very prominent

Nowadays blood tests can be done on days twenty-eight to thirty-seven after mating to diagnose pregnancy.

Ultrasound is the most common way to diagnose pregnancies, and is very accurate. Whilst it

Lottie saved from the pound and ready to drop!

can diagnose pregnancy it can be very difficult to tell the number of pups if there are more than six. It is also a very useful tool to monitor a difficult pregnancy and the size of the developing foetuses. If they are extremely large your vet may predict that a caesarean may be necessary for your bitch.

In the later stages of pregnancy the foetal heartbeats can also be detected through a stethoscope.

Care of the Pregnant Bitch

This can be a confusing time for your bitch, as one instinct tells her she wants to stay close to you, while her natural instinct tells her to start digging a whelping den away from prying eyes, often outside in the garden. The bitch should not be discouraged from this, but now is a good time to be preparing the whelping room and encouraging her to spend more time there so she feels relaxed when her time comes.

Around week six of the pregnancy, food should be gradually increased. Your bitch should be fed four or five times a day, little and often, as she will struggle with large meals due to the increase in the size of her abdomen. Resist the temptation to over-supplement her, as too much calcium and vitamin D can cause skeletal disorder in the pups. A good commercial diet should supply all she needs unless advised otherwise by your vet.

During pregnancy, the cyclic growth of hair is changed and all hairs that make up the coat will go into the growth phase. Ensure she is brushed daily and her coat kept clean, but do not use any insecticidal sprays or shampoos. If your bitch has a long coat it may be necessary to cut the hair away from around the teats and vulva ready for whelping. This will keep her cleaner during whelping and therefore more comfortable, and will prevent the newborn pups from getting a mouthful of hair rather than nipple.

Your bitch should continue to be exercised throughout her pregnancy, but steady lead walking is a good idea as the pregnancy progresses. She will not want to go far the further she gets into the pregnancy, so let *her* determine how long or how far. Avoid over-heating her by walking in the sun now she is pregnant, and avoid chilling her by letting her jump into a pond if that is her style. Remember she will also need to urinate more often now, as her abdomen puts pressure on her bladder.

Be aware of her interactions with other animals in the home, as she will now be giving off a different scent they may find confusing, and her getting fed more often may cause jealousy and upset. Fighting is the most common cause for a bitch to suffer an abortion.

Consult with your vet as to the best worming programme for your bitch during pregnancy as you do not want a heavy worm burden on your pups. Some worms can migrate in the pregnant bitch to infect the pups in the uterus and through her milk. Prevention will ensure healthy pups that should thrive.

• **Pregnancy duration for a German Shepherd is stated as sixty-three days from mating. Many adhere to this timescale, but whelping can occur anywhere from between 54 days and 72 days.**

PREPARING FOR WHELPING

You should already have considered where you are going to set up the whelping room, ensur-

THE WHELPING KIT

The following are the very basics required for when the pups are being born:

• Old, soft clean towels for drying the pups
• Small box with a covered hot water bottle in case you need to move pups away from mum whilst delivering further pups
• Scales to weigh pups
• Pen and paper to note times of birth and weights
• Flashlight for examination if needed or if there is a power cut!
• Somewhere to dispose of soiled materials and placenta
• Substitute milk and bottles in case mum cannot or will not feed
• Your vet's phone number

Remember that you need to keep the area sterile and avoid cross contamination, so consider surgical-style gloves and antiseptic hand dispensers for yourself and anyone else who needs to enter the room.

ing that the room can be heated but does not overheat and is in a quiet place with no through traffic. The ideal room would be on the ground floor with easy access to a wash basin or sink, and direct access to the garden for when the pups are ready to explore.

Consider the flooring. If carpeted, you will want to protect this. Many people suggest stockpiling newspapers to use, but this can cause continual clearing up and rearrangement as they are walked over. Old sheets may be a better option. There are also beddings that can be purchased in rolls or mats which can be washed and reused easily. If you are using a floor with cold tiles, this form of bedding is probably preferable to keep the pups warm unless of course it is a hot summer when they may appreciate a cool area on which to lie, as will your bitch.

Bear in mind you will need to keep watch as her whelping date becomes due. Is there space for you, or can you watch through a window without disturbing her? Alternatively you might consider the use of a camera, which can be purchased at quite reasonable cost. This can be the comfortable way to monitor your bitch, and later the pups, especially if she is more comfortable alone with them.

There are many suggestions on building a whelping box. Cardboard boxes can be used which can be disposed of when soiled and may be better than a wooden box, in which any dirt and thus infection can be ingrained. It is also advised to create a hood to give the bitch the feeling of a cave, though this is very rarely done in practice. You can, of course, purchase a ready-made whelping box. It is advised to have a heated pad or heat lamp in one area of the whelping box for pups to be kept warm whilst mum continues to deliver, because at this stage of their life they are unable to regulate their own body temperature.

The important thing is to ensure that the whelping box is large enough for your bitch to stretch out fully with room for the pups around her. It should be raised on all sides so that the pups do not fall or roll out, but not so high that your bitch struggles to get in and out. You should be able to keep the area clean and free from infection easily.

10 WHELPING AND WEANING

WHELPING

There is no fixed time as to how long whelping will last: one bitch could produce a whole litter within an hour, whilst another could take twenty-four hours or longer. German Shepherds as a breed tend to whelp quite easily.

Whelping is described as a three-stage process, but in fact there is a stage before, the preparatory stage, when the levels of progesterone – the hormone that maintains pregnancy and which prevents the uterus from contracting while the foetus grows – in the blood fall, and oestrogen takes over again. The production of prostaglandin is stimulated allowing whelping to begin.

These hormonal levels are triggered by rising cortisol levels produced by the developing pups, and during this time, the bitch's body temperature will drop. Breeders will therefore take their bitch's temperature a few times a day to pinpoint that drop in temperature, which can be as low as 97°F for a few hours. This usually indicates that the bitch will whelp within the next twenty-four hours.

Stage One

The foetuses actually trigger whelping, because towards the end of pregnancy they become crowded in the uterus and increasingly stressed, stimulating immature cardiac and respiratory systems to become ready to perform at birth. Your bitch will be restless during this time and may refuse food, and may vomit. She may pant heavily whilst sleeping on and off. This behaviour pattern could last for up to twenty-four hours or, if you are lucky, stage one could be over before you even realize it has happened. On average, a German Shepherd will take six to twelve hours on stage one of whelping.

Some bitches shred their bedding, which is now considered to be a reaction to the pain rather than preparing the nest as previously thought, and she may well repeat the shredding between the arrival of pups. Some breeders recommend leaving down some newspaper purely for this.

Just before whelping, the mucoid discharge from the vulva seen during pregnancy will increase in volume as the mucoid plug sealing the cervix dissolves, and the cervix will dilate so the pups can move down the uterus, down the vagina and into the world. If the cervix has not dilated this is when whelping can become difficult.

At this point you should warn your vet of the imminent arrivals in case his help is needed.

Stage Two

The foetuses usually lie on their backs in the uterus and must rotate into position so they can pass through the birth canal head first, therefore meeting the open cervix centrally. The foetus should still be in its amniotic sac (a double-layered water bag), which aids their journey by the pushing, squeezing and relaxing process of the uterine muscles.

Recent evidence suggests that foetuses are born from each uterine horn alternately, so if a foetus arrives at the cervix in an awkward position or starts to move up the opposite horn rather than through the cervix, both mum and pup are in immediate trouble. It can also risk the pups to follow, as once the placenta has separated from the uterine walls it is urgent the foetus is born quickly, and that once in the outside world they can take their first breath unaided as soon as possible.

Your bitch should have stopped panting and become quieter, but you should see abdominal contractions as she presses down towards her hind end. The first visible sign of an imminent birth will be the appearance of the amniotic sac, which will look like a black bag of fluid. This

LOTTIE – 1

I was asked to foster Lottie, a German Shepherd bitch who had been taken in as a stray by a pound. It was discovered she was pregnant so they asked for rescue help. Having a room I could use away from the other dogs made me the ideal candidate, even though I had no breeding experience apart from what I had read in books and seen on the television.

Lottie arrived one hot summer Saturday, emaciated and heavily pregnant. She had a quick trip to my vets who scanned her, and said it could be any day or up to two weeks until she was due to whelp, and it looked like six pups. Lots of semi-moist puppy food was fed to her numerous times throughout the day to help her get more strength and nutrients, whilst rushing round collecting together a whelping kit, especially as we were concerned about her being able to feed the pups.

Two days later Lottie was out in the garden with my own two dogs, and I noticed through the window that she looked constipated, so went out to check her. But no: Lottie was giving birth to pup number one with my two dogs watching in fascination right in the middle of the lawn!

A quick move into the birthing room, and I spent the rest of the afternoon in wonder and amazement as she produced six gorgeous little pups without any need of my assistance. She had obviously done this before! She did it all by the book, breaking the cords, licking the pups and feeding them, eating the placenta: what more could I ask for!

She had politely started at 2pm and finished at 8pm the same day, and had been totally happy for me to be present and handle the pups from the start to weigh them and check them. My only job had been to offer encouragement and praise throughout. All this from a dog I had only known for forty-eight hours!

Lottie.

water bag has served as an outer membrane for each foetus to aid its passage, and may well burst before passing through the cervix, producing a gush of fluid. This bag does not contain the pup but one should follow very soon. Your bitch may stand, crouch or lie down to give birth, and when the head appears the rest of pup should slide out very quickly after.

If there is a lapse in contractions once pup has appeared, you may need to help by providing some gentle traction. Your hands should be thoroughly scrubbed or surgical gloves worn, and lubricated. Pup should still be enclosed in the inner, allantoic membrane, so take between your first and second fingers with the back of your hand upwards and pull gently downwards as your bitch strains. Hopefully this will only be necessary for the first pup, which will have enlarged the passage for the others to follow.

Do not panic if pup arrives hind feet first, as whilst it makes it slightly more difficult as the widest part of pup is coming last, it is not the

Pups one and two, Laura and Carl taking their first meal in the outside world.

end of the world. A breeched birth is when pup presents rump first with their hind legs tucked underneath. Where pup is not lined up straight or has a leg tucked behind, it is often possible to use your forefinger to get them into position. Always lubricate. Often a slight rotation of pup can help, but whatever your assistance, beware of pulling too hard on an exposed head or limb, and always coincide gentle pulls with the bitch as she pushes. You can encourage your bitch to push by stroking your fingers against the inside of her vulva.

Many bitches new to whelping may be surprised and shocked at the birth of their first puppy, however when it makes its first cry, maternal instincts usually kick in. Do not intervene unless your bitch is tiring towards the end of the litter, when you may need to assist in opening the amniotic sac so the pup can breathe. Normally your bitch will tear the sac with her teeth and consume it, and she then shreds the umbilical cord with her side teeth. She will then ensure the resuscitation of the pup by licking and pulling and turning it to stimulate its breathing. This is an important bonding stage for mum, and will help her maternal instinct throughout the lactation period.

Only if your bitch neglects the pup should you intervene immediately, tearing off the membrane and holding the pup upside down to drain fluid from its lungs. Clean the mouth and nose of mucus with a gauze swab to clear the airways as fully as possible. Vigorous rubbing with a warm towel should start puppy breathing. Once pup is comfortable you will need to ease the blood within the umbilical cord down towards pup, and then cut the cord with sterilized scissors, or tear it as far from the pup as possible. You should not apply anything to the end of the cord or to pup's naval.

If pup is still not breathing, hold its head between your first two fingers with its body in the palm of your hand, and swing pup upside down quite vigorously beside you. This should clear its airways fully and stimulate it into taking its first breath. Make sure pup is dried so as not to lose heat, either by offering to mum to lick or with a towel.

Mum should 'nose' the pups towards her teats, and once they are suckling, they are on the road to life.

Stage Three

It is normal for the placenta to arrive with the first pup, but it may well come with the second pup's arrival. The placenta is full of blood and high in nutrients, so it is usual for the bitch to eat it; it is now also thought that this may help stimulate the flow of milk. If your bitch has to deliver by Caesarean she will miss out on this nutritious snack, so it is a good idea to ask the vet to save the placenta so you can offer it to her when she is conscious.

At this stage the whelping area can become quite wet and messy, so your job now is to try and keep it as clean and dry as possible so that the new-born pups do not get wet and cold. The pups' suckling action is said to stimulate contractions, so pups already born should be allowed to continue suckling. Also, some bitches may become upset if their pups are moved away, and this is the last thing mum needs during delivery.

All done (or so I thought)! Laura, Carl, Ben and Charlotte.

135

LOTTIE – 2

Lottie popped them out like clockwork. Laura arrived at 14.15pm, followed by Carl at 15.30pm and Ben at 16.25pm. It seemed we were on a nice hourly cycle! But at 16.40pm out came Charlotte, who had obviously been bursting to get out. I had been weighing the pups soon after each birth, and was amazed at the difference in them: Laura weighed 430g, and the weights then dropped in order of birth down to Charlotte who weighed just 235g.

After another hour of watching and waiting, I decided that the scan must have fooled them and in fact that was it, so left Lottie to being a mother whilst I caught up on the other daily chores. Imagine my surprise when I walked back in an hour later and found number 5 had arrived! Mary arrived at 19.45pm weighing 410g, followed by Tina at 20.30pm weighing 360g.

Otherwise my only task was moving the new-born pups back to the teats, as they seemed to keep heading back to her hind end as if they wanted to go back!

Deciding how long is safe between births can be a skill, as is deciding when may be the time to ask for veterinary assistance. Is the bitch in trouble or just resting? How long a bitch takes to whelp can vary greatly, but the general consensus is that a reasonable time is around two to two and a half hours. Your vet should already have been advised that your bitch has begun whelping, so will be on stand-by if required, but it is you who are observing and who must decide if help is needed. If your bitch appears to be straining to no effect then she may well need help, but if she is asleep with her new-born pups she may well be taking an extended rest before going through it again. Of course it may well be that she only has a small litter, especially if it is her first, but hopefully she has been scanned and the vet has given some indication of the number of pups to expect.

As pups are born, be sure to record details for identification, and times of arrival so you can keep track of how long it is between arrivals. Also note any pups that may have needed your assistance in case of health problems in the following days. And remember to offer mum a drink whilst she is whelping, as she may well be thirsty but not want to get up.

The later arrivals, Mary and Tina.

There were six in the bed and the little one said, roll over!

It is a good idea to have mum and pups checked by your vet the day after whelping: he can check that her uterus is empty and contracting in size, and that there are no signs of infection or any other form of complication.

DEALING WITH COMPLICATIONS

Primary inertia: If stage two has not commenced after twenty-four hours, or if a green vaginal discharge is seen, this is known as primary inertia and your bitch should be examined by your vet.

Secondary inertia: This follows a prolonged and unproductive labour where due to an obstruction known as dystocia, birth cannot take place and the bitch becomes exhausted.

Dystocia

Dystocia is due to either a problem with the mother, or with puppy size or position.

Abnormalities of the uterus: Abnormalities include poor contraction of the muscles of the uterus, abnormalities associated with foetal or maternal fluids, or twisting or rupture of the uterus. Sometimes the uterine muscles never start to contract properly and a Caesarean operation must be performed to deliver the puppies. In other cases labour may develop normally but is prolonged and the muscles of the uterus become exhausted before all the puppies have been born. Intravenous solutions containing glucose and drugs may help to stimulate contractions of the uterus, but a Caesarean operation may still be necessary.

Disorders of the birth canal: Previous damage to the pelvis such as healed fractures can make the birth canal narrow. Some bitches have abnormalities of the birth canal, or an unusually small vulva opening, which may require a partial episiotomy (surgical incision) in order for the puppies to be delivered vaginally.

Puppy abnormalities: Abnormalities include puppies that are too large, or in an abnormal position, presentation or posture. Puppy oversize can occur with prolonged pregnancy in abnormally small litters and is a common cause of dystocia. The normal position of a puppy before delivery is with the foetal backbone lying along the top of the womb. A mild dystocia may arise if they are lying the other way up. In most breeds puppies can be born normally in either anterior (head first) or posterior (back feet first) presentation. It is only a transverse (sideways) presentation that is associated with dystocia, and this is rare. Deformed puppies may also become stuck in the birth canal. If the puppy is not in the correct position it is not easy to correct this with the use of forceps or traction because of the small size of the birth canal of the bitch. If a puppy is stuck in the birth canal then a Caesarean operation is needed in most cases.

Caesarean

If a Caesarean is required for your bitch and it is necessary to take her to the vet's having delivered some pups, ensure these are left in a warm, heated box. They will be fine without food for a few hours, and modern anaesthetics mean that mum will be awake fairly quickly after the operation and will be able to return to them.

She may be a little slow to accept the pups, partly because she has not gone through the natural birth process, and partly due to the anaesthetic effect. Pups may also seem a little drowsy because of the transmission of anaesthetic to them through suckling.

The wound should not hinder her caring naturally for the pups, but of course must be kept clean and dry. Only the mildest of antiseptics should be used, if any, so as not to harm the pups. Take advice from your vet.

PROBLEMS POST-WHELPING

Most post-whelping problems are seen within the first few hours after whelping. Sometimes conditions occur that mean the bitch is unable to feed her pups, and they will have to be hand reared and fed milk replacer. If this is the case it is important that the puppies receive colostrum to ensure they have a good immune system.

Eclampsia (Milk Fever)

Eclampsia is caused by hypocalcaemia (low blood calcium levels) in the dog. The lactating bitch is more susceptible to blood calcium depletion because her body cannot keep up with the increased demand for calcium as dogs lack the ability to quickly move calcium into their milk without depleting their own blood levels of this mineral.

Litters do not need to be large to cause eclampsia. It does tend to be the small breed dogs that are at a higher risk.

Whilst eclampsia is a very serious disorder the signs are fairly easy to recognize. Your bitch may:

- appear restless and nervous
- walk with a stiff gait and may even wobble or appear disoriented
- become unable to walk, and her legs may become stiff or rigid
- develop a fever, with body temperature over 40°C
- develop muscle tremors
- have an increase in her respiration rate
- suffer seizures and death if no treatment is given

If you suspect your bitch has eclampsia you must get veterinary advice immediately, and pups should be prevented from feeding from mum for at least twenty-four hours. They will need to be fed with a milk replacement. A blood test can quickly establish eclampsia, and it can be quickly corrected by your vet through the use of intravenous calcium supplementation.

Haemorrhage

If your bitch experiences a heavy significant

flow of blood any time after whelping, call your vet immediately. This is a very serious emergency.

Retained Placenta and Pups

Signs of retained placenta or pups may follow whelping immediately, or several days later. Symptoms include:

- persistent vomiting
- dehydration
- lack of appetite
- depression
- weakness
- green vaginal discharge

Seek advice from your vet immediately.

Metritis

Metritis is an inflammation of the uterus and is usually associated with infection. Uterine infections are emergencies that can be fatal if not treated quickly. Metritis sometimes follows after a long or difficult labour. Symptoms include:

- fever
- weakness
- depression
- dehydration
- dull eyes
- reduced milk production
- foul-smelling discharge from the vagina

This is a serious condition that requires veterinary intervention immediately.

Mastitis

Mastitis refers to swelling, inflammation and infection of the mammary gland, and is typically caused by three kinds of bacteria: E coli, Staphylococcus or Streptococcus. Mastitis is most often seen in dogs during the first two weeks after delivery. Symptoms include:

- The affected mammary glands are typically hot, swollen, firm to hard and may be painful to the touch
- Severely infected glands may be black in colour or even rupture, leaking a foul-smelling pus discharge

Mastitis is fairly easy to treat but can be deadly if left untreated. Seek veterinary advice immediately.

Maternal Damage to Pups and Neglect

In rare cases the bitch can cause damage to her own puppies. In some cases this is accidental, in that when the bitch breaks the umbilical cord she can get too close to pup's umbilical area with her teeth and cause damage. It has also been known for a bitch to overlick the pups, and this can also cause damage to them. Other cases can include the bitch biting or eating her puppies.

Some bitches may be completely non-maternal and totally disinterested in their pups. You

CHECKLIST

Stay with your bitch throughout the whelping process, observing from a distance unless your intervention is required.

Remember to keep your vet up to date once whelping has begun.

Allow the bitch to do as much for herself as she can.

Two hours is about normal between births.

Keep the whelping area clean and dry.

Keep your bitch hydrated throughout.

will have to hand rear them unless you are lucky enough to know of a bitch having a phantom pregnancy who may well adopt the litter as her own.

Some bitches, especially with first litters, may be scared of their pups, which will mean you will have to give them the confidence and encouragement they need for their maternal instincts to kick in.

Some bitches, especially working bitches, may be very protective of their litter, so to begin with observation only is possible. Handling and inspection of the pups should only be done when the bitch is out on a toilet break or short walk.

It is for these reasons it is so important to observe the new family carefully for the first few days after birth, especially if it is the bitch's first litter. If she does struggle or harms any of her litter, you should not breed from her again and she should be spayed as soon as the vet deems it possible.

CARE OF THE NEWLY WHELPED BITCH AND PUPPIES

During the lactation phase the pups make the most demand on the bitch so it is essential that a good nutritious diet continues to be fed, which is easy to digest. If the litter is large, you should get up at least once during the night to check on the litter and give your bitch a feed. Also ensure she is getting plenty of fluid so if she is reluctant to leave the whelping box regularly offer her water.

For the first few days after whelping your bitch is unlikely to want to leave her pups for long and will not require any form of exercise. To start with, all she will need is access to the garden for toilet breaks, though after a few days she may appreciate short walks to give her a change of scene.

Try to groom her daily to keep her clean and comfortable – and of course by doing so you are ensuring a clean environment for the pups as well. It is important to keep the whelping area as clean as possible, which is why modern bedding such as Vetbed (a polyester bedding with a latex backing) is ideal. The bedding can be regularly changed and can be washed numerous times, so always have at least two sets of bedding, if not more, on hand.

The first thirty-six hours are critical for the pups. They are born with an immature brain and nervous system, and with their eyes and ears tightly closed. Their body temperature is low, so they must gain heat from their mum. This is why it is important to ensure the whelping area is kept warm, especially in the colder months of the year. You will see the pups twitching and jerking in their sleep, with reflex actions known as 'activated sleep', which serves to develop and exercise the nerve and muscle system.

Sleeping gives the pups time to develop their brain and nervous system.

Healthy new-born pups are quiet and sleepy, and should be warm to the touch. They should be firm and plump, and they have a smell all of their own. A happy litter will make contented, low murmur-type noises with the occasional sharp cry if they get squashed or pushed off a teat. You will see that the pups, when suckling, make paddling motions with their paws on mum's mammary glands, so ensure their nails are kept trim to prevent her from being scratched, because if

A nice even-sized litter at the end of week one.

she gets sore this may put her off allowing the pups to suckle.

Mum will stimulate her pups to urinate and defecate by licking their bottoms, and she will do this up to about twenty days of age. You can be lulled into a false sense of how easy it all is, as your turn at cleaning up has not yet come! If she is reluctant to do this task, a little sunflower oil or honey on the pups' fur can encourage her. It is possible that her tongue is sore or that she has a mouth ulcer, so do check.

Healthy pups should gain weight steadily, but they should double their birthweight within a week of birth. Daily weighing is a great idea if mum allows, and of course this gives you an opportunity to check each pup over. Always check the umbilical area daily for any signs of infection. Remember to keep notes, as this will be useful for any future health problems that may crop up with a pup, and it is also a good guide if you plan to breed from mum again in the future. By seven weeks you should

WEIGHT CHECKS OF LOTTIE'S PUPS

	Laura	Carl	Ben	Charlotte	Mary	Tina
Day 1	430g	309g	286g	235g	410g	360g
Day 2	430g	325g	300g	275g	425g	400g
Day 3	400g	325g	325g	250g	435g	400g
Day 4	425g	375g	350g	300g	450g	425g
Day 5	425g	350g	325g	325g	475g	425g
Day 7	550g	500g	450g	400g	625g	500g
Day 14	810g	700g	640g	640g	850g	790g
Day 35	2.26kg	2.06kg	2.16kg	2.06kg	2.35kg	2.36kg
Day 56	4.90kg	5.00kg	5.15kg	4.80kg	5.30kg	5.20kg
Day 69	6.40kg	7.10kg	7.5kg	6.5kg	7.2kg	7.4kg
Day 176	-	-	-	15.6kg	-	16.4kg

have an evenly sized litter, as the pups that were smaller at birth tend to catch up quickly when weaned.

Distinguishing Pups

Distinguishing pups can be difficult, and of course they are much too young to be wearing any form of collar. However, there are ways of identifying them:

- A few strands of coloured wool, plaited
- Trimming an area of coat in a specific place
- Coloured paper collars which you may be able to obtain from your vet
- A small blob of felt tip, coloured or in a specific position if it will show up

Remember, though, that any type of fastening around the pups' necks must be checked regularly as you do not want any entanglements, and as they grow they must not be restricted.

I was lucky with Lottie's pups in that it was obvious from the day they were born that they were not full German Shepherds. I had a variety of colours and all had distinct markings, so I noted them down as they were born, which enabled me to track each pup carefully.

Such was our amusement, we took a DNA swab from Laura, the first pup born, to try and identify what breeds might be present to get an idea of what size they might make. As expected, the result came back that Laura was 50 per cent German Shepherd, and strongly suggested that dad/s were lurcher, two types of sight hound and two types of terrier.

It may well be that Lottie mated with a Heinz 57, or maybe she mated with multiple males whilst in season. This is something we shall never know, as at that time she was a stray on the streets.

Care in Week One

The first two weeks after birth should be a quiet time to allow the maternal bond to be established between mum and pups. Visitors should be kept to a minimum, and only gentle handling of the pups should take place at this time to check on their progress.

Day One

Ensure that all pups suckle on the first day, as the bitch's colostrum (first milk) is rich in antibodies, which enable the pups to withstand infection for their first few weeks of life until they are vaccinated.

Check pups for obvious abnormalities and consult with your vet if unsure.

It is a good idea to have your vet check over mum and pups. If you are lucky your vet will make a house call, but you should have established this prior to whelping so are prepared if you need to go to your vet.

Ensure the pups are all getting enough to drink, especially if the litter is large. Smaller or weak pups may need to be supplemented by bottle feeding.

Day Three

If dew claws are present on hind legs, it is advised to have them removed at this age as they can tear very easily. It is not the end of the world if this is not done, as they can be removed later in life, but then the procedure will involve a general anaesthetic. Many young rescue dogs come into us with hind dew claws, and very often they are moving with a strange gait to avoid catching themselves. We will ask the vet to remove the dew claws at the same time as neutering so they only have to undergo one operation. Front dew claws are usually left and rarely cause a problem.

Care in Week Two

Pups' eyes will open around days ten to fifteen, so this is the time to check them for abnormalities.

Their ears will also be opening around this time, and their hearing skills will start to develop.

At two weeks of age pups should receive their first worming treatment specifically for roundworm. Your vet will prescribe the most suitable product, and it is easy to administer with a small syringe.

Care in Week Three

At two to three weeks of age the pups will be becoming more mobile, and at twenty-one days they will be quite lively and will begin wandering

Eyes beginning to open.

outside the whelping area. This is when you will have the never-ending task of cleaning up after them, as mum has done her job on getting their systems working!

The pups are now learning about their social group, recognizing their mum and littermates, and also their humans.

This is the ideal time to start socialization and habituation, with frequent handling and exposure to household noise and events. Start to introduce them to other family people and ani-

mals. Allow your other animals to wander around their pen, ensuring mum is not upset by this, or do it when she is out on a walk.

It is better to introduce new things to the pups too early rather than too late. Their perception develops much more quickly than their reactions, so they are often learning long before we realize it.

CONGENITAL DEFECTS

Congenital defects are inherited, and include the following:

Umbilical hernia: A hernia is the protrusion of a part of the body organ through an abnormal opening in the surrounding tissues. An umbilical hernia is when part of the abdominal organ protrudes through an incompletely closed umbilical ring. A small umbilical hernia is likely to disappear as pup grows.

Inguinal hernia: An inguinal hernia is the protrusion of the abdominal organ through the inguinal canal of the groin, the canal through which the testes descend in males. It can also be seen in bitches. Often the hernia in a bitch contains one or both uterine horns, which would cause problems if she was bred from. Both can be corrected by surgery.

First days outside in the playpen.

Cleft palate: A cleft palate is the result of both halves of the hard palate in the roof of the mouth failing to fuse together. It is more common in short-nosed breeds.

Harelip: Harelip is an inherited condition that is not often seen now. It is sometimes seen together with a cleft palate. Harelip is the result of a failure of the upper lip to join properly in the midline. It can be corrected surgically.

Under-/overshot jaw: It may not be possible to identify an under-/overshot jaw until four months of age when the second teeth are through. This defect can be corrected but dogs that have this condition should not be used for breeding.

DEALING WITH PROBLEMS DURING REARING

25 per cent of the litter may die during the first week, so if pups have made it to week two they stand a good chance of survival until they meet their next hurdle, which is weaning. It is at this time that any digestive defects may become apparent.

Fading puppy syndrome: From days five to fourteen pups can fade and die for no apparent reason. Causes are usually hypothermia, infection, lack of food, lack of colostrum, trauma from the bitch, roundworms or stress. It is very hard to accept, but often a pup suffering fading puppy syndrome cannot be saved.

Breathing problems: It may be that a pup's lungs did not expand effectively at birth and you hear a wheezing and rattling noise as they breathe. Consult your vet immediately as a spell in an oxygen cage may help.

Juvenile pyoderma: Also known as milk rash or nappy rash, tiny spots often appear on the lower abdomen, groin, hindquarters and back. There will be pus in these spots. It is predominantly caused by the bitch not cleaning the pups sufficiently, however it is less prevalent nowadays since newspaper is not used as much. In extreme

cases antibiotics may be needed, so consult your vet.

Conjunctivitis: A slight discharge may be seen even before a pup's eyes are open, so it may be necessary to open the lid to drain the pus. Consult your vet.

BOTTLE FEEDING

If you have to bottle feed there are some simple rules to follow:

- Avoid if at all possible
- It is preferable not to alternate between the bitch's milk and the bottle, so if she is struggling to feed a large litter consider taking some of the pups off the bitch altogether
- Have all required equipment ready 'in case'
- Use a high protein/high fat formula – your vet will be able to advise the most suitable product
- Keep all equipment sterilized
- Keep the pups clean

WEANING

Care at Week Four

At week four, weaning can begin. You should start by feeding pups soft food several times a day. Remember to use a plastic or metal bowl that they cannot destroy, and the shallower the bowl the better, so the pups can reach in easily. Feeding time is a messy business as they will climb into the bowls, walk through the food, put it all over each other and spread it around. Pups will still be suckling at this time.

You should feed four to five small meals a day using a good commercial food with the right balance of nutrients.

Pups should also be wormed again at four to five weeks. It is best to consult with your vet for an ideal worming programme for your pups, as exact timings will depend on the products used.

Following advice from my vet, Lottie's pups

Feeding time can be a messy affair!

were wormed at two weeks, five weeks, eight weeks, ten weeks and twelve weeks of age, and then every three months thereafter.

At this stage the pups' play behaviour and problem-solving behaviour start to develop, so now is the time to give them some challenges. They need things to carry, pull, climb on, move around and tug with each other. It is good for the pups to have different surfaces to walk on, as they learn a lot through their feet. Start moving their pen into different rooms, and if the weather allows, maybe it can be set up outside and they can get their first feel of grass under their feet.

By giving them a changing environment and stimulating their mind and senses, they will develop strength, coordination, agility and sharing. Pups that miss out on these important lessons can grow up to be poor learners and unable to deal with frustration, which results in behavioural or temperamental issues.

Mum will also start to be firmer with them now, so don't panic as she is also teaching them how to overcome frustration. She will show this by telling them off if they are too rough with her

Exploring new things with their teeth is always fun.

or standing up and walking away if they are suckling on her teats. This could be because the pups first teeth are now through, but also because she is helping along the weaning process.

It is good for the pups to be meeting new people in their home now, and they should be handled by other family members and visitors. This is the time when prospective purchasers should start to visit, so use it to the advantage of the pups.

It is also beneficial to try and spend some 'one to one' time with each pup, taking them away from mum and the rest of the litter: this will reduce separation problems in the future by developing their independence whilst bonding with humans. Use it as a time to give them a groom with a soft brush to desensitize them to being groomed as they grow up. Get them used to being touched all over, and examine them thoroughly as a vet would.

Care at Weeks Five to Seven

This period is the most crucial time for the pup's brain development, and they are at their most curious. Whilst they should now be willing to approach people, it is also the time that their natural fear starts to be defined by their environment. This increase in fearfulness is a gradual

Independence is good.

process, so it is important to continue to introduce new sights, sounds and smells to them.

In the wild this stage would have started in a wolf pup at around nineteen days. The average dog will get to this stage at around forty-nine days, whilst the German Shepherd starts at around day thirty-six, being one of the more reactive breeds and of course a much more direct descendant of the wolf.

Continue to teach the pups to be away from their mum and siblings, to continue the bond with humans. Now pups should be eating properly, start using different bowls and your hand to feed them. This will ensure they are not fussy about only eating from a particular bowl, and also ensure there are no food aggression problems with people in the future. They will see the hand as literally feeding them, so not a threat in any way!

Continue grooming and handling.

Pups can start to wear a light collar to accustom them to the

Collars don't have to be scary.

feel, though it is best not to leave it on when they are unsupervised.

If you are able to, it is a good idea to start taking the pups out for short car journeys to accustom them to the motion of a car. You can also take them out to watch things in the world go by, but remember to carry them as they are not yet fully vaccinated.

The above are guidelines and you must remember that each pup is an individual and treat them so! Some will be fast learners and others will take more time.

Also consider the following:

- It is advised that pups go to their new homes between six and eight weeks of age, this being the best window in their development to adjust to a new family home
- Pups' first primary vaccinations are due at seven to eight weeks of age, therefore do you give the first vaccination, or do you trust the new owners to properly vaccinate the pup? If you give the first initial vaccination it must be followed with a second primary vaccination from the same manufacturer, so what happens if the new owner's vet uses a different brand to your own vet: does the pup have to start all over again? This is further complicated by the fact that some of the more up-to-date vaccinations require four weeks between

the two injections, unlike the traditional two weeks that used to be the norm

I wanted to ensure that all Lottie's pups got the proper start, so they had their first primary vaccination at eight weeks of age and their second primary vaccination at ten weeks of age: then they were allowed to go home with their new families. It was stressed to their new families that pups should not go out into public places unless they were carried for another week until the vaccinations had taken full effect, and that any animals they interacted with in their new homes were already fully vaccinated.

The pups were also microchipped on their first visit to the vets, and I ensured that all microchips were registered initially to myself and then to the new owners so there was traceability.

Care of Your Bitch after Weaning

While the pups are being weaned, mum will start to spend less time with them, so ensure she has a bed away from them but has access to them at all times.

She will appreciate longer walks, and now is a good time to start to help her get her figure back. As the pups should have stopped suckling you should also be adjusting her diet accordingly to get her back into her normal routine. Remember not to change it suddenly, however, but make it a gradual process over a number of days.

TIME TO LEAVE HOME

Care at Week Eight

A lot of the preparations have been discussed in Chapter 9 'Breeding and Pregnancy', and also in Chapter 2 'Choosing Your German Shepherd', but of course as the purchaser.

By week eight you should have prospective owners for all the pups, and all the necessary paperwork in place and prepared ready for the pups to leave home.

Buyers should have been visiting from four weeks of age, and deposits taken to secure the purchase of their pup.

All buyers should have been fully vetted by yourself, and where possible home checks car-

Ready to leave home.

ried out. Remember vets are a good place to get a reference on owners, so do not be afraid to ask for their vet's details and tell them you will be contacting them for a reference as they may need to give their authorization for the vet to speak to you.

The litter should have been registered with the Kennel Club, and pedigree certificates prepared for new owners, with all other relevant documentation such as copies of health certificates for mum and dad.

Contracts of sale should already have been shown to buyers and prepared ready, including any endorsements and after support. You should also allow in the contract for the return of a pup. This may relate to the new owner having a vet health check within so many days of purchase, and if a health problem is found, pup can be returned with a full refund, or if they simply realize they have made a mistake and want to return the pup you may want to include that the pup will be taken back and their money refunded, less a percentage.

Puppy care information packs should have been prepared for all new owners, ensuring that the following advice is covered:

- Tendencies or potential traits in the breed and/or puppy
- Socialization, exercise and training given and needed

Who, me?

- Feeding advice and diet sheet
- Worming and vaccination information, as in what has been done and what will be required and when
- Grooming advice

It is also normal to have arranged insurance for the pups, enabling you to give the new owner a period of free insurance for their pup. The new owners will then be given the option to take out a full insurance policy with this insurance company to continue the pup's cover.

It is best to arrange for the pups to leave home over a period of a few days, as not only will it mean you can spend more time with each new owner, but mum could become quite distraught if all the pups disappeared at the same time.

If you have done your job correctly the pups will leave home healthy and happy, socialized and habituated.

They will have learnt about being a dog from their mum and their litter mates.

They will have had an education from you.

Now it is time for them to learn to be a family dog in their own home.

THE RESPONSIBLE BREEDER

Remember, a responsible breeder will always include in the contract of sale that if for any reason the owners find themselves in a position where they need to rehome their new pup at whatever age, they should approach you, the breeder, first for help and advice.

You may wish to insert that you will take the dog back, or it may be that you offer them help to find a new and good home for the dog.

A good breeder should have a network of people who would be looking for one of their pups or dogs, so finding a new home should not be too difficult.

A good breeder will exhaust all avenues of their networks and connections before having to approach a breed specific rescue.

Too often rescues are contacted by people who have purchased a German Shepherd pup from a breeder and have not been properly screened, so in fact they should never have had the pup in the first place, having no experience of the breed, and having failed to carry out the necessary research. The breeder is not interested in taking back the pup or helping to secure the pup a new home, so these poor dogs are sold on through internet sites in an attempt by the purchaser to claw back some of the purchase money, probably to another inexperienced family. And so it goes on!

More responsible people will contact a rescue and ask for help, seeing the pup's welfare as being more important than trying to get back some money, and of course rescues like our own will help.

The dogs that are sold on the internet sites usually end up with us at some point as they have missed out on all the proper socialization and have become a problem dog. We then have to try to undo the problems and start over with them.

This is infuriating for rescues that become overwhelmed with dogs simply because of irresponsible breeders.

11 COMMON AILMENTS AND DISEASES

BONES, MUSCLES AND JOINTS

Bone Infections (Osteomyelitis)

In dogs, bone infections can be either acute (sudden) or chronic in nature. While most bone infections result from bacterial infections, they can also be caused by fungal infections. Acute bone infections appear almost immediately and typically occur as the result of bite wounds or bone fractures. Chronic bone infections may persist for months before being recognized, and are often caused by the staphylococcus bacteria or even fungal organisms. With bone infections, the bloodstream is often the main carrier, so any type of infection can permeate to the bone.

Some of the signs and symptoms of bone infections in dogs are:

- lameness
- fever
- generalized weakness and fatigue
- appearance of pain while walking
- lack of desire for normal activities
- swelling of the limbs

Treatment begins with identifying the underlying cause. In acute cases, cleaning, drainage, surgical trimming of the dead tissue and antibiotic administration will be required. If antibiotics are not effective, ampu-tation may be required if the infection is life-threatening to the dog.

Fractures

Any break or crack in a bone is called a fracture. When repairing a fracture the vet's aim is to replace the fractured ends of bone into their normal position and then immobilize the bone for four to six weeks. Depending on the bone and type of fracture there are several methods available:

- cage rest
- external casts
- surgery to perform internal fixation with plates and/or pins

Bone Tumours

Bone tumours are more common in giant breeds but are known to occur in German Shepherds. The most common sites for a tumour are the radius, humerus and femur. They can be very painful

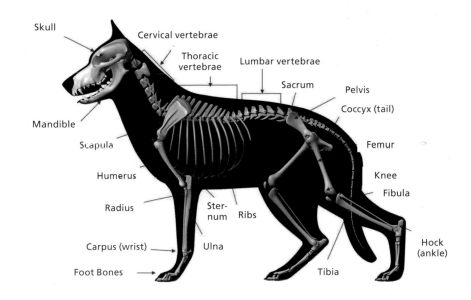

Skull
Cervical vertebrae
Thoracic vertebrae
Lumbar vertebrae
Sacrum
Pelvis
Coccyx (tail)
Mandible
Scapula
Femur
Humerus
Knee
Fibula
Radius
Sternum
Ribs
Hock (ankle)
Carpus (wrist)
Ulna
Foot Bones
Tibia

The skeleton.

and tend to be malignant therefore spreading to other parts of the body early on.

Amputation of the limb can remove the primary tumour, but as it may have already spread to other areas this is often not a feasible option. Radiotherapy and chemotherapy are rarely successful.

Sprains

A sprain is inflammation of an overstretched joint, which becomes hot, swollen and painful, thus making the dog lame. Sprains are normally treated with rest, cold compresses and a mild pain-killing drug.

More severe sprains may require support bandaging and anti-inflammatory drugs.

Cruciate Ligament Rupture

In the vast majority of dogs, the cranial cruciate ligament ruptures as a result of long-term degeneration. The precise cause is not known, but genetic factors are probably most important, with certain breeds being predisposed to this injury. Other factors, such as obesity, individual conformation, hormonal imbalance and certain inflammatory conditions of the joint, may also play a role, and when seen in a German Shepherd the affected dog is usually middle-aged or older. However, ruptures can also occur as a result of a severe sprain.

Limping is the most common sign of injury. This may appear suddenly during or after exercise in some dogs, or it may be progressive and intermittent in others. Some dogs are simultaneously affected in both knees. It is important from an insurance point of view for your vet to clarify if they believe it is cruciate disease that has caused the rupture, or if the rupture has occurred from injury. It can be the difference between one claim for both legs, and a separate claim amount for each leg.

Diagnosis is usually based on examination by an experienced orthopaedic surgeon, along with x-rays or MRI scans. Non-surgical management is seldom recommended, except where the risks of a general anaesthetic or surgery are considered excessive; the cornerstones of non-surgical treatment are bodyweight management, physiotherapy, exercise modification, and anti-inflammatory pain killers. Dogs heavier than 15kg have a very poor chance of becoming clinically normal with non-surgical treatment.

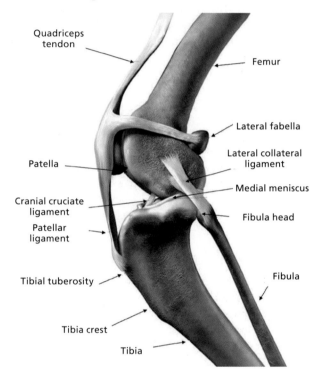

The knee structure.

Surgical treatments are categorized into techniques that aim to replace the deficient ligament, and those that render the ligament redundant by cutting the tibia and realigning the forces acting on the stifle joint.

Ligament replacement techniques: These do not change the biomechanics of the cruciate ligament, which means a future rupture could occur.

Treatments that render the cranial cruciate ligament redundant: There are surgeries that alter the geometry of the affected knee joint in such a way that the cruciate ligament becomes redundant. There are several variations in technique, all of which involve reshaping the top of the shin (tibia) by cutting the bone and fixing it in a new position.

- **Tibial plateau levelling osteotomy (TPLO):** This surgery involves the creation of an arcuate cut in the top of the tibia and rotation of the plateau segment until the previous slope in the bone is no longer present. The bone is subsequently fixed in this new position using a bone plate and screws
- **Tibial tuberosity advancement (TTA):** This surgery follows the same principle as TPLO, with a cut being created in the tibia to allow a change in geometry. The mathematical principles behind TTA are more complex than those behind TPLO

Because bone healing is more efficient than ligament healing, these repairs have a reputation for being significantly more robust than surgeries designed to replace the damaged ligament. The major practical benefit is a very reliable return of limb use, with all dogs expected to start weight-bearing on the operated limb in one to three days. The mechanical advantages of TPLO and TTA, coupled with the rapid return to function, is especially important for heavy dogs, athletic animals, animals presenting with mild lameness (where ligament replacement could make them significantly lamer initially), and in animals with cruciate ligament injuries affecting both stifle joints. The decision as to whether TPLO or TTA is most appropriate is made based on the anatomy of the individual.

Arthritis or Degenerative Joint Disease (DJD)

DJD can be common in the German Shepherd, especially where it follows hip or elbow dysplasia. The result is a thickening of the joint capsule, the formation of abnormal new bone around the edges of the joint, and sometimes wearing of the joint cartilage.

The joint becomes enlarged and painful and has a reduced range of movement. DJD is more common in older dogs and is usually a problem in the hips, stifles and elbows. There is no cure, and treatment is usually with anti-inflammatory drugs with the aim of providing pain relief.

Glucosamine as a food supplement can help joints last longer and is considered by many owners as a preventative measure as their dog gets older.

Spondylosis Deformans

Spondylosis deformans is a degenerative, non-inflammatory condition of the spinal column characterized by the production of bone spurs along the bottom, sides and upper aspects of the vertebrae of the spine. These bone spurs are simply projected growths of bone, usually grown in response to ageing or injury. Older, large-breed dogs such as the German Shepherd are at highest risk for developing spondylosis deformans.

Typically, patients with spondylosis deformans will not show outward symptoms of early abnormal bone growth. A neurologic examination should be performed to rule out a spinal condition requiring surgery. Again, there is no cure, and treatment with anti-inflammatory drugs may be required to provide pain relief. Acupuncture may also provide pain relief for some animals.

Osteochondritis Dissecans (OCD)

This is a developmental disease that occurs in rapidly growing medium to large breed dogs typically between six and nine months of age, and may occur more often in male dogs.

Dogs that are affected with OCD typically limp or are lame in the affected leg or legs. During an orthopaedic examination, when pressure is applied to the affected joint, or when the joint is manipulated, the dog will often cry out in pain. The affected joint may be swollen and warm to the touch. In some cases, the lameness may be mild and intermittent, while in other cases the dog may be in constant pain, and avoids bearing weight on the affected leg.

The results of a lameness examination may be suggestive of this condition, especially if the shoulder is the affected joint. If it is one of the

Hydrotherapy is great for rehabilitation.

other joints, such as the stifle (knee), hip or elbow, other bone conditions must also be considered, including hip dysplasia and elbow dysplasia.

The OCD lesion can vary in severity, ranging from a crack in the cartilage to a cartilage flap, to a completely detached fragment of cartilage that is floating around in the joint. If the defect is a crack or a very small flap of cartilage, it may heal if the patient has strict rest and activity restriction for several weeks. Anti-inflammatory drugs will be prescribed and possibly supplements to promote joint health. Physiotherapy is often recommended to maintain the joint's flexibility and mobility. If the lameness does not improve following this conservative approach, or if the lesion is more severe, surgery will be required by opening the joint, or by arthroscopy. Whatever the surgical technique, the remainder of the cartilage surface will be inspected and any other areas of defective cartilage will be debrided or removed.

Hip Dysplasia
(*See* Chapter 12, 'Breed Specific Ailments and Diseases'.)

Elbow Dysplasia

Elbow dysplasia is a condition caused by the abnormal growth of cells, tissues or bone. The condition is characterized by a series of four development abnormalities that lead to malformation and degeneration of the elbow joint. It is the most common cause of elbow pain and lameness, and one of the most common causes of forelimb lameness in large breed dogs. The age for onset is typically four to ten months, with diagnosis generally being made around four to eighteen months.

Not all affected dogs will show signs when they are young, and an acute episode of elbow lameness due to advanced degenerative joint disease in a more mature dog is common. Symptoms are as follows:

- Intermittent or persistent forelimb lameness that is aggravated by exercise; it progresses from stiffness, and is noticed only after the dog has been resting
- Pain when extending or flexing the elbow
- Tendency for dogs to hold the affected limb away from their body
- Fluid build-up in the joint
- Grating of bone and joint with movement may be detected with advanced degenerative joint disease
- Diminished range of motion

This condition is primarily of genetic cause, although environmental factors such as obesity during puppyhood may influence whether an animal with the genes coding for elbow dysplasia will develop a clinical problem.

The pattern of abnormal development is not the same in all affected elbow joints. In order to offer the optimal treatment for a dog with elbow dysplasia, it is essential to identify and neutralize the abnormal forces acting on the affected elbow:

- Elbow incongruity due to a relatively short radius – it can be transient or permanent
- Coronoid process overloading due to conflict with the radius – in some affected elbow joints, stress fractures of the coronoid process of the ulna could be the consequence of repetitive impact from the adjacent radial head
- Ulnar notch incongruity – in some cases the notch of the ulna is excessively elliptical, or simply the wrong shape relative to the humerus, resulting in severe overload of the extremities of the notch

Every dog with elbow dysplasia is affected by some degree of elbow osteoarthritis at the time of diagnosis. This can be the consequence of a loose fragment acting like a 'stone in a shoe' within the joint, or of untreated elbow incongruity such as radio-ulnar or humero-ulnar conflict.

Surgical treatments for elbow dysplasia include:

- Arthroscopic fragment removal
- Sliding humeral osteotomy (SHO) – used in some dogs with advanced elbow dysplasia with severe secondary osteoarthritis
- Total elbow replacement (TER) – performed as a last resort where other treatments will be ineffective

Panosteitis

We have all heard the term 'growing pains', and when this term is applied to dogs, more often than not it is referring to panosteitis. Growing pains in children involve leg pains of unclear origin that generally resolve when the child enters its teen years. Panosteitis in dogs is a specific, painful bone condition involving the long leg bones of large breed dogs generally between the ages of five and eighteen months. The condition can be quite painful during its flare-ups, but ultimately resolves permanently when the pup outgrows it. As in humans with growing pains, the cause of panosteitis is not clear cut.

Diagnosis of panosteitis is relatively straightforward. In panosteitis, there is a slight predisposition of males over females. The lameness can shift from one leg to another, and can be accompanied by fever. Painful episodes typically last one to three weeks but recur, often changing legs, until the puppy outgrows the condition. In panosteitis, characteristic cloudiness in the bone marrow cavities is visible on x-rays.

Treatment is aimed at relieving the pain until the puppy outgrows the problem.

What causes all this to happen in the first place is unclear and open to speculation. There is some evidence of an infectious cause: a normal dog will develop panosteitis if it receives a bone inoculation of marrow from an affected dog. Another theory is that the recent trend in high-protein dog foods is to blame, the idea being that protein accumulation in the bone marrow leads to swelling inside the bone. Because the bone is a rigid structure and cannot expand, pressure is exerted on the blood vessels leading to tissue death, inflammation and the panosteitis phenomenon. Since there is a breed predisposition for panosteitis, this implies a genetic basis. It has often been noted that most of the breeds predisposed to panosteitis are also the breeds predisposed to the genetic blood-clotting disorder called Von Willebrand's disease.

THE NERVOUS SYSTEM

The nervous system consists of two parts:

- The central nervous system, which includes the spinal cord and the brain
- The peripheral nervous system, consisting of the nerves that are found throughout the rest of the body

The brain is divided into three main sections:

- The brain stem, which controls many basic life functions
- The cerebrum, which is the centre of conscious decision-making
- The cerebellum, which is involved in movement and motor control

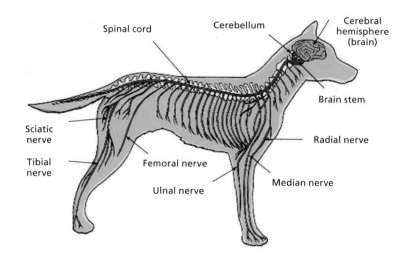

The nervous system.

Canine Distemper Virus

Canine distemper virus is a highly infectious viral disease of dogs which can cause mild signs in some individuals, but which may be fatal in others. Dogs less than one year of age are most commonly affected. However, those animals that have not been vaccinated or have weakened immune systems are also susceptible. Canine distemper is related to the virus causing measles in man. Some strains of the virus may be more pathogenic than others. However, vaccination offers protection against all strains.

The early signs of disease are primarily respiratory, with runny eyes and nose, and coughing. This is followed by depression, loss of appetite, vomiting and subsequently diarrhoea. In the later stages of the disease, dogs may develop thickening of the foot pads, known as 'hard pad', and nose. Dogs which survive may go on to show serious neurological signs including seizures (fits).

It is essential to vaccinate your dog according to your vet's recommendations. Pups that are born to vaccinated dams usually have antibodies from their mothers (maternal antibodies) that protect them against infection during the first few weeks of their lives. The pup is in danger after the level of maternal antibodies declines, and that is when it should be vaccinated.

There is no specific treatment for canine distemper, although supportive therapy in the form of intravenous fluids are often given to correct the fluid loss due to vomiting and diarrhoea.

Vestibular Syndrome

The vestibular system is responsible for maintaining normal balance and has central components located in the brain, and peripheral components located in the inner and middle ear. Vestibular syndrome refers to a sudden, non-progressive disturbance of balance. It is more common in older dogs. It is also referred to as 'old dog vestibular syndrome' and 'canine idiopathic vestibular syndrome'.

Symptoms include the sudden onset of loss of balance, disorientation, head tilt, irregular jerking eye movements and vomiting. Many dogs will become reluctant to stand or walk. Most dogs will lean or fall in the direction of their head tilt.

Causes of vestibular disease include middle or inner ear infections, drugs that are toxic to the ear, trauma or injury, tumours and hypothyroidism (underactive thyroid). When no specific diagnosis is found, the condition will be called idiopathic vestibular syndrome. These cases are distinguished by the sudden onset of symptoms and the subsequent rapid improvement without medical intervention.

Treatment is directed at the underlying cause if identified. In severe cases, supportive treatment such as intravenous fluids and hospitalization may be required until the pet can eat and walk on its own. If the pet is seriously disoriented or ataxic (stumbling, unable to stand or walk), it may be given sedatives to help it relax. Antibiotics will be used in cases

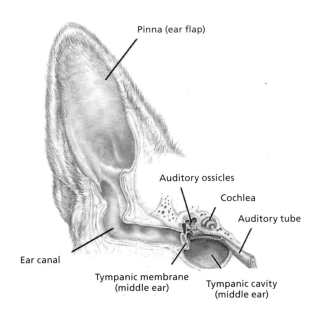

The ear structure.

suspected of having middle or inner ear infections.

The clinical signs associated with vestibular disease are often most severe during the first twenty-four to forty-eight hours. Many pets begin to improve within seventy-two hours. Most patients are completely recovered within two to three weeks, although some will have residual symptoms such as a head tilt or mild 'wobbling' for life.

Epilepsy
See Chapter 12 'Breed Specific Ailments and Diseases'.

Canine Degenerative Radiculo Myelopathy (CDRM)
See Chapter 12 'Breed Specific Ailments and Diseases'.

THE HEART AND CIRCULATION

The cardiovascular and circulatory systems of a dog are extremely intricate, and can naturally be affected by a wide range of health problems.

Heart disease in dogs can be brought on by a wide range of reasons, including bacterial infections, viruses and parasites. Some breeds are more susceptible to degenerative heart disease than others.

Heart Attack
Heart attack in dogs is uncommon, but collapse or fainting may occur due to inadequate cardiac functions.

Heart Murmurs
Acquired disease: A heart murmur may be as a result of wear and tear on, or inflammation of the heart valves, problems of rhythm and rate or disease of the heart muscle. Signs of heart failure may include:

- not wanting to go on walks
- lethargy
- excessive panting
- enlargement of the abdomen due to fluid accumulation
- poor digestion and weight loss
- coughing

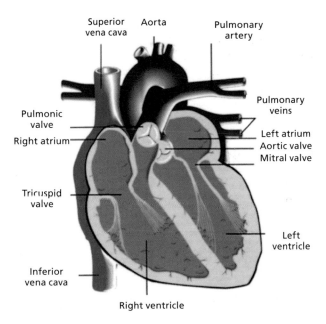

The heart.

Congenital heart disease: Usually due to valve defects or a hole in the heart. Signs of the disease may include the sudden death of a puppy, or weakness and failure to grow at a normal rate. Congenital heart defects are present at birth, and can be hereditary as well as caused by environmental factors. Since a lot of heart defects in dogs are hereditary, responsible breeding is very important to keep down the number of dogs with heart defects.

Congestive heart failure: This is the name given to any disease where the heart of the dog is unable to put out sufficient amounts of blood. Congestive heart failure can be caused by several different diseases (including bacterial infections and heartworm), sudden injury, heat stroke, electric shock, high blood pressure, or developmental heart abnormalities. Congestive heart failure is called congestive since the malfunctioning of the heart causes fluid retention in the lungs and other parts of the body.

Heart Block

Heart block is an acquired problem, also known as 'atrioventricular block'.

The canine heart has four chambers. The top two are called the atria, and the bottom two the ventricles. The heart's 'natural' pacemaker is called the sinoatrial (SA) node or sinus node, a small mass of specialized cells in the heart's right atrium. It produces electrical impulses that make the heart beat. For the heart to beat properly, the signal must travel from the SA node down a specific path to reach the ventricles. As the signal goes from the atria to the ventricles, it passes through conducting tissue called the atrioventricular (AV) node.

Sometimes the signal from the heart's upper chambers to its lower chambers is impaired or doesn't transmit. This is 'heart block' or 'AV block'. This does not mean that the blood flow or blood vessels are blocked. Heart block is classified according to the level of impairment:

First-degree heart block: This is when the electrical impulse moves through the AV node more slowly than normal. Heart rate and rhythm are normal, and there may be nothing wrong with the heart. As such, most cases are found incidentally, requiring no treatment and offering a good prognosis.

Second-degree heart block: This occurs when some signals from the atria do not reach the ventricles. This causes 'dropped beats'.

- Type I second-degree heart block, or Mobitz Type I: Electrical impulses are delayed more and more with each heartbeat until a beat is skipped
- Type II second-degree heart block, or Mobitz Type II: Less common than Type I but generally more serious

Third-degree heart block (complete AV block): The heart's electrical signal fails to pass from the upper to the lower chambers. Complete heart block may be a medical emergency with potentially severe symptoms and a serious risk of cardiac arrest. Treatment is to implant a pacemaker as soon as possible.

Blood-Clotting Defects

Platelets are the cell fragments necessary for proper formation of blood clots, also known as thrombocytes. When a dog develops a platelet disorder that causes dysfunctional platelets or low levels of platelets, its blood will not be able to clot as it should, which can lead to anything from unusual bruising to severe blood loss. An abnormally high level of platelets is normally asymptomatic, but it may increase the risk for thrombosis (the formation of a clot inside a blood vessel). Congenital clotting defects arise if a puppy is born with abnormal blood platelets or clotting factors.

Haemophilia A: The most common and severe inherited coagulation disorder in animals and human beings. In dogs, as in other species, the disease arises as the result of spontaneous mutation. Once haemophilia appears in a family, the defect can then be transmitted through many generations. Normally only males are afflicted, and whilst it is possible for a female to have the disorder, it is extremely rare – however, they can carry haemophilia and pass it on to the next generation. It has become normal amongst reputable German Shepherd breeders to ensure that any male they use at stud has been tested and proven clear of the disease.

Von Willebrand's disease: Another inherited disease that decreases the blood-clotting ability in dogs. The symptoms of Von Willebrand's disease in dogs are somewhat similar to the symptoms displayed by haemophilia A. Von Willebrand's disease is a blood disease caused by a deficiency of an adhesive glycoprotein in the blood required for normal clotting at the sites of small blood-vessel injuries. The best way of preventing Von Willebrand's disease is to never allow any dogs with the disease to breed. Your dog can be tested.

Anaemia

Anaemia develops when the number of red blood cells in the bloodstream is reduced. Since they are responsible for the transport and delivery of oxygen throughout the body, a deficiency in red blood cells can be potentially catastrophic to the entire system. There are many causes and types of anaemia, ranging from simple blood loss or the destruction of red blood cells within the body as part of a specific disease process, to the inability of the body to produce enough red blood cells.

Signs of anaemia include tiredness, exercise intolerance, decreased appetite and pale gums, though dogs with mild cases may not have any signs at all. A severe anaemic may need a transfusion, and in all cases the underlying cause of the problem must be treated.

Tumours of the Spleen

The spleen, which is a reservoir and filter for blood, is a relatively common site for tumours, especially in older dogs. Tumours of the spleen can bleed slowly into the abdomen or can rupture suddenly, causing collapse. Usually enlargement of the spleen is not cancerous. In some cases, the enlargement may be due to blood accumulating as a result of poor circulation or bleeding within the spleen (haematoma). Cancers of the blood vessels are also common in the spleen. Some are benign (non-spreading) and others are malignant (spreading).

Surgical removal of the whole spleen is the treatment of choice for these tumours. However, although benign tumours will only affect the spleen, most malignant cancers will already have spread before diagnosis and surgery. With malignant cancer, removal of the spleen does not cure the disease but may slow the progress, however from experience the time gained is short and must be balanced against putting an older dog through a major operation.

Chemotherapy is used to induce remission and prolong life in lymphoid, blood and mast cell cancers, however it rarely cures the disease. Significant remission is more likely for smaller and more rapidly dividing tumours. The drugs used are toxic to organs with dividing cells such as the intestine, bone marrow and skin. Some also affect other organs such as the liver to induce malaise. The optimal chemotherapy protocol for splenic tumours has not been determined. Side effects should also be considered.

A common malignant tumour which can be heart, splenic or located in the subcutaneous tissue of the skin, is haemangiosarcoma (*see* Chapter 12 'Breed Specific Ailments and Diseases').

THE RESPIRATORY SYSTEM

The most important function of the respiratory system is to deliver oxygen into the blood, which distributes it throughout the body, and to remove carbon dioxide from the blood. The exchange of oxygen and carbon dioxide occurs in the alveoli. When this exchange fails or becomes inefficient because of disease, the animal can become seriously ill. The upper airways also provide for the sense of smell, and play a role in temperature regulation in animals such as dogs that use panting as a way to help keep cool.

Both very young and older animals are at increased risk of developing respiratory disease compared to healthy adult animals. At birth, the respiratory and immune systems are not fully developed, which makes it easier for disease

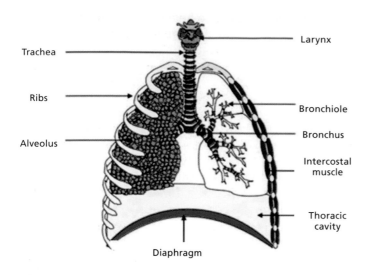

Labels: Trachea, Ribs, Alveolus, Larynx, Bronchiole, Bronchus, Intercostal muscle, Thoracic cavity, Diaphragm

The lungs.

organisms to enter and spread within the lungs. In aged animals, a decrease in the animal's ability to filter out particles and fight off infection may render the lungs more vulnerable to airborne disease organisms and toxic particles.

Lung and airway disorders are often caused by direct infection with viruses, bacteria, fungi or parasites, as well as by immune-mediated reactions or inhalation of irritants or toxic substances. Trauma (such as being hit by a car) may lead to the collapse of a lung or airway.

Signs of respiratory disorders are:

- discharge from the nose (mucus, pus or blood, depending on the cause)
- coughing that may be dry or may include mucus or blood
- rapid breathing (not always a sign of disease, such as in healthy animals after exercise)
- laboured or difficult breathing; shortness of breath
- shallow breathing
- signs of pain associated with breathing in or out
- noise (such as grunting) associated with breathing

Rhinitis

The most common upper respiratory tract malfunction is rhinitis, which is the inflammation of the mucous membranes of the nose. It is often associated with sinusitis, or inflammation of the lining of the sinuses. If the nasal passages deteriorate and fail to function properly, a major filtration function is removed. This exposes the lungs to much heavier loads of dust and micro-organisms.

Rhinitis is caused by viruses, bacteria or fungi and may also be part of a disease such as distemper or kennel cough. The usual symptoms will be sneezing and/or a nasal discharge. Another cause can be the inhalation of a foreign object, such as a dog inhaling a grass seed when sniffing; the dog may start sneezing violently and paw at their face. Another form is allergic rhinitis, which occurs seasonally in association with pollen production, and year-round in association with house dusts and moulds.

In mild cases or those that are recent in onset, treatment to relieve signs may be effective. Your vet may prescribe antibiotics if bacterial infection is present or suspected (antibiotics are not effective against viruses). Fungal rhinitis and sinusitis can be treated with antifungal therapy once the particular fungus has been identified.

Laryngeal Paralysis

Laryngeal paralysis is a disease that affects older dogs. The condition occurs when the cartilages of the larynx do not open and close normally during respiration. It is an acquired problem in large breeds. The vocal cords become paralysed and obstruct the airway. Signs include a dry cough, voice changes, and noisy breathing that slowly progresses to obvious difficulty in breathing during stress and exertion, and eventually to collapse. Initially treatment is directed at relieving the signs of airway obstruction. Severe obstruction may require the placement of a tube into the trachea (tracheotomy). Surgery to correct the problem is often successful.

Laryngitis

Laryngitis is an inflammation of the larynx, which may result from upper respiratory tract infection or direct irritation from the inhalation of dust, smoke or irritating gas, or foreign objects. It can also be caused by the trauma of a breathing tube placed during surgery, or as a result of excessive barking. Laryngitis may accompany infectious tracheobronchitis and distemper in dogs.

A cough is often the first noticeable sign of laryngitis. The cough is harsh, dry and short at first, but becomes soft and moist later and may be very painful. Swallowing is difficult and painful. The build-up of fluid and swelling of the larynx may develop within hours, causing an increased effort to inhale, and high-pitched breathing arising from the larynx. The respiratory rate may slow as the animal's effort to breathe increases. Visible mucous membranes, such as the gums in the mouth, become bluish from lack of oxygen, the pulse rate increases, and body temperature rises. If the swelling obstructs the airways, affected dogs may be unable to cool themselves down in hot weather. Untreated animals with significant obstruction eventually collapse.

Identification and treatment of the primary cause of the laryngitis is essential. Procedures that may be recommended to speed the animal's recovery and provide comfort include inhalation of humidified air, confinement in a warm, clean environment, feeding soft or liquid foods, and the avoidance of dust. Cough-suppressing medications and antibiotics may also be used to treat this condition.

Tracheobronchitis

Tracheobronchitis is an acute or chronic inflammation of the trachea and bronchial airways, which may also extend into the lungs. It often occurs in dogs already affected by respiratory disease or a disorder of the lungs or airways. Other causes of tracheobronchitis in dogs include parasites, diseases of the mouth and pharynx, chronic coughing related to heart or lung disease, smoke inhalation, and exposure to chemical fumes.

Spasms of coughing are the most prominent sign. The act of coughing is an attempt to remove accumulations of mucus and secretions from the respiratory passages and is most severe after rest, or with a change of environment, or at the beginning of exercise. The dog's temperature may be slightly increased. The acute stage of bronchitis passes in two to three days, however the cough may persist for several weeks. Severe bronchitis and pneumonia are difficult to tell apart, and bronchitis often extends from the bronchial tubes into the lung cells and results in pneumonia.

In mild cases or those with a recent onset of signs, supportive therapy may be effective, but treatment of the underlying disease (if present) is also needed. Rest, warmth and proper hygiene are important. If bacterial infection is present, antibiotics may be prescribed. A persistent, dry cough may be controlled by a prescribed cough suppressant.

Infectious Tracheobronchitis (Kennel Cough)

Kennel cough results from inflammation of the upper airways. It can be a mild disease that normally improves on its own, however, it can progress to fatal bronchopneumonia in puppies or to chronic bronchitis in weakened, ill or aged dogs. The disease spreads rapidly among susceptible dogs housed in close confinement such as veterinary hospitals or kennels.

A number of viral and bacterial organisms can cause kennel cough. There are two main causes: bordello, which is a bacterial infection, and the para-influenza virus. Stress and environmental changes such as extremes of ventilation, temperature and humidity appear to increase the dog's susceptibility to the disease as well as its severity.

Chronic bronchitis in middle-aged and older dogs may become worse following sudden changes in the weather or other environmental stresses. Animals with foreign bodies in the airway or developmental abnormalities such as deformities of the larynx may tend to develop bronchitis.

The most common signs are spasms of harsh, dry coughing, which may be followed by retching and gagging. The severity of the cough usually diminishes during the first five days, but the disease persists for ten to twenty days. Affected dogs have few, if any, additional signs except for some loss of appetite. Body temperature and white blood cell counts usually remain normal. Development of more severe signs, including fever, pus-containing nasal discharge, depression, loss of appetite and a productive cough, especially in puppies, usually indicates the presence of an additional infection such as distemper or bronchopneumonia. Stress, particularly from adverse environmental conditions and a poor diet, may contribute to a relapse during recovery.

Kennel cough is highly contagious, so isolation of patients is needed. The dog's recovery may be hastened by good nutrition and rest. Cough suppressants are sometimes prescribed to control persistent, non-productive coughing. Antibiotics are usually not needed except in severe chronic cases.

Vaccines are available for kennel cough and are insisted on by many commercial boarding kennels these days.

Pneumonia

Pneumonia is an inflammation of the lungs and airways that causes breathing difficulties and deficiency of oxygen in the blood. There are many possible causes. The most common cause of pneumonia is a viral infection of the lower respiratory tract. Parasitic invasion of the bronchi can also result in pneumonia.

Signs of pneumonia include lethargy, loss of appetite, and a deep cough. Laboured breathing, 'blowing' of the lips, and bluish mucous membranes may be evident, especially after exercise. Body temperature is moderately increased. Complications such as pleurisy or infection by additional organisms may occur.

Animals with pneumonia benefit from a warm, dry environment. If the mucous membranes are very bluish (indicating poor oxygen in the blood), your vet may administer oxygen. Antibiotics are usually given, although the treatment may be modified based on the results of laboratory cultures, so that the drugs given best match the type of infection found.

Aspiration pneumonia: A lung infection caused by inhalation of foreign material. The severity of the inflammation depends on the material inhaled, the type of bacteria inhaled, and the distribution of foreign material in the lungs.

Fungal pneumonia: Also called mycotic pneumonia, this is a fungal infection of the lung that leads to the development of pneumonia. Often these fungi are found in dogs with a compromised immune system, but they can cause disease in healthy animals as well.

Tumours

Tumours of the nose: It is suggested that the occurrence of a tumour of the nose is slightly higher in males and in older dogs. In dogs, virtually all these tumours are cancerous (malignant). Chronic nasal discharge containing mucus, pus, or blood is the most common sign initially. Deformities of the face and mouth will result from the destruction of bony or soft-tissue nasal and sinus structures. Late in the disease, central nervous system signs such as disorientation, blindness, seizures, stupor and coma may develop if the tumour extends into the upper skull. The recommended treatment largely depends on the tumour type and the extent of disease. Treatments such as aggressive surgical removal of the tumour provide a more favourable outlook when diagnosis is made early.

Tumours of the larynx and trachea: Rare in dogs. The most common signs of tumours of the larynx include laboured breathing when inhaling or after exercise, high-pitched noisy breathing, voice change (hoarse bark or loss of voice), and coughing. The tumour mass may be seen by your vet during examination of the larynx or trachea with an endoscope. Definitive diagnosis can be made after a biopsy. Treatment involves surgically removing the tumour.

Primary lung tumours: Also rare in dogs. Virtually all are malignant (cancerous). Primary lung tumours have variable signs, which depend on the location of the tumour, the rate of tumour growth, and the presence of previous or current lung disease. The most common sign in dogs is a chronic, non-productive cough. Surgery to remove the portion of the lung containing the tumour is the recommended treatment in most cases, however if the lymph nodes are involved or multiple tumours are found, survival time is short.

Metastatic lung tumours: Tumours that originate in another part of the body and then spread to the lungs. These are more common than primary lung tumours. The severity of signs depends on the location of the tumour, and whether the lesions are single or multiple. The diagnosis and treatment is similar to that for primary lung tumours. Because the spread to the lung occurs late in the clinical course of a malignant tumour, the outlook is poor.

Pulmonary Contusions

Pulmonary contusion, or a haemorrhage of the lung, occurs when the dog's lung is torn and/or crushed during direct trauma to the chest, thus impeding its ability to breathe, as the rupture of a blood vessel in the lung fills the air sacs with blood. Dogs suffering from capillary damage may also develop pulmonary fluid in the lungs, as well as haemorrhage.

Symptoms include:

- coughing up of blood or blood-tinged fluid
- respiratory distress, or abnormal respiratory effort after a blunt trauma to the chest
- cyanotic (blue-tinged) or pale mucous membranes

Causes include:

- blunt trauma
- motor vehicle accidents
- physical abuse
- coagulation/clotting disorder

Oxygen support is crucial in the treatment of pulmonary contusions. Since the lungs are unable to function fully, additional oxygen can help lessen their burden and reduce the amount of work required of them. Pain control is important since breathing rates generally increase with pain, and increased breathing rates can delay healing. Many dogs with severe lung damage are also in shock, and appropriate fluid and possible steroid treatment may be needed. Cage rest with minimal exercise is crucial in lung healing. Generally, improvement will be seen within forty-eight hours, but it may take up to ten days for the dog to recover fully. Be aware that despite aggressive medical care, some lung traumas are so severe that the dog may not survive.

Ruptured Diaphragm (Diaphragmatic Hernia)

Diaphragmatic hernias occur in dogs when the abdominal organ such as the stomach, liver or spleen moves into an abnormal opening in the dog's diaphragm, the sheet of muscle separating the abdomen from the ribcage area. This can occur because of an acquired injury from a trauma such as a car accident, or because of a defect at birth (congenital).

Signs of a diaphragmatic hernia include irregular heartbeat, laboured breathing (especially after a forceful blow) and symptoms of shock. The abdomen may move rapidly (palpitate) or feel empty. Reactions such as vomiting, diarrhoea and bloating can occur because of damage to the bowel or stomach. Other symptoms that initially appear to be caused by a diaphragmatic hernia include a gathering of excess fluid in the space around the lungs, or abnormally fast breathing due to other causes.

In congenital cases, the symptoms may not be evident immediately. Gradual symptoms include muffled heart sounds or heart murmurs, abdominal defects, and trouble breathing. Signs may occur suddenly with damage to the bowel, spleen or liver.

The only treatment to repair the diaphragmatic hernia is surgery. Surgery is performed on an emergency basis if the stomach is herniated into the chest cavity and becomes distended with gas. This can prevent lung expansion. A needle can be used through the chest wall to decompress the stomach, and then surgery can be performed. Surgical repair of the diaphragmatic hernia is typically performed by entering the abdominal cavity along the ventral midline, retracting the abdominal organs back into the abdomen, and suturing the tear in the diaphragm. A tube is placed to remove air, blood or fluid that may accumulate in the chest cavity.

The prognosis for dogs with a traumatic diaphragmatic hernia is variable depending on other injuries incurred.

THE DIGESTIVE SYSTEM

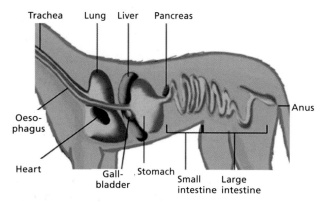

The digestive system.

The Mouth

Dental disease: Problems to do with the teeth and gums might include the following:

- *Dental caries (tooth decay)* – not common in dogs unless they are allowed access to sweet or sugary foods
- *Periodontal disease* – inflammation and erosion around the roots of the teeth
- *Dental tartar* – forms on the teeth surfaces and irritates the adjacent gum causing pain, bad breath, gum recession and tooth loss. Can be prevented with a good diet, large chews and hard biscuits
- *Tooth fracture* – can result from a trauma or from enthusiastic stone chewing
- *Epulis* – a benign overgrowth of the gum which requires surgical removal

Salivary cysts: May occur as swellings under the tongue or neck as a result of a ruptured salivary duct.

Mouth tumours: Often highly malignant, growing rapidly and spreading to other organs. First symptoms may be bad breath, increased salivation, bleeding from the mouth and difficulties in eating.

The Intestine

Gastritis: Inflammation of the stomach, which can be the result of an unsuitable diet, scavenging or infection. The dog repeatedly vomits food or yellowish fluid and froth, sometimes with blood spots.

Obstruction of the oesophagus: Leads to regurgitation of food immediately after eating, and may be caused by a small bone or other foreign object. Diagnosis will be confirmed by an x-ray or endoscopic examination. Treatment must be immediate.

Megaesophagus: This is caused by a defect in the wall of the oesophagus due to a faulty nerve control, which leads to ballooning, retention of swallowed food and regurgitation before the food reaches the stomach.

Obstruction lower in the gut: May be the result of items such as stones, corks, buttons. Tumours can also lead to obstructive vomiting. Diagnosis is by x-ray or explorative surgery.

Intussusception: This condition is telescoping of the bowel, which can follow diarrhoea, especially in puppies. Surgery is essential.

Gastric dilation and volvulus (GDV): *See* Chapter 12 'Breed Specific Ailments and Diseases'.

Dietary diarrhoea: Can occur as a result of sudden changes in diet, scavenging, feeding of unsuitable foods or stress (going to a new home).

Malabsorbtion: An uncommon condition which is caused by defective absorption of digested food. Affected dogs have a ravenous appetite, pass bulky, soft faeces and are underweight.

Enteritis: Inflammation of the small intestines, which can be caused by an infection such as parvovirus, severe worm burden or food poisoning. Continued diarrhoea leads to dehydration, so fluids may need to be given by your vet intravenously.

Colitis: Inflammation of the large bowel (colon). Symptoms include straining and frequent defecation, with watery faeces with mucous or blood.

Inflammatory bowel disease (IBD): *See* Chapter 12 'Breed Specific Ailments and Diseases'.

Canine parvovirus: Affects the bowels causing a sudden onset of vomiting and diarrhoea, often with blood, and severe depression. Death is usually due to dehydration, so prompt replacement of fluid and electrolyte loss is essential. Antibiotics are usually given to prevent secondary bacterial infection. Prevention by vaccination is essential.

Bowel tumours: Most likely to cause vomiting, but lymphosarcoma causes diffuse thickening of the gut lining, which may lead to diarrhoea.

The Pancreas

Acute pancreatitis: This is an extremely painful and serious condition requiring immediate treatment and intensive therapy. It is usually life threatening.

Exocrine pancreatic insufficiency (EPI): *See* Chapter 12 'Breed Specific Ailments and Diseases'.

Diabetes mellitus: One of the functions of the pancreas is to manufacture the hormone insulin, which controls body sugar levels. If insulin is deficient, blood and urine glucose levels rise, both of which can be detected by tests. Affected dogs have an increased appetite and thirst, weight loss and lethargy. Like people, if left untreated, your dog may go into a diabetic coma.

Pancreatic tumours: Relatively common and are usually highly malignant. Symptoms vary from vomiting, weight loss and signs of abdominal pain to acute jaundice. The prognosis is not good, and death is fairly rapid.

The Liver

Acute hepatitis: Not common due to vaccinations.

- Infectious canine hepatitis: Affects the liver. In severe cases the dog may go off its food completely as a first sign, followed by depression and collapse. Some dogs may die suddenly. Recovery is unlikely from this form of disease
- Leptospirosis: In addition to causing severe and often fatal disease in the dog, leptospirosis is infectious to humans. Leptospira canicola causes acute kidney disease. Leptospira icterohaemorrhagiae causes an acute infection of the liver, often leading to jaundice. There is not a successful treatment.

Chronic liver failure: Can be due to heart failure, tumours or cirrhosis. Affected dogs usually lose weight and become depressed, go off their food and may vomit. Diarrhoea and increased thirst are other symptoms. The liver may increase or decrease in size, and there is sometimes fluid retention in the abdomen. Jaundice is sometimes apparent. Diagnosis depends on symptoms and blood tests, x-rays or ultrasound examinations, and possibly liver biopsy.

THE URINARY SYSTEM

Acute kidney failure: The most common infectious agent causing acute nephritis (inflammation of the kidney) is leptospirosis, more specifically *leptospira canicola*. It is also infectious to humans. This disease is not treatable, and vaccination is a must for prevention.

Chronic kidney failure: This is more common in older dogs, and occurs when persistent damage to the kidney results in toxic substances starting

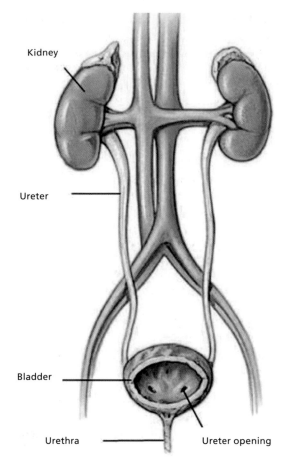

Kidney

Ureter

Bladder

Urethra   Ureter opening

The urinary system.

to accumulate in the bloodstream. A symptom is increased thirst.

Cystitis: An infection of the bladder, cystitis is more common in bitches because the infection has easy access through the shorter urethra. The clinical signs include increased frequency of urination, straining and sometimes blood in the urine. Treatment with antibiotics usually resolves the problem.

Urinary calculi (stones): These can form in either the kidneys or bladder. Blood may be seen in the urine.

Kidney stones: Small kidney stones can enter the ureters, causing severe abdominal pain. Blood

may be visible in the urine. Surgical removal is necessary.

Bladder stones: Calculi or bladder stones are common in both sexes. In the bitch they are larger and straining is usually the only clinical sign. In the dog the most common sign is unproductive straining due to urinary obstruction. Blood may be seen in the urine. They can sometimes be dissolved by feeding a special diet, but surgical removal may be required.

Bladder tumours: These tumours can occur, but are uncommon in dogs. They cause frequent straining and bloody urine, or can cause incontinence by occupying space within the bladder.

Incontinence: Incontinence occasionally occurs for no apparent reason. Hormones or medicine to tighten the bladder sphincter can help. Other causes are:

- hormonal imbalance
- weak bladder sphincter
- urinary tract infection
- urinary stones
- spinal injury or degeneration
- protruding intervertebral disc
- prostate disorders
- the presence of other diseases that cause excessive water consumption, such as diabetes, kidney disease, hyperadrenocorticism
- congenital abnormalities
- anatomic disorders
- certain medications

THE REPRODUCTIVE ORGANS

The Male Dog
Retained testicle (cryptorchidism): Occasionally one or both testicles may fail to descend into the scrotum, and remain somewhere along their development path. Surgery is required to remove retained testicles as they are very likely to develop cancer.

Tumours: These are fairly common but fortunately most are benign. One type of testicular tumour, Sertoli cell tumour, produces female hormones leading to the development of female characteristics.

Prostate disease: More common in the older dog. Usually a benign enlargement occurs where the prostate slowly increases in size. Castration normally helps.

Infection of the penis and sheath (balanitis): An increase and discoloration occurs in the discharge from the sheath, and the dog licks his penis more frequently. Treatment by antibiotics is required.

Paraphimosis: A prolonged erection of the penis, which is unable to retract back into the sheath after mating. The exposed penis should be bathed in cool, sterile water to reduce its size, and lubrication should make it possible to pull the sheath forward over the penis.

The Bitch

Pyometra: A serious disease more common in the older bitch where the womb becomes infected; unless it is diagnosed early and treated by removal of the womb, it can lead to death. Early spaying can prevent this.

Mastitis: An infection of the mammary glands which usually occurs in lactating bitches. The glands become swollen, hard and painful.

Mammary tumours: Common in the older bitch that is entire. Most are benign, but where malignant they can grow rapidly and spread to other organs. Early surgical removal of any lumps is advisable because of the danger of malignancy.

False or pseudo pregnancy: False pregnancy can occur in bitches about eight to twelve weeks after oestrus, at the stage when the bitch would have been lactating had she been pregnant. Treatment by hormones may help, as would having the bitch spayed.

THE ANAL AREA

Anal sac impaction: Quite a common condition, the anal sacs are scent glands and little used in the dog. If the secretion slowly accumulates in the gland instead of being emptied during defecation, the sac will become full and itchy. Your dog may drag his anus along the floor or bite himself around the base of the tail. The anal sacs should be emptied by your vet, because if left, an abscess can form.

Anal furunculosis: *See* Chapter 12 'Breed Specific Ailments and Diseases'.

THE SKIN

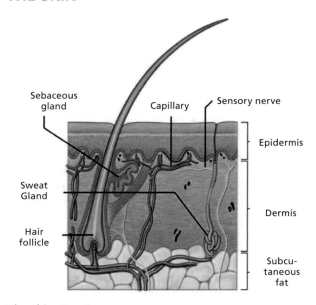

The skin structure.

Skin Conditions that Itch

Fleas

Fleas are the most common cause of skin disease in dogs, and often dogs become allergic to them. They are dark in colour and fast moving. They will feed off a dog, and then jump off into your carpet or bedding to lay their eggs, which can number around fifty a day. Fleas live for about three weeks, but in that time can leave another 1,000 to take their place. They can jump from animal to animal, and also to humans – however, we are not their first choice as host, so they often use a human as a carrier.

Preventative measures are better than having to treat a flea infestation. There are many 'spot-on' treatments available, along with flea collars. Check with your vet for a recommendation, and bear in mind that the cheaper product available in your local supermarket could be much less effective as compared to the more expensive product your vet supplies. Some products can be purchased on line without a prescription through reputable pet drug suppliers, and may work out more cost effective.

Lice

These pests are less common. They are small, whitish insects that crawl slowly around the hair where they also lay their eggs. They spend their whole life on the dog, and again can be prevented with products recommended by your vet.

Sarcoptic mange

Caused by a mite called Sarcoptes, which burrows into the skin, thus causing intense irritation to your dog, and hair loss. Mange is very contagious. The mange mite will spend its entire life on the dog. Again, preventative measures can be taken, but for the affected dog your vet will prescribe an antiparasitic shampoo, and in worse cases, antibiotics.

Bacterial infections

Common in dogs, and often secondary to another skin disease such as mange, or allergies.

Pyoderma

Can be an acute, wet, painful area of the skin; also known as 'wet eczema' or 'hot spot'. A more persistent infection may appear as ring-like sores. Veterinary treatment must be sought.

Furunculosis

Characterized by the presence of boils that recur; it is often referred to as 'canine acne'. The condition is caused by infection that affects the hair follicles and causes small abscesses under the skin that are filled with pus. A dog can get this infection under his chin, in his groin and anal areas (anal furunculosis), and between the toes (interdigital furunculosis).

Contact dermatitis

An itchy reddening of the skin, usually of the abdomen, groin, armpit or feet, where there is least hair to protect the skin. It can be an allergic reaction to materials such as wool or carpets, or to an irritant such as oil or disinfectant.

Lick granuloma

Also known as 'acral lick dermatitis'; typically it results from the dog's urge to lick the lower portion of one of his or her legs. The lesion can initially be red, swollen, irritated and bleeding, similar to a wet eczema. The dog's incessant licking of the lesion eventually results in a thickened, firm, oval plaque. The most common cause appears to be psychological, related to stress, anxiety, separation anxiety, boredom or compulsion.

Skin Conditions that Do Not Itch
Demodectic Mange

Sometimes just called 'demodex' or 'red mange', this is the most common form of mange in dogs. It is caused by the Demodex Canis, a parasite that lives in the hair follicles of dogs. All normal dogs (and many humans) have a few of these mites on their skin. As long as the body's immune system is functioning properly, these mites cause no harm. Demodectic mange most often occurs when a dog has an immature immune system, allowing the number of skin mites to increase rapidly. As a result, this disease occurs primarily in young dogs. Adult dogs that have the disease usually have defective immune systems. Demodectic mange may occur in older dogs because function of the immune system often declines with age.

A dog with demodectic mange usually does not itch severely, even though it loses hair in patches. The hair loss usually begins on the face, especially around the eyes. When there are only a few patches of hair loss, the condition is called localized demodectic mange. If the disease spreads to many areas of the skin, it becomes generalized demodectic mange. It is not contagious like Sarcoptic mange. However, if left untreated, it can rapidly spread causing open red sores leading to infection.

Ticks

Ticks are external parasites from the arachnid family that feed on the blood. They are most active in the warmer weather, and live in tall grass where they may attach to dogs walking through. These parasites prefer to stay close to the head, neck, feet and ear area. In severe infestations, however, they can be found anywhere on a dog's body. Ticks are visible to the naked eye. If you do spot a tick, it is important to take care when removing it. Any contact with the tick's blood can potentially transmit infection to your dog or even to you. Treat the area by rubbing with alcohol, and pluck the parasite with tweezers, making sure you have got the biting head and other body parts. You can also buy a tick-removal tool from your vet. Some complications associated with ticks in dogs, apart from irritation to the skin, are:

- blood loss
- anaemia
- tick paralysis

Ticks can also transmit diseases such as Lyme disease, and all of these can cause serious complications and are potentially fatal without prompt and proper treatment. Ticks can be prevented with regular treatment as recommended by your vet.

Ringworm

Although the name suggests otherwise, ringworm is not caused by a worm, but a fungus. This highly contagious infection can lead to patchy areas of hair loss, and can spread to other animals and humans. Symptoms of ringworm include lesions that typically appear on a dog's head, ears, paws and forelimbs. These lesions can cause patchy, crusted circular 'bald spots' that sometimes look red in the centre. In mild cases of ringworm there may be just a few broken hairs, while in bad cases the bald spots can spread over most of a dog's body. It is also possible for a dog to carry the fungus and not show any symptoms whatsoever. Puppies less than a year old are most prone to infection, but malnourished, immune compromised and stressed dogs are also at a greater risk than healthy animals.

Because transmission of the ringworm fungus can occur via contact with infected animals and bedding, dishes and other materials in the environment where infected hair or scales may collect, ringworm can quickly spread where there are many dogs in a close environment such as kennels. Veterinary advice should be sought immediately.

Hormonal Skin Disease

Skin diseases caused by hormonal abnormalities in dogs are difficult to diagnose. The thyroid gland, adrenal glands, pituitary gland, testicles and ovaries all produce hormones. If excessive (hyper) or deficient (hypo), these hormones produce changes in the skin and hair coat. Most hormonal problems that affect the skin produce hair loss that is evenly distributed on each side of the dog's body. The skin may be thicker or thinner than normal, and there may be changes in the colour of the skin or coat hair. These diseases are not usually itchy.

When any of the hormone-producing glands malfunction, they affect other body functions besides the skin. Hormonal skin diseases in dogs can be much more serious than just a skin problem. Some causes of hormonal skin disease, such as hypothyroidism and adrenal gland problems, can be diagnosed by special blood tests and effectively treated. Others may be more difficult to diagnose and treat. Skin changes related to the sex hormones can be successfully treated with neutering if this has not been performed previously.

Tumours and Cysts

Tumours affecting the skin or the tissue just under the skin are the most commonly seen tumours in dogs. However, hormonal abnormalities and genetic factors may also play a role in the development of skin tumours. All of the various layers and components of skin have the potential to develop distinctive tumours, and distinguishing a tumour from an inflammatory disease can sometimes be difficult as they are so diverse in appearance. They are usually small lumps or bumps, but they can also occur as hairless, discoloured patches, rashes, or non-healing ulcers.

Treatment for a particular tumour depends largely on the type of tumour, its location and size, and the overall physical condition of the dog. For benign tumours that are not ulcerated and do not impair the dog's normal routine, treatment may not be necessary. This may be the most prudent option, especially in aged dogs.

There are several treatment options for cancerous tumours and benign tumours that inhibit normal activities or are cosmetically unpleasant. For most tumours, surgical removal is the most effective option. It is also probably the least costly option and the one with the fewest side effects. If malignancy is suspected, tissue surrounding the tumour will also be removed to increase the chance that none of the tumour cells are left behind. For tumours that cannot be completely removed, partial removal may prolong the life of the dog. Radiation treatment or chemotherapy may also be used to provide your pet with a better outcome, but the side effects must be considered.

Sebaceous Cysts

Sebaceous cysts occur when a pore or hair follicle gets clogged. This can happen because of dirt, infection or scar tissue, or even normal sebum that becomes too thick to get out of the pore's opening. As long as these cysts are small and closed off from the outside air, it is fine for them to be left alone as they are harmless. Usually in the beginning stage they stay white, raised and small; when touched, they will feel like a small, circular or oval bump underneath the skin. They are common with dogs, and are also known as epidermoid cysts. Normally your dog will ignore a cyst and go about his or her daily life as if it wasn't there, and it will gradually get smaller until it goes away completely. If the cyst doesn't bother your dog, you might think of leaving it alone and waiting for it to heal on its own. The exception to this is if the cyst is cut open allowing in bacteria that will cause infection. Your dog may then need a treatment of antibiotics, or in severe cases the cyst may need to be surgically removed.

Warts

A dog wart is the singular form of papillomas, meaning only one visible bump in an isolated area. Warts usually occur on the ageing skin of older dogs. Warts can trigger an 'itch' response, making the dog lick or scratch the area, which also makes it bleed or get infected. Papillomas are benign (non-cancerous) canine tumours that commonly occur in clumps. They can often be found on young puppies, where they tend to take on a unique appearance, mirroring tufts of cauliflower. These papillomas are viral in nature, but tend to clear up after a few months as the puppy's immune system matures.

Perianal Adenomas

A fairly common tumour that arises from the sebaceous glands surrounding the anus. It is particularly common in entire older males. These tumours ulcerate when quite small and produce small bleeding points. The size and location of the tumour will dictate whether surgical removal is carried out.

Haemangiosarcomas

See Chapter 12 'Breed Specific Ailments and Diseases'.

Panniculitis

See Chapter 12 'Breed Specific Ailments and Diseases'.

THE FEET

Interdigital Eczema

It is very common for dogs to lick and groom their feet, especially after an injury, whether this is because a thorn has become embedded, or due to a graze or bruise caused by an accident. The problem with this kind of licking is that the affected area becomes wet, which can then lead to feathering and then infection (especially on the foot pads and feet). The condition will then be exacerbated by the dog's constant licking, which will simply perpetuate the infection and inflammation. It is not uncommon for the dog to become lame.

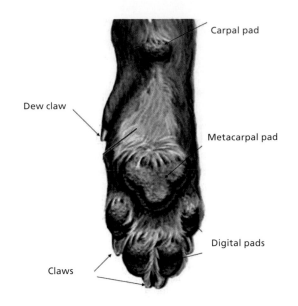

Carpal pad

Dew claw

Metacarpal pad

Digital pads

Claws

The foot.

Treatment for interdigital canine eczema involves the foot (paw) being thoroughly cleaned, with the hair clipped. Of course if there is an injury or thorn in the foot or pad this will need to be seen to first of all. The foot should then be dried and bandaged, which should help stop the dog from continually licking the affected area.

Interdigital Cysts and Abscesses

Interdigital cysts are common in some breeds of dog. They are soft to firm fluid-filled swellings that form in the web of skin between the toes. They sometimes rupture and discharge fluid or pus, and sometimes open sinus tracts form. Interdigital abscesses may form as a result of a foreign body such as a grass seed penetrating the skin.

The underlying cause of interdigital cysts is usually unknown and in fact they are not true cysts, but they form as a result of inflammation. Bacterial infection is thought to be a secondary complication if it is not associated with a foreign body penetration.

The common signs are:

- matted hair over the interdigital space
- pigmentation of the skin and hair between the toes (red-brown-black)

- soft to firm swelling(s) in the web of skin between the toes
- discharging sinus in the interdigital skin
- increased licking or biting of the feet between the toes
- lameness

Your vet will need to identify and remove any foreign object, and may need to surgically explore the site. Surgical removal of the swellings is usually only considered if the dog does not respond to prescribed medical treatment.

Interdigital Furunculosis

Interdigital furunculosis is characterized by the presence of painful nodule lesions in the interdigital webs of the affected dog's paws. Interdigital furunculosis can be caused by a bacterial infection; it can also be due to the presence of short bristly hairs on the webbing between the toes – these hairs are often forced into the hair follicles when the dog walks, which can cause inflammation and secondary bacterial infections. Foreign material that attaches to the paws can also get embedded in the skin and cause interdigital furunculosis.

Antibiotics are generally given for a period of time. The affected area should be kept clean, and the hair in the region should be trimmed to allow the discharge to be cleaned. Antibiotic skin washes are very effective. Surgical removal of foreign bodies in the case of interdigital furunculosis may be required. You must keep the affected area well ventilated and dry. Proper hygiene along with a nutritious diet that boosts the immune system can help your pet fight furunculosis successfully.

Foreign Body in the Pad

The most common foreign body is a sharp fragment of glass or a thorn. Your dog is usually very lame and the affected pad is painful to the touch. Often an entry point will be seen. If you cannot see the object to remove yourself, your vet may be able to remove it with digital pressure, but in some cases surgical removal of the object may be required. Bathing the pad in a warm saline solution can help draw the object to the surface and will clean the wound, thus preventing infection.

Nail Bed Infections

Dogs' feet are often exposed to bacteria and fungi in dirt and grass. A split or torn nail opens up the nail bed to germs, and fungi such as ringworm eat keratin (the non-living part of the claw), which can weaken and infect the nail.

The infection attacks the nail root where it grows out of the toe. The skin around the claw swells, turns red and crusty, and may smell bad. In severe cases the nail becomes brittle or powdery, deformed, or even loosens in the flesh. Pus collects in the area. Pets with nail-bed infections may limp, and often lick the area, which will be sore or itchy.

Neglected infections can lead to more serious complications such as disease of the bone, so it is best to consult with your vet, who will prescribe a suitable antibiotic treatment for the infection. The affected area must be kept clean and dry.

THE EYES

Entropion

Entropion is a genetic condition where a portion of the eyelid is inverted or folded inwards. This can cause an eyelash or hair to irritate and scratch the surface of the eye, leading to corneal ulceration or perforation. It can also cause dark-coloured scar tissue to build up over the wound (pigmentary keratitis). These factors may cause a decrease or loss of vision. Diagnosis of entropion is fairly straightforward through examination. Any underlying causes or irritants should be dealt with prior to attempting surgical correction.

Third Eyelid

Prolapse of the Harderian Gland

Also known as 'cherry eye', this is a condition which usually develops during the first year of life. All dogs have three eyelids: an upper, a lower, and a third eyelid that is usually out of sight. The third eyelid acts like a windscreen wiper and helps protect the eye, but sometimes it can prolapse or pop out altogether, and a mass of red tissue will be seen in the inside corner of the eye. If one eye has cherry eye, the other eye could be predisposed to it as well. If the condition is left untreated, it may go away on its own in two or three weeks, but in other cases it leads to further eye diseases.

The exact cause of the prolapse is unknown, but it is considered to be as a result of a weakness of the connective tissue around the gland. The gland starts to move and becomes irritated; irritation leads to swelling, clear or mucous discharge, bleeding and ulceration. Left untreated, this may result in conjunctivitis. Eyelids may become inflamed from dermatitis, a bacterial, parasitic, or fungal infection, a metabolic or immune system problem, cancers, trauma or sun damage. It is also a common congenital defect that can be passed from one generation to another.

Treatment involves a surgical procedure where the prolapsed gland is pushed back in its pocket. The complete removal of the third eyelid is also an option, but this type of surgery adversely affects the stability of the tear layer of the eye.

Eversion of the third eyelid

Occasionally in young dogs the edge of the nictitating membrane rolls outwards due to a kink which irritates the eye. Surgical removal is necessary.

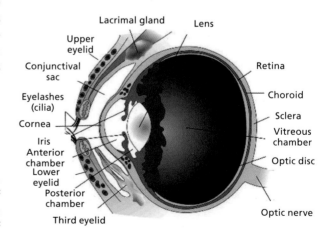

The eye.

Conjunctivitis

Conjunctivitis, also known as 'pinkeye' or 'red eye', is as common in dogs as it is in humans. It is an itchy inflammation of the tissue that coats the eye, called the conjunctiva. Conjunctivitis can happen at any age, by itself, or because of another eye problem. While just one eye is typically affected, conjunctivitis can spread to both.

Allergic conjunctivitis: This allergic reaction is often seasonal and is not contagious.

Viral conjunctivitis: Caused by a virus, spreads easily, and can take up to three weeks to get better.

Bacterial conjunctivitis: This type is also very contagious.

Your vet should be consulted, and will probably recommend bathing your dog's eyes in warm, sterile water. He may prescribe antibiotics and/or anti-inflammatory drops or ointment depending on the cause.

Keratitis

Keratitis, or 'cloudy eye', is an inflammation of the cornea in which the cornea becomes cloudy, resulting in loss of transparency. The signs are excessive tearing, squinting, pawing at the eye, avoiding light, and protrusion of the third eyelid. There are different types of keratitis, all of which are serious diseases and can lead to partial or complete blindness. All types of keratitis should be treated by your vet, who can prescribe antibiotics and/or inflammatory drugs as required.

Ulcerative keratitis: This is a painful corneal inflammation that occurs as a complication of keratoconjunctivitis sicca or corneal ulcer. The cornea appears dull and hazy, then cloudy, and finally milky white and relatively opaque.

Infectious keratitis: This occurs when a bacterial infection complicates ulcerative keratitis, keratoconjunctivitis sicca, or corneal ulcer. In addition to eye pain, infectious keratitis is characterized by a discharge from the eye. The eyelids are swollen and matted. This might, at first, suggest conjunctivitis, which could seriously delay diagnosis and treatment, but conjunctivitis is not usually accompanied by signs of a painful eye.

Corneal Ulcer

The cornea, the transparent part of the eye, forms a cover over the iris and pupil; it also admits light to the inside of the eye. A corneal ulcer occurs when deeper layers of the cornea are lost. These ulcers are classified as superficial or deep. If your dog's eyes are tearing excessively, or it is squinting, there is a possibility of a corneal ulcer (or ulcerative keratitis).

Although initially painful, uncomplicated ulcers should heal with appropriate treatment fairly quickly. Ulcers that persist beyond this period of time, or progress quickly, are more complicated:

- Some fail to heal due to external causes, and display ongoing trauma, possibly due to unresolved foreign bodies embedded within the eyelid or conjunctiva, and abnormally placed eyelashes
- Others fail to heal because they are secondary to other ocular diseases such as dry eye, glaucoma or inflammation (uveitis)
- Some become deeper or progress due to secondary bacterial or fungal infections. These ulcers may rapidly worsen, with resultant perforation of the cornea. They may exhibit a phenomenon known as 'melting', in which the support substance of the stroma is degraded by bacterial or inflammatory enzymes and the tissue dramatically softens, weakens and loses its supportive strength and may lead to severe inflammation within the eye and result in rupture of the eye with loss of vision

Pannus

See Chapter 12 'Breed Specific Ailments and Diseases'.

Cataract

Your vet should be able to determine the severity of your dog's condition and may suggest corrective surgery. Cataract is a progressive disorder

Cataract refers to the cloudiness in the crystalline lens of the eye, varying from complete to partial opacity. When the eye lens is clouded, it prevents light from passing to the retina, which can cause vision loss. Most cases of cataracts are inherited, but other causes can include:

- diabetes mellitus
- old age
- electric shock
- inflammation of the eye's uvea (uveitis)
- abnormally low levels of calcium in the blood (hypocalcemia)
- exposure to radiation or toxic substances

which, if not treated quickly, may lead to blindness in one or both of your dog's eyes. This is especially the case with diabetes mellitus-related cataracts, because they progress very rapidly in dogs. The rate of progression of this disease depends on the underlying cause of the cataract, its location, and the age of the animal. Surgery is often not recommended for dogs with non-hereditary forms of cataract.

THE EARS

Aural Haematoma

Ear haematomas, also known as 'auricular haematomas' or 'aural haematomas', occur when blood accumulates in the flap (or pinna) of the ear. They are characterized by a swelling of the ear flap. In most cases only one ear will be affected, however it is possible for both ears to have haematomas. The swelling may involve the entire ear flap, or it may cover only part of the ear flap.

The most common cause of an ear haematoma in dogs is an ear infection or other irritation within the ear. Ear infections cause irritation to the ear, resulting in shaking of the head which in turn causes the development of the haematoma. Less commonly, allergic skin disease, immune disorders or blood clotting deficits can be the cause of ear haematomas.

Many different treatments exist. The fluid within the haematoma can be drained, but it is likely to recur and may need to be drained numerous times. Many vets prefer to lance the haematoma and drain the fluid under anaesthetic. In most cases, a drain is placed in the ear to keep additional fluid from building up within the ear flap; alternatively, sutures or other devices may be placed through the ear flap to discourage additional accumulation of fluid and recurrence of the haematoma.

Otitis (Infection)

Otitis externa is a chronic inflammation of the dog's external ear canal. Otitis media, meanwhile, is an inflammation of the dog's middle ear. Both of these terms are used to describe clinical symptoms, and are not diseases in themselves; they can affect dogs of any age or breed.

Otitis externa and otitis media can be caused by a variety of things. The primary causes are parasites, food allergies, drug reactions, foreign bodies such as grass seeds, accumulation of hair, dead skin build-up (keratinization), and auto-immune diseases. Other factors that may contribute to the onset of the inflammatory conditions include bacterial infections, mixed infections caused by bacteria and fungal species, and progressive changes in the environment of the outer ear canal.

Otitis externa causes the glands lining the canal to enlarge and produce excessive wax. Gradually the outer skin (epidermis) and the inner skin (dermis) produce excessive fibrous tissue (fibrosis), and the canal becomes narrowed. Otitis externa causes pain, itching and redness, and when the condition is chronic, it often results in a ruptured ear drum (tympanum) and otitis media.

The most common symptoms of otitis externa and otitis media are pain, head shaking, scratching at the external ear flaps, and bad odour. Your dog may exhibit redness and swelling of the external ear canal, scaling skin or obstruction of the ear canal. Signs such as tilting the head, anorexia, loss of coordination and occasional vomiting may indicate the development of otitis media, or otitis interna, if the infection and inflammation spreads to the inner ear.

Treatment

Treatment usually involves outpatient care unless the inflammation or infection has moved into the inner ear. In most cases of otitis externa, a topical treatment following a complete cleansing of the external ear is an effective resolution to the problem. In severe cases where the presence of infectious organisms has been confirmed, antibiotics and antifungals may be prescribed. Corticosteroids may also be used to reduce the animal's pain and the swelling. With the proper therapy, most cases of otitis externa will resolve within a few weeks; otitis media, on the other hand, takes considerably longer to be resolved.

ALLERGIES

The following conditions and behaviours are symptomatic of a dog suffering an allergic reaction:

- Scratches his ears
- Licks or chews his feet or body
- Has a reddish discoloration of the hair on the paws or between the toes
- Rubs his face against the furniture or floor
- Has a rash, bumps, pimples or open sores on the skin
- Has red or watery eyes
- Has ear infections
- Has sneezing fits and/or a runny nose
- Vomits or has diarrhoea
- Coughs or wheezes

All dog breeds can be affected by allergies. Allergies usually affect dogs over two years old, although they have been reported in dogs as young as five months old. This means that dogs that are affected by allergies often suffer for their entire lives, and symptoms often become worse with age.

Airborne Allergy (Atopy)

An allergy to particles your dog inhales is called atopy and is very common. Common allergens include tree pollens, grass pollens, weed pollens, moulds, mildew and house dust mites. Many of these allergies occur seasonally, such as grass pollens, whilst others, such as moulds, mildew and house dust mites, are year-round problems. When humans inhale these allergens they usually develop respiratory signs (hay fever), whereas dogs develop itching of the face, feet and armpits.

One of the most important courses of action is to minimize your dog's exposure to things to which he is allergic. For example, if a dog is allergic to pollen, he should be kept inside when pollen counts are high or the grass is being mowed. Air filters can also help remove many airborne allergens to keep the home environment clean. Some vets may recommend allergy shots if specific allergens have been identified.

Flea Allergy

Flea allergy, or 'flea dermatitis', is a very common allergy in dogs. Most dogs will have minor irritation and itching from a flea bite. A dog with flea allergy, however, will have a severe reaction to a single flea, and they will often bite and break the skin and even remove large patches of their own hair. The most common area of the body affected by flea allergy is the base of the tail or the hind legs.

Treatment of flea allergy includes strict flea control. Fleas can be very difficult to kill, but with modern flea medicine and home treatment options, your vet can help you rid your home and dog of these pests – but remember, 'prevention is better than cure'.

Food Allergy

Food allergies are more common than originally thought, and it is now known that food allergy and atopy often occur together. Food allergy can strike at any age, and allergies can develop to any protein or carbohydrate in the food. Allergies to beef, pork, chicken, turkey, eggs, soy, corn and wheat seem to be the most common. Common symptoms of food allergy include itching of the face, feet, sides of the body, legs and anal area. Affected dogs will often have ear yeast infections and skin infections that respond to antibiotics, but which recur as soon as the antibiotic is finished. Some dogs with food allergy will also have increased bowel movements and soft stools.

Food allergies should not be confused with food intolerances, which generally cause more severe vomiting and diarrhoea.

Treatment of food allergy involves feeding your dog a diet that does not contain the allergen. To achieve this, your vet will perform a 'diet trial'. A commercial hypoallergenic diet or home-made dog food is prescribed and fed for eight to twelve weeks. If a positive response is seen after this trial, your vet will advise you as to how to proceed.

Contact Allergy

This is the least common type of allergy and is caused by something your dog comes in contact with, such as carpet, bedding, plastic, cleaners, detergents, lawn chemicals, grasses, or other things. The area of the body affected is the contact surface, such as the stomach, bottom of the feet, muzzle or elbows. Treatment involves identifying and removing the allergen.

Diagnosis of Allergies

If you suspect your dog has an allergy, you should see your vet. Vets will usually make a preliminary diagnosis and treatment plan, based on the following information:

- Season(s) of the year when your dog has the most symptoms
- Which parts of the body are the most itchy
- Response of the itch to medications (for example shampoos, antihistamines, steroids)

If the initial treatment does not give your dog relief, your vet may recommend more specific 'allergy testing'. This is done by either taking a blood test or performing intradermal skin testing. Blood tests are reasonably reliable for detecting airborne allergies, but not as good for food or contact allergies. Skin testing is considered more accurate and involves shaving a patch of hair on your dog's side, and then injecting small amounts of allergens under the skin; a positive test is diagnosed if there is a reddening or welting of the skin after injection. Those allergens can then be mixed together by a laboratory and injections given weekly at home over several months to help diminish the dog's reaction to the allergens.

Treatment of Allergies

In addition to specific treatments listed above for each allergy type, your vet may recommend the following skin treatments to give your allergic dog relief during his most itchy times:

Shampoo: Frequent bathing with a natural shampoo removes pollens, debris and other allergens from the coat, which could be absorbed through the skin. Your vet may prescribe a medicated shampoo or conditioner that contains anti-inflammatory ingredients if your dog needs additional relief.

Anti-inflammatory allergy medication: Steroids, antihistamines or cyclosporine may be prescribed, as they dramatically block the allergic reaction in most cases. These medications create almost immediate relief from skin irritation and severe itching associated with most types of allergy.

Antibiotics: Often the itch of allergy is made worse by bacterial or yeast skin infections. Your vet may recommend the use of oral antibiotics or anti-yeast medications to treat these infections.

Home treatment: There are additional things you can do at home to minimize your dog's itchiness or allergy symptoms:

- Try to minimize your dog's exposure to the suspected allergens
- Feed your dog a high quality dog food with the correct supplements to ensure it has no dietary deficiencies
- Use stainless-steel feeding dishes and clean them regularly
- Brush your dog's coat regularly to distribute the natural oils and prevent mats that can further irritate itchy skin
- Use flea preventative regularly, as allergic dogs tend to be even more sensitive than normal dogs to flea or insect bites
- Wash your dog's bedding with hypoallergenic detergent in very hot water

12 BREED-SPECIFIC AILMENTS AND DISEASES

Dogs of all breeds, shapes and sizes will at some point in their life contract an ailment or disease that will need veterinary attention. In this chapter we are going to concentrate on the ones that mostly affect the German Shepherd dog.

ANAL FURUNCULOSIS

Anal furunculosis, or 'perianal fistulas', occurs mostly in middle-aged or older dogs. It is a chronic progressive inflammatory disease where lesions appear, very often becoming infected and ulcerated in the area around the anus.

Why Does it Occur?

There are a number of theories over the years regarding the causes; these include the wide base tail of the German shepherd and increased number of sweat glands in the region of the anal canal. During recent research some similarities have been made with the human condition Crohn's disease. Tests have suggested that anal furunculosis lesions develop due to the dog's immune system lacking in the defences that would normally protect the perennial skin and the bacteria present in that area. This leaves the immune system exposed to more than normal levels of bacteria, and it then becomes over-activated, which can lead to a marked level of inflammation and ulceration in the anal area.

Diagnosis

Many owners first notice their dog licking under the tail and around the anal area far more than usual; also the dog may have difficulty passing his motions, or you may see blood in his poo and smell an unfamiliar odour.

To be 100 per cent sure an examination by your vet is required; in most cases just lifting the tail will be enough for the vet to confirm the diagnosis, although in severe cases this will cause more pain as it will pull on the affected skin and your dog may well object – so mild sedation may be necessary to confirm the condition.

Treatment

There are various treatments on the market, and many different views on what works best for each dog; below are a few favoured combinations.

Cyclosporine A: This drug will reduce the activity of the immune cells involved in aggravating the condition.

Cyclosporine A used with Ketoconazole: By using the two together the amount of Cyclosporine can be reduced. Not all dogs will tolerate this combination.

Metronidazole, oxytetracycline and prednisolone can also be used; this is a combination I have used on several occasions with outstanding results, as the case study will explain.

Surgery

In a very few cases where the lesions have not responded well enough to any other treatment, surgery is an option, where the remaining lesions that have shrunk as much as possible are removed. Surgery generally involves removing the active lesions, scar tissue as well as the anal glands on one or both sides. Surgery should only be an option when nothing else has worked.

Prognosis

Statistics show that in around 95 per cent of cases following medication improvement is seen, and lesions are up to 100 per cent reduced in size.

CASE STUDY: TED

Ted was a six-year-old German Shepherd dog who came into rescue in September 2013 already on a high dose of Cyclosporine (Atopica). He had been on this dose for some time, but with the vet's advice we lowered the dose and he seemed fine for a while. Ted then went into foster care, where his foster

mum thought it would help to wash the area every day (the area needs to be monitored and cleaned only if needed, dogs will do this naturally) – but all this did was break down any new skin trying to establish itself, and aggravated the area, causing the lesions to expand – and before we knew it they were very large and infected again.

The vet suggested increasing the level of Atopica to shrink the lesions, but after several weeks of more meds and still the daily cleaning the situation had not improved; so we slowly weaned him off his meds and I decided to take Ted into my home and try a new combination. Ted arrived with me in February 2014 and we started him on the Metronidazole combination mentioned in the main text. This treatment was given for approximately three months, with three weekly vet visits and monitoring of the area only: no cleaning unless really needed.

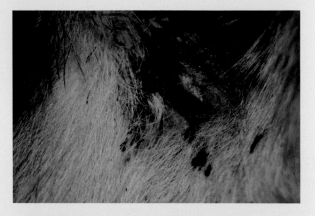

Large lesion.

I am very happy to say that as you can see from the photograph the results were outstanding, as the lesion completely closed up and shrank to a quarter of its original size.

Ted was now ready to be rehomed, and I am very happy to say this happened in May 2014, and I am even happier to say that this was with a very low dose of Prednisolone, from which he was gradually weaned. The lesions have not reopened and he is 100 per cent in remission.

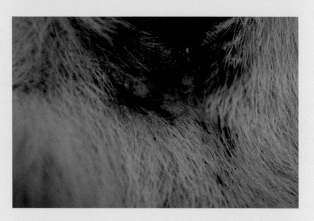

The same lesion after the new treatment regime.

Up to 85 per cent of dogs will go into complete remission with the use of medication.

In approximately 40 per cent of dogs in remission the lesions can reappear. If this is the case it will probably happen six to eight months after the 'all clear'. Normally a much lower dose of previous treatment is needed to combat this.

A very low percentage of dogs do not respond to one or more of the treatments mentioned in this chapter.

All treatments carry side effects, but in most cases are relatively minor; however, always speak to your vet about these first.

EPILEPSY

Epilepsy means repeated seizures due to abnormal activity in the dog's brain. There are said to be two types: acquired and idiopathic.

Acquired epilepsy has an identifiable source

such as a head trauma where there may be scar tissue; idiopathic has no real known source, but it has been suggested that an imbalance of the chemicals that transmit electrical impulses in the brain could be to blame.

- **If the seizure occurs because of a problem elsewhere in the body, like the heart, which stops oxygen reaching the brain, then this is not epilepsy**

What Happens During a Seizure?

A lot of dogs will sense when a seizure is about to happen and will often seek out the security of their owner for comfort.

Once a seizure starts the dog is actually unconscious so therefore cannot hear or indeed respond to you. In most cases dogs will now become stiff, fall over on to their side and demonstrate running motions with their legs; some may cry out and also lose control of their bowels and bladder. In general, most seizures will last from one to three minutes. It is worth making a note of the start and finish of the seizure to be able to give your vet as much information as possible, because they will often seem longer than they actually are.

After a seizure, dogs will behave in a number of different ways, but the vast majority will be disorientated for at least ten to fifteen minutes before returning to normal. Some may ask to be let out into the garden, or to go for a drink of water. If your dog has had more than one seizure you may start to see a pattern forming before and after each seizure.

Most seizures seem to occur when your dog is at rest, and very rarely during exercise; or they can be triggered by stress. In many cases a pattern will start to form, but in some animals seizures will continue to be unpredictable, which is most stressful to both dog and owner.

Are Seizures Harmful?

If your dog suffers repeated seizures then it is likely that the brain will incur some damage and also that further seizures are likely. The damage to the brain is cumulative, and after a large number of seizures it may well result in early senility.

- **Early senility in dogs can lead to a loss of learned behaviour such as house training. Many other behavioural changes may also appear without warning**

Some dogs may bite their tongue and there may appear to be a large amount of blood; however, don't worry as the dog cannot swallow his tongue. It is very rare for the dog to injure himself during a fit.

If the seizure goes on for longer than ten minutes the dog's body temperature will rise, and this can in turn cause damage to other internal organs such as the kidneys or liver as well as the brain. After a very severe seizure a dog may be left in a comatose state.

Treatment

Before treatment is given it would be helpful for your vet to have some history of the seizures your dog has been having. If he has only had one, your vet may advise waiting, as the drugs that may be prescribed are designed to make fits less frequent. To administer the correct dose as much information as possible will be needed, and if your dog has only had the one fit you may be giving him medication he does not need.

Diazepam

Diazepam is very effective at stopping seizures, which is why it is often given as a suppository during a fit to try to stop the fit. It is often prescribed for dogs who suffer prolonged fits. However, this drug is very quickly removed from the dog's body and he can become tolerant of its effects if it is given on a too regular basis.

Bromide

Bromide is one of the oldest anticonvulsants in human medicine, although it is very rarely used these days. This drug needs to be given only once a day as it stays in the body for quite a long time, and is eventually removed through the kidneys. So it can be used on dogs with liver conditions, but obviously not dogs with kidney disease.

Bromide is normally administered in liquid form with food, because if it is given on an empty stomach it can cause nausea. Raised salt levels in your dog's food can alter the effectiveness of the drug. You may see your dog's appetite raised when he is given bromide, and also he may be sleepier than normal.

Bromide is often used alongside phenobarbitone, especially for dogs that suffer from having groups of seizures (cluster seizures).

Phenobarbitone

Also known as phenobarbital, or sold under its manufactured name of Epiphen.

This is also an anticonvulsant drug, quite possibly the most common for preventing seizures. It is mostly prescribed to be given twice a day, and it works very effectively, but it must be administered regularly as missing a dose can affect the levels of the drug in the bloodstream, making it ineffective, which may lead to a seizure.

Phenobarbitone is usually given in tablet form, which makes it very easy to give the correct dose, and maximizes its impact. The drug is broken down in the liver, and with prolonged use can cause some side effects. Regular blood tests enable your vet to monitor any effects on your dog's liver and to act accordingly

Will the Seizures Ever Stop?

It is highly unlikely for an epileptic dog to stop having fits altogether, but with the correct medication they can normally be controlled so that it affects the dog's normal lifestyle as little as possible. Please do not be tempted to stop your dog's treatment because you think he does not need it any more, as this is highly likely to trigger the onset of the fits again. As long as your dog has regular check-ups with your vet to monitor the drugs he is on, there is no reason why he should not live a full and happy life.

GASTRIC DILATION AND VOLVULUS (GDV)

More commonly known as 'bloat' or 'gastric torsion'.

Mainly affecting large breed dogs, particularly ones with a deep chest cavity such as the German Shepherd, this is potentially a life-threatening condition if veterinary help is not sought immediately. The stomach fills with gas, often caused by the dog gulping his food down and taking in too much air, which can ferment the food in the gut. Often if the dog burps this can relieve the pressure, but if this is not the case, gas continues to build up, causing the stomach to blow up like a balloon and often tilting it on to its side, making it even more difficult for the gases to escape. This is when the bloat escalates and you need to get the dog to a vet immediately. If at this point the stomach twists on itself it is known as a GDV.

Signs to Look For

One of the first signs of bloat will normally be restlessness, with the dog pacing back and forth, over-salivating, and making numerous attempts to vomit but only producing white frothy foam. You may also

Typical playful pups.

notice the abdomen becoming swollen and fairly firm to touch – though by this time you need to be on the way to the vet. The dog's breathing will become more erratic, and he may collapse.

- **Time is of the essence with this condition: from seeing the first symptoms your dog could very well be dead within the hour if you do not act *quickly*.**

The distended stomach presses on to the diaphragm and other surrounding organs, causing problems for the proper function of both circulatory and respiratory systems, making it difficult for the dog to breathe and for the heart to pump blood around the body efficiently At this point the dog will very quickly go into shock. If the stomach does get twisted its blood supply is greatly restricted. The spleen may also be affected. With a lack of blood supply the walls of the stomach and spleen may well start to die.

Once you have arrived at the vet, the dog will need to be attached to an intravenous drip to replace fluids to help with the shock. A tube will be passed down the oesophagus into the stomach to release some of the gas and reduce pressure on surrounding organs. In some cases this is not possible, as the stomach may have twisted making entry impossible, in which case emergency surgery is needed to empty the stomach.

However this condition is dealt with, it is extremely serious. Statistics say that around three dogs in twenty will not survive even with surgery. Many dogs will have other organ damage, and the damaged organ may need to be removed to save the dog's life.

In almost all cases a precautionary procedure is performed to fix the stomach in place. This is called 'gastropexy'. If this is not done it is thought that eight out of ten dogs that have suffered an attack of bloat will have a further attack.

At the time of surgery a tube can be placed with one end inserted into the stomach and the other end passing through the stomach wall and out of the body wall where it is fixed, allowing any gases to escape easily. This tube can be left in place for a week, and is easily removed without

Always be around after feeding time to monitor your dog.

further surgery at the vet's discretion when he is happy with the dog's progress.

PREVENTION IS BETTER THAN CURE

Remember: prevention is always better than cure, so do not allow your dog to bolt his food, avoid letting him drink excessive amounts of water after a meal, avoid strenuous exercise for up to one hour either side of a meal, and if possible do not give one large meal, but split it into two or more. Grain-based complete foods will be harder to digest as they encourage fermentation.

CANINE DEGENERATIVE RADICULO MYELOPATHY (CDRM)

CDRM is a progressive disease affecting the spinal cord. It is of unknown origin, and normally occurs in older dogs from around the age of seven years.

The first signs are often loss of co-ordination of the hind limbs, causing the dog to fall over and become very weak in this area, eventually leading to paralysis in the hind limbs.

What are the Causes?

As previously mentioned, there is no real known origin, but the myelin sheaths around the spinal neurons just start to slowly disintegrate; as this happens the nerves become exposed and start to degenerate so the communication system between the spinal cord and the brain becomes disrupted. CDRM has many similarities to the human disease multiple sclerosis. Although there has been no known pattern of inheritance, it seems primarily to attack pedigree dogs; a genetic component is suspected.

Signs to Look Out For

Clinical signs appear gradually and worsen with time, and it can take months or years for full spine and pelvic paralysis to take place. The following signs might indicate CDRM:

- Dragging of the rear paws and possible knuckling over of the toes
- Sores appearing on the toes
- Excessive wear on the toenails
- Swaying gait of the hind limbs
- Difficulty in getting up
- Unexplained lameness
- Difficulties with balance
- Incontinence of bowels and bladder
- Hind-leg stiffness

Although there is no actual cure for CDRM, the earlier you can spot one or more of the above signs and get your dog to your vet, the better, because early diagnosis and prompt treatment, such as physiotherapy and swimming, can help delay the progression of the disease.

The gene responsible for CDRM has been found in forty-three different breeds, all pedigree, but the only breed to have a unique form of the disease is the German Shepherd, known as 'German Shepherd Dog Myelopathy' (GSDM). There is no sensory loss with other forms of CDRM as there is with GSDM.

Before CDRM is established as the cause, all other spinal dysfunctions should be ruled out, as damaged discs or spinal tumours will give off similar symptoms.

Summary

Sadly, CDRM is a non-reversible progressive disease with no known cure: to date there are no

Hind-leg stiffness is a common symptom.

known proven drugs that can be used to halt its progression. Nonsteroidal anti-inflammatory drugs may be used to alleviate any pain.

However, as there seems to be very little pain involved for the dog with CDRM, the administration of drugs is a moot point.

Exercise is encouraged as long as the dog is happy and capable, and physiotherapy and swimming can also be helpful.

This disease has very little rhyme or reason to its progression, thus for some dogs it may be slower in its advancement than it is for others – which makes it even harder to accept.

In the later stages of the disease wheels can be used, depending on the owner's preference: there are many websites that offer help and advice on the subject.

PANNICULITIS

In panniculitis the layer of fat underneath the skin which normally provides warmth, protection and energy, becomes inflamed. It is not a common condition.

It may be caused by an infection, either bacterial or fungal. In other cases sterile nodular panniculitis (SNP) is a descriptive term for the lesions or lumps that appear without the evidence of infection.

Other causes are also considered, such as recent vaccines, trauma, systemic illnesses such as an auto-immune disease or pancreatitis, or it could be that the dog has a vitamin C deficiency.

The inflammation of the skin results in bumps or nodules forming under or on the skin surface; these can be soft or hard in texture, and may be sore and painful to the touch.

The lumps will often rupture, releasing an oily discharge which can be clear, or a yellow/brown colour, and may also contain blood.

Treatment

If the cause is infection, then treatment with antibiotics is paramount, and the sooner this is given the better. If, however, the cause is unknown (idiopathic), then immunosuppressive drugs can be used, such as steroids. The addition of vitamin E to the dog's daily food will be beneficial.

As in most cases of Panniculitis the cause is somewhat unknown so there are no particular precautions that an owner can put into place to prevent any further outbreaks.

EXOCRINE PANCREATIC INSUFFICIENCY (EPI)

What is EPI?

EPI is a disease affecting the pancreas, a small organ found close to the stomach which plays a major role in the digestion of your dog's food. When functioning correctly it produces vast volumes of enzymes that are released into the gut, when your dog has a meal, to help maximize digestion as the food leaves the stomach.

If your dog suffers from EPI the pancreas is unable to produce sufficient enzymes, so food is poorly digested and the dog does not get the full amount of goodness from his diet and it is passed out as greasy, foul-smelling faeces. Although the dog will be consuming enough food for his age, weight and size, he will only be gaining a small portion of the nutrients he needs.

In certain breeds of dog, the German Shepherd being one, EPI can be hereditary, even though the parents showed no outward signs of having the disease. EPI occurs due to atrophy, which means the tissues of the pancreas are withering away. Recent studies have also shown that EPI contracted in later life may be the result of long-term pancreas damage due to pancreatitis.

Signs to Look Out For

The most obvious sign is that of weight loss over several weeks, despite an increased appetite and maybe more food than normal being fed. Always check your dog's faeces so you know if they change. With EPI they can often be greasy and smelly, and diarrhoea is common. Even with all the above symptoms your dog may appear well in himself, although sometimes the coat may become dull and brittle to touch.

When visiting your vet and presenting the above symptoms, EPI may be suspected straightaway, but to be on the safe side and to get an accurate diagnosis it can be confirmed with a blood test.

Treatment

The treatment of EPI in theory is quite straight-forward. If there is insufficient production of digestive enzymes these will need to be replaced in a supplement, available in powder or enteric coated capsules.

Some people prefer to go down the natural route and feed a raw form of pig's pancreas to supplement the pancreas that is not working correctly. Many have found this works really well as a replacement of conventional medication.

You may need to make changes in your dog's diet to restrict fat intake. Early signs of improvement may be seen in as little as a few days in your dog's faeces, which should appear firmer and less smelly, though it may take up to several months for your dog's weight and appetite to return to normal.

Long Term Outlook

As with many conditions, the earlier you can spot the signs mentioned above, the sooner the correct treatment can be given, and good results will be seen.

Most cases of EPI are very manageable with the correct treatment, and dogs not only maintain

Continued weight loss should be monitored.

their optimum bodyweight but some even put more weight on.

However, once EPI has been diagnosed it will stay with your dog for life and therefore will also need treatment for ever.

INFLAMMATORY BOWEL DISEASE (IBD)

The symptoms for IBD are very similar to colitis, irritable bowel syndrome, regional enteritis, chronic colitis, lymphocytic/plasmacytic inflammatory bowel disease, granulomatous enteritis or spastic bowel syndrome, depending on whichever is the more predominant symptom. Very often if the dog has a bad case of internal parasites the symptoms will be very similar too.

Irritable bowel syndrome (IBS) is often mistaken for irritable bowel disease at the time of diagnosis as many of their symptoms are the same. This may also mean that there will be a delay in the dog receiving the correct treatment.

IBD occurs when inflammatory cells attack the dog's healthy cells and cause inflammation. If the inflammation is associated with ulceration it increases the risk of developing certain cancers. Ulcerative colitis is one such condition associated with colon cancer in dogs. IBD may also develop due to Crohn's disease, which involves the inflammation of parts of the gastrointestinal tract.

IBS is a syndrome and may result in inflammation throughout the dog's body. It is associated with stress, so dogs in high perfomance activities can be more susceptible. Dogs suffering from IBS do not develop ulcerative colitis or internal bleeding.

Dogs with IBS should be fed a diet that is easily digestibile and high in fibre.

Most dogs will at some time in their life suffer from an upset tummy due to either eating something they shouldn't have, or raiding the bins. They will suffer the consequences with either vomiting or loose stools for a few days, but then the body will right itself – though with IBD this will continue for a longer period.

The most common sign is loose stools over a period of time, often with diarrhoea and possible straining. If you monitor your dog over a week or

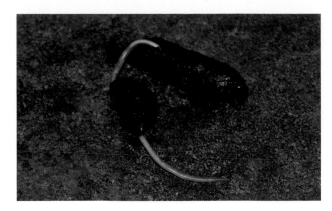

A strict worming programme should be adhered to.

so you will have some history to give to your vet to help with diagnosis.

In all forms of IBD, the dog's defence cells build up in the walls of the digestive system. This happens if the dog has been eating things he should not have eaten, and his body is protecting itself. In many cases it can just be that the body is attacking things in the intestines that are no threat to the dog at all.

What are the Causes?

Some types of IBD are genetic to certain breeds. Lymphocytic/plasmacytic (LPIDB) is the most common. LPIDB describes the type of cell the vet will see if a biopsy is performed; a certain number of these cells are always present, but it is not good news if they are present in much larger numbers.

The second most common form is Eosinophillic IBD. This can often be more severe than LPIBD, but because a suspected cause is food allergies, when a change of diet is made improvement is seen. In a lot of cases dogs are not actually allergic to the foodstuffs, they simply cannot digest or absorb certain nutrients in that particular food, which leads to an upset tummy and possible diarrhoea.

Chronic intestinal infections caused by bacteria, fungi or protozoa can also cause diarrhoea. If given the correct antibiotics this will improve, but there will often be an underlying intestinal problem that caused the organisms to get out of control. However, salmonella and campylo-bacter can give off IBD-like symptoms and with no underlying disease.

What Tests Can My Vet Do?

Normally your vet will start with a simple faecal sample to rule out parasites, and a blood test to rule out pancreatic, liver or any other systemic disease.

In a lot of IBD cases the bloods will come back as normal. If the problem has been very severe or of long standing, the blood protein level may be low due to its loss from the inflamed intestines; also the globulin (protein found in blood serum) may be higher than normal. If the dog has been vomiting for a while, then the potassium levels will need to be checked.

When the tests come back as normal your vet will check your dog's diet and use medication such as Metronidazole, which kills several bacteria that can cause diarrhoea. Your vet may also recommend other medications that slow down, soothe and coat the intestines.

If the above treatments do not work and the symptoms persist, your vet may well suggest an x-ray or abdominal ultrasound to rule out other causes. The only definite diagnostic procedure is to do an intestinal biopsy which will require your dog to be anaesthetized and small pieces of tissue removed from the intestines. This procedure can be very expensive and you will more often than not be referred to a specialist.

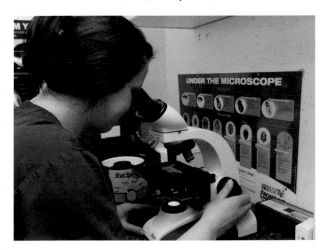

Faecal and blood samples can be taken.

Treatment

The main aim is to try to reduce the inflammation in the intestines. Steroids such as Prednisolone are very effective in doing this, but they do have side effects, so should only be given in small doses, as they will suppress the whole immune system throughout the body and not just treat the intestines. This will not cure IBD but will help to manage it.

There are many hypoallergenic diets on the market that should be free from as many preservatives, additives and colouring agents as possible. Diets that contain a source of protein from one of the following – cheese, duck, rabbit or venison – are best, and even using one of these it will still take up to several months to see an improvement.

For true IBD there is no cure, but when you have found the correct treatment or combination that suits your dog and stabilizes his condition, he will be able to live quite happily with it.

HIP DYSPLASIA

What is hip dysplasia, and what are its causes? Hip dysplasia is an inherited condition, and it is determined by the individual genetic (genotype) make-up of each dog. In a breeding programme a puppy will receive genes from both mum and dad, so there is a need for hip scoring of the parents (this will be covered in more detail later in this chapter).

Hip dysplasia occurs when the ball and socket joint of the hip does not fit together properly; this results in rubbing, which in turn then damages the surfaces of the joint, more often than not, causing lameness, and arthritis in later life.

Normal function relies on a good fit of the ball – which is the head of the femur – into the socket (acetabulum). The surfaces of the head of the femur and acetabulum are covered with smooth articular cartilage, whereas the joint is encased in a special type of connective tissue called the joint capsule, which produces a fluid that lubricates and nourishes the articular cartilage.

Although the cause of hip dysplasia is thought to be primarily inherited, a lot also depends on the start in life a dog gets, namely its diet, welfare and exercise (too little or too much are both as bad).

Normal hip development is determined by the fit of the hip joint and the dog's lifestyle, which also makes a contribution.

Signs

In most cases there are no extreme signs, usually just a mild lameness, which may in time worsen, is displayed. On first standing a dog may show signs of stiffness or soreness, and it may be reluctant to go for walks. It may display bunny hopping, or show an abnormal gait, whereby the legs move more together rather than swinging alternately. The dog may not want to jump or climb stairs or stand on its hind limbs. There will be a lack of muscle or wasting away of the muscle mass in the hip area.

Most affected dogs will appear normal when they are puppies and adolescent, but may develop some of the above signs later in life. If the condition is more severe, signs will be seen earlier as hind leg lameness or weakness. Lameness will be more visible if one hip is more severely affected than the other, but in many cases dogs will have similar changes in both hips so may just appear stiff. If this is an older dog many owners may not even notice.

Diagnosis

Take your dog to the vet for an x-ray, which will show the development of the joint, and how equal the wear and tear is on each hip, and the vet will suggest the best course of action.

If the dog is over twelve months old your vet may suggest having the hips scored, although

HIP SCORING

Hip scoring cannot be performed on a dog, certainly under the Kennel Club scheme, until it is twelve months old. Each hip is scored separately, and that is then put against the scoring system of being either 0 up to 53. Thus the lowest combined hip score of a dog can be as low as 0 or a maximum of 106. The breed average to date is nineteen for both hips.

this does not seem to be common practice if an x-ray will suffice.

Once the x-ray has established the condition of the ball and socket joint, the vet will also assess the dog's movement and decide if its quality of life is being affected. The vet will be able to judge a lot from watching the dog move, how lame it is, how difficult or compromised its movement is when running, and he will also note how the dog places its feet. All the above factors will reveal any problems. In some cases the x-ray may have shown very little, but the x-ray only looks at bone, not cartilage, and the dog may therefore still be in considerable pain, so this needs to be taken into account.

BEWARE MISDIAGNOSIS

There are a few other conditions that have the same symptoms as hip dysplasia, and they need to be ruled out during diagnosis. Lower back problems, cruciate ligament tears and damage, arthritic conditions in the hind limbs, and elbow dysplasia are difficult to diagnose as the dog may only have an unusual gait, and it can easily be diagnosed with hip dysplasia by mistake.

Treatment
While there is no cure for hip dysplasia, there are many treatments that will alleviate the symptoms and reduce the amount of pain the dog is suffering. As this is an inherited degenerative condition it will change as the dog gets older, so any treatments given will need to be reviewed throughout his life. Maintaining your dog's ideal weight is also critical, as an overweight dog will struggle a lot more.

If the condition is relatively mild, then very often all that is needed is to bring the symptoms under control with the correct medication to help the body with the inflammation, pain and joint wear. For a lot of dogs this will be suitable for many years.

In more severe cases, when medication is not enough to stabilize the symptoms, there are two types of surgery regularly used. The first is to reshape the joint to reduce pain and/or help movement; however, this can only be offered for smaller breed dogs, so for a German Shepherd the other option would be a complete hip replacement. This is where the hip is replaced with an artificial hip joint, and is very similar to the operation given to people. This will prevent the arthritis caused by HD in later life.

Multi-functioning drugs which reduce inflammation and pain are prescribed. These are typically non-steroidal anti-inflammatory drugs (NSAIDs) such as Rimadyl or Metacam, which are both also used to treat arthritis. Both of these drugs carry side effects, so always follow your vet's advice.

- **If dogs are to be on any medication for very long periods it is advisable to have twice annual blood tests to check how their body is coping.**

PANNUS

Pannus, or 'chronic superficial keratitis', is an auto-immune condition affecting the cornea or clear part of the eye. It occurs primarily in middle-aged dogs. Pannus is thought to be a hereditary condition that develops as the pet ages. Predisposing factors, such as increased exposure to ultraviolet light, high altitudes and smoke, may contribute to the development of pannus and can certainly exacerbate the condition.

Signs

At first, a non-painful, elevated pink mass appears on the cornea, most commonly on the lateral or outer surface. Both eyes are usually affected, but one may appear worse than the other. The third eyelid commonly appears thickened and inflamed. There is a variation of pannus that only involves the third eyelid, called nictitans plasmacytic conjunctivitis or plasmoma. As pannus progresses, the lesion will flatten and spread out, will become pigmented or dark in colour, and scarring will spread over the cornea. In advanced cases, visual impairment may result due to the inability to see through the dark pigment covering the cornea. If the condition is not treated, the pet will become blind.

Treatment

Treatment involves using topical corticosteroids or other immune modulating drugs. Antibiotics are sometimes required in cases that have developed a secondary infection. Treatment will not cure the condition, but will halt its progression and may reverse some of the changes. The treatment of pannus is for life. It is important that your vet's instructions are carefully followed and medications are consistently administered. Regular check-ups and vigilance are imperative since the condition often relapses throughout life.

Advanced stages can lead to blindness.

HAEMANGIOSARCOMAS

Haemangiosarcoma in dogs is a malignant cancer that arises from the blood vessels. It occurs more commonly in older dogs, and is almost exclusive to the canine. There are several breeds of dog that seem to be at a greater risk for haemangiosarcoma, and they include German Shepherds, Golden Retrievers and Boxers.

In dogs, haemangiosarcomas generally occur in the following locations: the spleen, the right atrium of the heart, and in subcutaneous tissue.

These tumours grow by infiltrating into normal tissues surrounding the tumour as well as displaying distant spread (metastasis). The disease does not cause pain, and the rate of growth in the early stages is relatively slow. Since haemangiosarcoma tends to spread aggressively, distant spread inevitably occurs before the disease is diagnosed. The eventual outcome for patients with this disease often follows the rupture of a large or rapidly growing tumour, which results in acute, severe haemorrhage, collapse, shock and death.

It is not known precisely what causes canine haemangiosarcoma but the observations that the disease occurs more commonly in dogs, and some breeds are at higher risk than others, lead us to deduce that heritable factors must contribute to risk.

Prognosis is not good. With early detection, and treatment with surgery and chemotherapy, survival times and quality of life may be improved, but there should be a balanced decision made against putting your dog through these treatments and how much longer they may extend its life, especially in the older dog.

Haemangiosarcomas of the Skin

The subcutaneous form of haemangiosarcomas in dogs occurs as a lump under the skin, with the overlying skin appearing normal or as a red or black raised growth. Some may be associated with exposure to the sun, so most commonly occur on areas of the body with sparse fur, such as the abdomen, or in areas of short white fur. Other haemangiosarcomas of the skin in dogs can be metastasis from other tumours. The only way to positively identify a skin or subcutaneous tumour as a haemangiosarcoma is by histopathology (examining the removed tissue under the microscope).

These tumours need to be surgically removed. A wide margin of normal tissue around the tumour is also removed to be sure all cancerous cells are eliminated. If the tumour has not spread below the skin, the prognosis may be favourable, and chemotherapy may not be required. The earlier the tumour can be removed after it is detected, the better the prognosis.

Because haemangiosarcomas can spread quickly, it is recommended that chest x-rays and ultrasound examinations of the chest and abdomen be performed to look for other tumours.

Haemangiosarcomas of the Spleen

A haemangiosarcoma of the spleen can often be detected through palpation. Commonly, the first symptoms are related to sudden blood loss into the abdomen when the tumour ruptures. Symptoms would include weakness or collapse of the dog, and the appearance of pale mucous membranes. Occasionally, dogs will have symptoms of chronic blood loss, which include pale gums, irregular heart rate, and generalized weakness.

Treatment generally means removal of the entire spleen. If the tumour has ruptured, surgery is considered an emergency. In addition, chemotherapy is recommended. As with haemangiosarcomas of the skin, chest x-rays and ultrasound examinations of the chest and abdomen should be performed to look for other tumours. It is quite common for a dog with haemangiosarcomas of the spleen also to have a heart-based haemangiosarcoma. In general, dogs that undergo just splenectomy only survive for about two months, whereas those that have chemotherapy as well, may survive for six months.

Heart-Based Haemangiosarcomas

The first signs of heart-based haemangiosarcomas are often related to bleeding from the ruptured tumour. The blood that is released collects between the heart and a tough capsule that surrounds the heart called the pericardium. When the pericardium fills with blood, it puts pressure on the heart and the heart is unable to fill with blood and pump blood properly. Signs may include difficulty breathing, fainting, weakness, or sudden death. On x-rays of the chest, the heart will appear enlarged and round because the pericardium has filled with blood.

As an emergency measure, a needle can be placed within the pericardium to draw off the blood and allow the heart to pump more efficiently. Surgical removal of the tumour may sometimes be possible, but survival time is generally only several months, and recovery from the surgery is often complicated. If chemotherapy is also used, survival time may be lengthened to up to six months.

Scans and x-rays are good for monitoring any tumours.

REFERENCES

Alleyne, Robert, *The Trouble-Free Dog* (Hale, 2008)

Brazil-Adelman, Mary Belle, *The German Shepherd Dog Handbook* (Barron's, 2010)

Evans, J.M. and White, Kay, *Book Of The Bitch* (Interpet Publishing, 2007)

Neville, Peter, Bower, John and Caroline, *German Shepherd An Owner's Guide* (Collins, 2011)

Roberts, Angie, *Raw Diet – Biologically Appropriate Diet For Dogs* (September 2014)

http://en.wikipedia.org
Wikipedia, *The History And Origin Of The German Shepherd Dog*

http://www.germanshepherdk9.com
German Shepherd k9, *Living With The High Drive Dog*

https://www.gov.uk/government/organisations/department-for-environment-food-rural-affairs
Department for Environment Food & Rural Affairs, *Dealing With Irresponsible Dog Ownership* (October 2014)

http://www.vetmed.vt.edu
VMRCVN Veterinary Teaching Hospital, *Nutrition For The Adult Dog*

http://www.mypetonline.co.uk
My Pet Online, *Vaccinating Your Dog* (March 2014)

http://www.petwelfarealliance.org
WSAVA, *Guidelines For The Vaccination Of Dogs And Cats* (Journal of Small Animal Practice, Vol 51, June 2010)

http://www.dogsnaturallymagazine.com
Rasmusen, Jan, *Titer Testing*

http://www.mountvets.com
Mount Vets Veterinary Hospital, *Parasite Control For Dogs*

https://www.dogstrust.ie
Dogs Trust, *First Aid*

http://www.petbloodbankuk.org
Pet Blood Bank, *Frequently Asked Questions*

http://healthypets.mercola.com
Becker, Dr, *Help Your Dog Overcome These 3 Common Allergies...* (15 September 2011)

https://www.vetstream.com
Watkins & Tasker Veterinary Group, *Whelping – Potential Problems*

http://www.medicanimal.com
MedicAnimal, *Canine Pregnancy: The 7 Most Common Problems During And Post Whelping*

http://germanshepherdplace.com/
Grooming your German Shepherd

http://www.pedigreedatabase.com/
Training The German Shepherd Dog For The Show Ring

http://www.germanshepherdguide.com/
Elements of Temperament

http://www.canineepilepsy.co.uk/
Epilepsy in dogs

http://www.dfordog.co.uk/
Bloat

http://www.quincysdogs.com/
Canine Degenerative Myelopathy

http://www.willows.uk.net/
Anal Furunculosis / Hip Dysplasia /

http://www.vetstreet.com/
Panniculitis

http://www.thekennelclub.org.uk
The Kennel Club, *The Canine Code*

The Kennel Club, *Choosing And Bringing Home The Right Dog For You*

The Kennel Club, *Find A Rescue Dog* (March 2013)

The Kennel Club, *Do You Know How To Look After Your Dog In Its Senior Years?* (March 2013)

The Kennel Club, *Why Should I Microchip My Pet?* (March 2013)

The Kennel Club, *Pet Insurance For Dog Owners* (March 2013)

The Kennel Club, *Do You Know Dog Law* (March 2013)

The Kennel Club, *Road Travel With Your Dog* (March 2013)

The Kennel Club, *Moving House With Your Dog* (March 2013)

The Kennel Club, *Travelling Abroad With Your Dog* (March 2013)

The Kennel Club, *How To Get Started With Dog Training* (March 2013)

The Kennel Club, *How To Get Involved In Fun Activities And Competitions With Your Dog* (March 2013)

The Kennel Club, *How To Register Your Dog With The Kennel Club* (March 2012)

The Kennel Club, *Puppy Farming*, Issue 4 (March 2013)

The Kennel Club, *Breeding From Your Bitch* (March 2013)

The Kennel Club, *Breeding For Health* (February 2014)

The Kennel Club, *Thinking Of Using Your Dog At Stud?* (March 2013)

The Kennel Club, *DNA Profiling And Parentage Analysis Services* (March 2013)

The Kennel Club, *Breeding From Your DNA Tested Dog*

The Kennel Club, *Health Screening And The Kennel Club* (March 2013)

The Kennel Club, *Kennel Club Endorsements* (March 2013)

The Kennel Club, *Thinking Of Showing Your Dog In The UK?* (March 2013)

The Kennel Club, *Veterinary Health Checks For High Profile Breeds Exhibitor Information* Version 2 (February 2012)

ACKNOWLEDGEMENTS

Before writing this book we questioned how much we knew to be able to put together a comprehensive and factual guide. Between us, the knowledge we have accumulated over the years from practical experience with the German Shepherd breed is quite immense. Much of this experience has come through fostering many dogs over the years, and therefore experiencing most of the issues that can come with them. Many were resolved with our own common sense, but when at a loss, we would ask for advice through the network of people we have established through rescue.

In areas we had not been involved in, such as competitions and breeding, we found the Kennel Club website to be a valuable source of information, and by talking to people involved in these activities, we were able to bring together a factual insight to share.

A big thank-you to Sally Litchfield BVetMed MRCVS for her professional input with the veterinary chapters, and for checking and double checking the accuracy.

Many of the photographs were drawn from our own intensive collections; however, we would like to thank the following people for allowing the use of their photographs to complete the visual impact:

Ruth Downing www.ruralpictures.co.uk

Rob Dray www.thatpetphotographer.com

Surrey Police Dog Training School

Woodside Wildlife and Falconry Centre in Lincoln

Netty Kirby from Draycore German Shepherds

A thank-you to Angie Roberts, too, for allowing us to reproduce her raw diet feeding plan.

And finally we must not forget our thanks to Nicky Chapman BvetMed, and Avril Darmoo, Lizzy's mum, for expertly proof reading our first attempt at writing a book.

INDEX

Index